CW00554756

WHEN
RUNNING
MADE
HISTORY

Sports and Entertainment
Steven A. Riess, *Series Editor*

Select Titles in Sports and Entertainment

Abel Kiviat, National Champion: Twentieth-Century Track & Field and the Melting Pot
Alan S. Katchen

The American Marathon
Pamela Cooper

Anything for a T-Shirt: Fred Lebow and the New York City Marathon, the World's Greatest Footrace
Ron Rubin

The Fastest Kid on the Block: The Marty Glickman Story
Marty Glickman with Stan Isaacs

Legends Never Die: Athletes and Their Afterlives in Modern America
Richard Ian Kimball

The 1929 Bunion Derby: Johnny Salo and the Great Footrace across America
Charles B. Kastner

(Re)Presenting Wilma Rudolph
Rita Liberti and Maureen M. Smith

The War of the Wheels: H. G. Wells and the Bicycle
Jeremy Withers

WHEN RUNNING MADE HISTORY

Roger Robinson

Syracuse University Press

First Edition 2018

18   19   20   21   22   23   6   5   4   3   2   1

For a listing of books published and distributed by Syracuse University Press,
visit www.SyracuseUniversityPress.syr.edu.

ISBN: 978-0-8156-3578-9 (hardcover)
        978-0-8156-1100-4 (paperback)
        978-0-8156-5443-8 (e-book)

Library of Congress Cataloging-in-Publication Data

Names: Robinson, Roger, 1939– author.
Title: When running made history / Roger Robinson.
Description: First edition. | Syracuse, New York : Syracuse University Press, [2018] |
        Series: Sports and entertainment | Includes bibliographical references and index.
Identifiers: LCCN 2018011324 (print) | LCCN 2018011601 (ebook) |
        ISBN 9780815654438 (E-book) | ISBN 9780815635789 (hardback : alk. paper) |
        ISBN 9780815611004 (pbk. : alk. paper)
Subjects: LCSH: Running—History.
Classification: LCC GV1061 (ebook) | LCC GV1061 .R54 2018 (print) |
        DDC 796.42—dc23
LC record available at https://lccn.loc.gov/2018011324

FOR KATHRINE SWITZER

"Rejoice, we conquer."

Contents

Illustrations

Acknowledgments

This book shows the influence of a lifetime of family, friends, colleagues, and mentors. I have named many of these people in the narratives, so I have not repeated them here. Most influential for the book itself are the magazine editors I have written for: Tim Chamberlain, Jonathan Beverly, Rich Benyo, and Scott Douglas most importantly, as well as Michael Jacques, Chris Gaskell, Marc Bloom, Gordon Bakoulis, Amby Burfoot, Sarah Lorge Butler, Jack Fleming, Christopher Young, and Michael Doyle.

To these I now add the judicious, supportive, and highly professional staff of Syracuse University Press, especially editor-in-chief Suzanne Guiod and series editor Steven Riess, who have provided constructive input and done much to alleviate the loneliness of the long-distance writer.

I am grateful to those who enabled me to be present at so many historic events: Hal Higdon (chapter 8); Television New Zealand (chapters 10 and 11); Horst Milde and the Berlin Marathon (chapter 12); Boston Athletic Association (chapter 13); Athletics Wellington and the Christchurch International Track Meet (chapter 16); the Safaricom Marathon, Lewa Wildlife Conservancy, and Marathon Tours (chapter 17); and *Running Times* (chapters 14–20). In addition, I am grateful to all the races that have made me their guest as runner and/or speaker. Special thanks to Jack Taunton and the Vancouver Marathon and to Dave Cundy and the Canberra Marathon, because both changed my life in good ways; and to AIMS (Association of International Marathons and Distance Races) for the privilege of being keynote speaker in Prague to honor the memory of Emil Zátopek.

The world of running writers, historians, and commentators is like a floating faculty of scholars, and these chapters contain information or ideas willingly shared by international experts, including all the editors named above, plus Budd Coates, Gary Corbitt, David Davis, Tom Derderian, Mike Fanelli, Bob Fitzgerald, Peter Gambaccini, Jim Gerweck, Hal Higdon, Creigh Kelley, David Martin, David Monti, Walt Murphy, James O'Brien, Larry Rawson, Toni Reavis, Mike Sandrock, Phil Stewart, Kathrine Switzer, Greg Vitiello, Ken Young, Alan Brookes, Dan Cumming, Rob Reid, Frank Stebner, Margaret Webb, Louise Wood, Richard Mayer, Len Johnson, Trevor Vincent, Pat Butcher, Myles Edwards, Ferdie Gilson, Hugh Jones, Peter Lovesey, Bruce Tulloh, Mel Watman, Lynn McConnell, Sam McLean, Barry Magee, and Jim Robinson.

I always learn from the friends I run with, most recently Norman Goluskin, Marty Krakower, and Dennis Moore (combined age for the four of us is 293 years, so plenty of wisdom). Special thanks to Russell Tregonning and Mark Aierstok, orthopedic surgeons of excellence; I owe it to their skill that I'm even on my feet. My replaced knees are named Russell and Mark in their honor.

Sincere thanks to those who provided the photographs (in many cases as a generous gift) that make this a pleasing book visually. Their credits are listed alongside the images.

And, for many kinds of influence or support, thanks to Joan Barker, Mike Barnow and Adrienne Wald, John Barrington, David Bedford, James Boorsinn, Ian Boyd, Margaret and Geoff Buttner, Jeremy Commons, Peter and Janette Coughlan, Jack and Char Coughlin, Rob de Castella, Debra Dicandilo, Sarah Dukler, Jon Dunham, Mel Edwards, Thom Gilligan, Jay Glassman, Kay Q. Ince, Lisa Jackson, Ross and Sally Jackson, Tim Johnston, Deena Kastor, Bill Keeler, Paul Kennedy, Bob and Lynn Kopac, Wesley Korir, Wendell and Sheila Lafave, Billy Lamb, Grant McLean, Peter Middleton, Jimmy Moran, Paul Morten and Anna Smith, Gerald and Trudy Mould, Frank Murphy, Dave Oja, Gabrielle O'Rourke, Richard Owen and Gabrielle Ruben, Carol and Richard Parker, Joe Philpott, John Pitarresi, Les and Peggy Potapczyk, Rhonda Provost, Chris Risker, Peggy Robinson, T. J. Robinson, Tom Robinson, Bill Rodgers, Allison Roe, Alan Ruben, Julia Santos Solomon, Nikki Slade Robinson, Barry Spitz, Alan Stevens, Rudy Straub, Prue Taylor, Glenda Teasdale,

Sue Tulloh, Horst von Bohlen, Jane Vitiello, Marty Wanless, Nick Willis, Richard Willis, and Edith Zuschmann.

As always, the deepest heartfelt thanks go to Kathrine Switzer, whose loving support, profound knowledge of our sport, and daily example of creative energy have been of the essence. To her, as we pass thirty years of marriage, this book of a lifetime in running is dedicated.

Introduction

When impoverished, war-shattered London struggled to put on the 1948 Olympic Games, and huge crowds chanted for the inspirational Emil Zátopek, hope was created for postwar recovery and the possibility of international friendship, despite the darkening shadow of the Cold War.

When Ethiopian Abebe Bikila ran serenely to Olympic marathon victory in 1960, barefoot on the ancient cobblestones of Rome, he heralded a new source of respect for a continent that had long been undervalued and exploited.

When 26,000 marathon runners lingered and hugged and wept for joy beneath the Brandenburg Gate in Berlin in 1990, they made a public affirmation of international goodwill that outshone the official fireworks for German reunification three nights later.

When Christchurch, New Zealand, was devastated by earthquake in February 2011, the first major public event staged in that sport-loving city was a track meet on a grass track, with Olympic medalists sharing the effort to revive the community's morale.

When an American man in 2014 won the Boston Marathon for the first time in thirty-one years, one year after bombs devastated the finish area, that race became a symbol for redemption and strength. At a memorial service, President Barack Obama used marathon running as a metaphor for all that is best in American and world society—our human qualities of courage, resilience, and generous communal spirit—bringing to world attention a connection of ideas that had long been familiar to runners.

On all these occasions, and others recorded in this book, running made history. At all of them, I had the (mostly) good fortune to be present.

During a lifetime of involvement in running, I've been witness or participant at many such moments when the sport has taken on a greater significance. This book is an eyewitness record of those moments, whether they be a single dramatic race, or several races that give access to a historical process.

The book is in part a history of running since 1948, but history written from the varied individual viewpoints of a single close witness or actual participant. The full historical record of the development and significance of the modern running movement needs to be written, but my personal involvement in so many key moments in so many different ways seemed unique, and an opportunity not to be missed. This is history from the field, not the library or website. Its interpretations are subjective, but intended to let the process of historical analysis begin with authentic eyewitness observation.

I compiled the chapters from what Charles Dickens called "the broken threads of yesterday." Although I have tried to fill some of the gaps, the subject is not my life story, but my observation. As witness and narrator, I move in age from nine to seventy-eight; I describe the races and explore their significance from my varied viewpoints as a child fan, runner, spectator, stadium public address announcer, television or radio commentator, reporting journalist, columnist, environmental advocate, author, husband (to a running icon), historian, and finally runner again, in a disconcertingly senior age group. Much of the behind-the-scenes material has, to my knowledge, never been written about before. The work on the spot of a stadium announcer, television commentator, or online journalist is something new to running literature. Writing from personal memory also enables me to introduce many of the people who will feature in the later histories: the pioneers who created modern running. I've been lucky to meet and become friends with many of them, and they pass (often very rapidly) through these pages.

One way that running makes history is by being so global. My book reflects the fact that my experience, my thinking, my friends, and the world's future, are international. England, New Zealand, and the United States have been my home at different times, and all feature in ways that I hope show my lasting gratitude. I've also run, raced, written, and/or given speeches or broadcasts about running on every continent except Antarctica (where I have no intention of going).

The eyewitness approach means that there are many omissions. Running has made history for more than two thousand years. I wasn't there to see Pheidippides run to Sparta and meet the god Pan, nor Stylianos Kyriakides win Boston for starving Greece in 1946, nor Roger Bannister break four minutes for the mile. I wasn't in Munich when the Olympic Games were desecrated by terrorists, I didn't run the first New York City Marathon and race through the city's streets in 1976, nor did I see Joan Benoit Samuelson win the first women's Olympic marathon. As a historian, I've researched and narrated all those events, but I wasn't there.

I wanted to show the astonishing world phenomenon of running as it was, and is, from ground level. I wanted to capture how it has felt to see my eccentric little minority sport grow into a booming world movement, and to see road running acquire a mass appeal unknown to the track and cross-country that were the dominant forms of running for the first half of my life. I wanted to capture how I've watched modern running emerge as a movement, a community, a culture, an industry, and an economic generator. Because I care so much, and because I'm proud of what my sport has become, I can't or won't be dryly objective when I describe how running takes a leadership role in things that have transformed society in my lifetime, including giving opportunity and recognition to women, older people, new immigrants, and minorities of all kinds; helping the environment; and beneficently taking over our biggest cities, stopping traffic, reducing crime, and spreading goodwill. I'm writing the first draft of this introduction in New York City two days before the marathon; that's how immediate the subject is to me.

It's an exciting and unprecedented subject. Today's elite packs and the huge fields behind them make modern road racing one of the greatest sports ever conceived. And it is more than a sport. There's no precedent for the surging mass of purposeful runners pouring over the Verrazano-Narrows Bridge, or up the Champs-Élysées, or past the Coliseum, Tower Bridge, Brandenburg Gate, or many similar iconic cityscapes in our big races. Most readers of this book will know the unforgettable experience of being part of such gatherings. I've often described them as "the biggest peaceful participant activity in human history." Each word there is chosen carefully. Perhaps some religious pilgrimages or political demonstrations have been bigger, but I don't think they count as being "participant" in the same way.

So, this book is not a wire-to-wire history of the running movement, although I've done a lot of research and have woven in a good deal of that momentous story, including some detailed timelines; enough perhaps to provide a useful starting point for other work. Mainly the chapters try to give insights into the ways running has connected with, contributed to, or even shaped the world's recent history. That seems an important subject, as well as undiscovered literary territory.

It's a personal book, and I should end on a personal note. As a little boy, I used to crawl through the hedge at the University of London athletic track at Motspur Park, near London, to watch the runners. Even then, I was fascinated by the 3 mi., the longest race, twelve laps around the black crushed cinders of the track. (At about age nine, I ran the full twelve laps one Sunday morning when the track was open to the public, and according to my mother spent the rest of the day in bed. The same thing still sometimes happens.) I loved the extended drama of a long race. I loved the way it tested judgment as well as mere speed. I loved the sense that every runner had succeeded if only he finished, even if he finished last, when we clapped for him the loudest. And I loved the feeling that somehow it had a significance beyond the result of who won and who lost.

I still do.

WHEN RUNNING MADE HISTORY

I

July 30, 1948, Olympic Games, London

Postwar

London 1948 was a gray world for a small boy. There was little money, sparse entertainments, few cars, not even much food. Legal rations allowed one egg a week, a scrap of fresh meat, no chocolate or ice cream for us kids. I still remember my first banana. My mother collected coal from the yard at the train station in my young brother's pram (baby carriage). Most evenings the lights and heat went off with power cuts. The classrooms where I started school were bleak prefabs, and across the school playing field ran the long, grassed ridge of the air-raid shelter. In my first year, age five, the whole school huddled down there after the sirens howled. All around our suburb were overgrown spaces, called bombsites, where falling bombs had destroyed houses. The tumbled bricks and high weeds made good places for boys to play.

There was not much color in our lives. We yearned for heroes. The cheap "Saturday morning pictures" cinema showed cowboy serials, and we played cowboys or war on the bombsites. We admired local footballers (soccer players) on the muddy recreation ground, and sometimes I crawled through the hedge at the nearby cinder running track, called Motspur Park, to watch the athletes of London University train and race. I idolized the sprinter McDonald Bailey and the tall 440/880 yd. runner Arthur Wint, both West Indians, who won every race they ran. Wint strode with such tall elegance and majesty; he looked unbeatable. Once I pilfered my mother's tape measure to check his giant stride by the spike-marks he left in the cinders. It was nine feet.

1. Lapping most of the field, Emil Zátopek wins his first gold medal in 1948. Associated Press.

I still have both signatures, Wint and McDonald Bailey, in a now-faded brown-and-gold autograph book.

I was not tall and majestic like Wint. I was for sure no sprinter like Bailey. I came dead last in every race at school, where there was nothing longer than 100 yd. The events I most enjoyed watching were the steeplechase, when all the little boys rushed over to cluster around the

2. Autograph of Olympic gold medalist Arthur Wint, 1948.

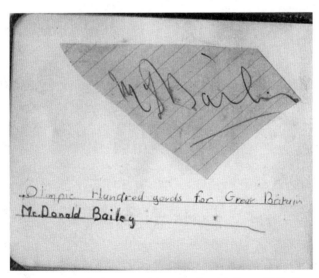

3. Autograph of Olympic 100 m finalist McDonald Bailey, 1948.

water-jump, whooping with glee whenever a runner splashily stumbled. We were ecstatic if one fell in. And, unlike my pals, I liked the 3 mi., with its long-developing drama.

That summer of 1948 I heard there was going to be something called the Olympic Games in London. It didn't mean much to me. There had been no Olympics since 1936, well before I was born. The Games were going to be at Wembley, somewhere across London, a long journey by bus and underground through sprawling bomb-scarred suburbs. My family had no money to buy tickets. I knew that some schools near Wembley were dormitories for the visiting athletes, who would be transported to their events by army lorries. But we were too far away.

Then, just before the Games, a neighbor from along Portland Avenue, Mr. Lutterloch, came around one day (we had no phone) to ask if I would like to go with him to the first day of track and field. He and his wife had no children, and sometimes he took me to sports events, usually swimming championships between insurance companies and banks. He worked for a shipping insurance company that never seemed to have much of a team. I suppose he missed having a son of his own. His wife wore heavy makeup and smoked. I remember him as a kind, soft-spoken man. I suppose there was a story, which I was far too young to understand.

So, on a hot day, Friday, July 30, 1948, I traveled across London with Mr. Lutterloch to this famous place called Wembley. I knew about it as the most important football stadium. I'd sat intent by the wireless when Manchester United beat Blackpool in that year's Football Association Cup Final at Wembley. I had little idea what it looked like. The Olympic Games had been opened the previous day by King George, but we had no television. No one I knew had a television. What excited me as we rode the bus and tube to Wembley was that I was going to see McDonald Bailey and Arthur Wint. Mr. Lutterloch said there would be a race called 10,000 m, which he said was even longer than 3 mi.

I'd never been in a place that huge. It held 100,000 people. Mr. Lutterloch had seats, but most of the crowd were standing. The infield was bright green, and the track black. I know now that it was made of crushed cinders from British fireplaces, and that the road to the stadium was built by Germans who had been prisoners of war, working with shovels and wheelbarrows. At the time, I was conscious only of the high terraces, the gleaming green grass of the infield, and the dark mass of the crowd. I'd never seen so many people. My brother told me later that we had all gone to Buckingham Palace for the VE Day (Victory in Europe) celebration in 1945, but I have no recollection of it.

That day at Wembley, we saw various heats, the high jump, and (a novelty for me) the women's discus. Most important, McDonald Bailey and Arthur Wint qualified for their finals.

I was eager to see the 10,000 m. Mr. Lutterloch told me the best long-distance runners all came from Finland, especially one called Heino, who was the fastest in the world. So, it seemed right that when the race began, Heino and another Finn took the lead, both wearing white and blue. They looked supremely in control, running almost in step, round and round. Twenty-five laps would seem endless to most children, but I was fascinated. The two Finns ran so calmly, with more than twenty runners straggling behind them. I cheered of course for the British runners, Jim Peters and Stan Cox.

After nine laps, the race suddenly changed. A man in red with white shorts moved up through the line of runners and then into the lead. He was a strangely awkward runner who seemed to be forcing himself along, not upright and graceful like the clockwork Finns, but scowling and writhing. Quickly, the immaculate Heino slid smoothly back to the front, and it seemed the brief challenge from the presumptuous nobody was over.

But then he astonished us again. Back to the front he came, still looking tortured. They were almost at halfway now, and this time he stayed in front and, incredibly, began breaking away. A French runner clung for a while, but soon he was twenty, thirty yards clear. It was amazing. The crowd was yelling louder than I had ever heard at football games.

Who was he? Mr. Lutterloch looked at his program.

"He's Zátopek," he said.

That was the first time I heard a name that became an important part of my consciousness for the rest of my life.

Gasping and thrashing, Zátopek pushed on, lap after lap, going farther and farther ahead. He was an image of strenuous effort, forcing himself to the very edge of the will. His will held the strain, but the other runners were broken in will and spirit. Mr. Lutterloch nudged me and pointed. Heino was walking off the track, his head hanging down.

The crowd began to chant the name of this new king of running.

"Zá-to-pek! Zá-to-pek! Zá-to-pek!"

I joined in with my squeaky little boy's voice.

"Zá-to-pek! Zá-to-pek! Zá-to-pek!"

This was fun.

Soon Zátopek was half a lap in front. Peters and Cox were well behind, in about seventh and eighth places. I was not going to see a British victory today. It was hard to know what I was seeing. Sports heroes in the 1940s were supposed to be well groomed and elegant. The great English cricketer and footballer Denis Compton (whose autograph also is in my book) appeared on posters on every train platform with his glossy black hair advertising a hair oil called Brylcreem. Zátopek didn't have much hair, and it certainly wasn't glossy. Nothing about him was groomed and elegant. Yet he was winning. The crowd knew we were watching a historic moment. We all saw the heroic greatness of it.

"Zá-to-pek! Zá-to-pek!"

He was lapping the back of the field now, and as he passed, he seemed to say something encouraging to most of them. His face was still grimacing, and his upper body pitched and rolled, but his legs! His legs were magical. His knees lifted high but turned over fast, like the pistons of the steam locomotives that rushed by on the railroad at the back of our house.

"Zá-to-pek! Zá-to-pek!"

The chant followed him round and round. Then the bell rang, and there were cries of anger and disbelief from the crowd. Officials had rung the bell a lap early. (Looking back, they were used to the twenty-four laps of the 6 mi. race, not the twenty-five laps of 10,000 m, and they lacked experience so soon after the war.) But Zátopek never faltered.

"Zá-to-pek! Zá-to-pek!"

Almost at the finish, as he was lapping a struggling runner in the blue of France, he patted him on the shoulder and smiled encouragingly. The crowd roared with delight. This was a nice man, a sportsman, not some impersonal machine. We cheered his last lap, every stride.

Emil Zátopek won that 1948 10,000 m in an Olympic record 29:59.6. He finished 47.8 seconds ahead of Alain Mimoun, another name we would come to know better. For me, it was the moment I discovered one of my few lifetime heroes. It was the moment I discovered something I wanted to do, and do well. I didn't want to be a soldier in another war—that didn't interest me. I didn't want to play football—I was too slightly built. Zátopek showed me running.

Looking back now from another century, another world, that race was a moment of revelation and transformation of things more important than a boy's aspiration, things I only understood years later. For the sport of running, it meant that no important distance race would ever be won again without intense, year-round training, and without the wholehearted commitment that Zátopek, in those still-amateur days, inspired runners all over the world to adopt. The old fussing about relaxation, style, gentlemanly demeanor, no running in winter, fear of "going stale," the nonsensical beliefs that training consists of giving things up and that rubdowns are more helpful than practice—all those were scattered among the cinders that Zátopek's spikes flung behind him.

Zátopek was one of the great pioneers. He stands historically with Alf Shrubb, Clarence DeMar, Paavo Nurmi, Woldemar Gerschler, and Arthur Lydiard, who all showed that the human body can benefit from a greater quantity and severity of training than was previously believed possible. Zátopek was also a good hero because he gave hope to runners like me, who had little natural talent or speed, showing us that sheer hard work can make you a better runner and that all the hard work can still be fun. Zátopek won that Olympic gold medal in London, and the silver in the rain-soaked 5,000 m, and four years later his legendary treble of gold medals at Helsinki, because he worked harder than any other runner, and because he was so courageous, so fiercely determined, so irrepressibly zestful, and so tactically inventive.

That race made history, beyond the history of running. Zátopek won it on the first day of the first Olympics after the world entered the Cold War era. He won it only four weeks after the Soviets imposed the blockade of Berlin. The Communist Iron Curtain had come down across Europe, and the world was again near the edge of war. Zátopek was wearing the red of a Communist nation, yet on the last lap of the race, when he was lapping Abdullah Ben Said of France (in fact a North African), Zátopek gave him that friendly pat on the shoulder and an encouraging smile. That gesture supplanted, or subverted, all political interpretations of sport. It disproved George Orwell's idea (from his 1945 essay "The Sporting Spirit") that sport is merely substitute war. It asserted in full view of a crowded stadium that the wartime era of dehumanizing the opposition was over.

"Great is the victory," Zátopek said later, "but the friendship of all is greater."

I didn't know all this as I cheered him at Wembley. I was a boy born in 1939. The only world I knew was the violence of war and the misery of its aftermath, even in victory. Our movie heroes were cowboys who used guns to win. But Zátopek showed that it's possible to combine victory with friendship—to win by scowling at yourself and smiling at your rivals.

To appreciate Zátopek the man, it's significant that the most famous photograph shows him not in a race but kissing his wife. It's significant that the most famous story about him is how he gave away one of his Olympic gold medals to a great runner who never won one, Ron Clarke of Australia. It's significant that he is revered now as a hero in the Czech Republic not only as a famous runner but because he was willing to use his fame, at great cost to himself, to protest the 1968 Soviet occupation of his country.

Although many runners since 1948 and 1952 have run faster than he did, it is Emil Zátopek who lives on as the most admired and inspirational runner the world has ever known. For me as a mature runner, twenty years after him, his best times served as markers. Running faster than Zátopek's best, as I finally did, felt almost like winning a gold medal.

For me as a boy, Zátopek and the London Olympic Games brought color, drama, and heroism into a gray world. In a context of deprivation, the athletes, organizers, and fans were courageously building toward a new world, one that was taking initiatives and creating opportunities in ways they didn't always understand at the time. One way was when a Dutch woman in a white blouse and orange shorts showed that a woman and mother could be an Olympic superstar. Fanny Blankers-Koen won gold medals in the 100 m, 200 m, 80 m hurdles, and 4 x 100 m relay. The rules inexplicably prohibited entering more than three individual events, a loss for Blankers-Koen, who was also world record-holder in high jump and long jump.

Another positive initiative was that a record fifty-nine nations took part in the London Olympic Games, and others, such as the USSR, were invited but chose not to attend. Only Germany and Japan were excluded, but they were under Allied occupation, and teams from there would hardly have been practicable given the devastation and deprivation in those nations. But their allies, who had been hostile to Great Britain in the war, such as Austria, Hungary, and Italy, were invited and welcomed. Such inclusiveness might fairly be called idealistic.

If I'd known any of that when I was nine, it wouldn't have seemed wrong. Walking to school in 1944, we used to pass a wired-off field where Italian prisoners of war (or perhaps ex-prisoners at that date) waved to us every day. Perhaps they missed their own kids. We always waved back. The Games were a communal achievement for postwar England and poor, shattered London. Cobbled together on a shoestring budget at two years' notice, they were the first international sports festival for a traumatized world. After six years of the destructive worst that humanity could devise, here was a united effort by humanity to construct the best. Here were excellence, achievement, friendship, and acts of imaginative creation (like Zátopek's). Here was the biggest crowd I had ever been part of, enthusiastically cheering for a great athlete from a foreign, potentially hostile nation and political system. There was patriotism, of course. Like every boy, I was patriotic. The first modern Olympic Games were created to foster nationalistic pride, something some of us now regret. But the focus of the London Games was on simple sport, not propaganda. The London Olympics did a lot to reclaim the Olympics from the Nazi propaganda of Berlin in 1936.

4. Autographs of Emil and Dana Zátopek,
c. 1984.

Sometimes sport gets dragged into the world's problems, as happened in 1936. Sometimes it can help the world rise above those problems, as happened in 1948. As we shuffled amid that great crowd out of Wembley Stadium, I knew little of the meanings that day would acquire in the context of history. I only knew I had a new hero. Forty years later, I got his autograph, too.

2

October 13, 1954, White City, London

Cold War

Prologue: First Four Minutes

Confession: I was not at Oxford on May 6, 1954. Chris Brasher used to say that he had met at least three thousand people who claimed, and probably believed, that they were among the two or three hundred who were present at the Iffley Road track the night Roger Bannister broke four minutes for a mile. But I was busy with schoolwork sixty miles away, and I was not yet delusional. We still had no television. The nearest I came to that epoch-making moment was two weeks later when my parents gave me a tabby kitten for my fifteenth birthday, and I named him Bannister. When I told Sir Roger thirty years later that I named a cat after him, he didn't seem nearly as impressed as I thought he should be.

I did get close to the mile story one evening in 1953 or early 1954, when I witnessed Bannister run a fast three quarters of a mile at the Motspur Park track. There were no crowds, no press attention. Bannister wanted it under the radar. But a fourteen-year-old local boy was watching.

By now I was a runner. As a Surrey County scholar at King's College School, Wimbledon, I had discovered cross-country on Wimbledon Common. I loved it. I loved the challenge of the distance and the weather and the terrain. There are steep hills and sharp gullies on the Common, as well as long, soggy tracks across what was then open space, since most mature trees had gone for wartime firewood. I also loved the mix of individual and team competition that cross-country provides. A modest talent, I was soon in the grip of the addictive allure of running: if

5. Chris Chataway beats Vladimir Kuts, 1954, bringing light to a dark world. PA Images/Alamy Stock Photo.

you work, you improve. And I made friendships that have survived more than sixty years.

We organized our own running program, with no teacher oversight. We read articles and planned our own training, the elected club captain picked our teams, we designed and ordered our uniforms, and the secretary corresponded with other schools to plan our racing schedule. The American system of paid coaches, rosters, walk-ons, and the possibility that an entire sport can be "cut" has always puzzled me. One race we arranged was against the adult runners of Thames Hare and Hounds, neighbors who also ran on Wimbledon Common. Their headquarters in those days were in an upper room above a Dickensian-era pub, with Victorian tin "hip baths" for postrun washing. Thames is the world's oldest adult running organization, founded in 1868, and that first race against

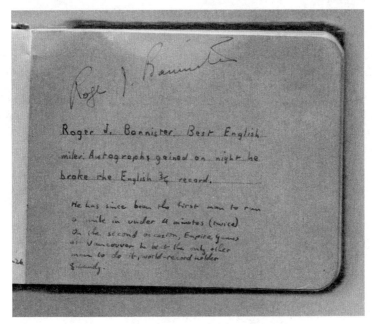

6. Autograph of Roger Bannister, 1954.

them introduced me to a club I have belonged to for fifty years, and to the long, colorful history of running, which has enthralled me ever since.

So, at age fourteen, as I leaned on the metal rail at Motspur Park and watched Bannister run his three laps at a 60-second average, I knew enough to understand that I was witnessing an important stepping stone to the first sub-four-minute mile. I secured his autograph after the run, and I added a teenage note about its significance. You might glimpse a future sports historian in that annotation.

Later that year, I did see major history made through running. I was fifteen.

October 13, 1954: It was billed modestly as "London versus Moscow." In those days, we sometimes had these track meets described officially as inter-city (e.g., "London versus Paris"), probably because it avoided the win-or-lose pressure of a full international contest. This one was portentous with national political significance. Red-scare McCarthyism was at its frenzied height in America, and the Iron Curtain (a term that Winston Churchill borrowed from H. G. Wells) divided Europe. Conscripted British men only three years older than me had fought Communists in Korea and were still fighting them in Malaya, or they were based in Germany to face the Soviet threat. With compulsory national service still in place, some such military action was likely to be my fate when I turned eighteen. Those were tense times when you lived close to the Iron Curtain.

This track meet was a Cold War face-off: the first time that runners from the Communist bloc had been seen in Britain, a public testing of rival values and social systems. The equivalent for America came ten years later with the USA versus USSR meet in Los Angeles on July 24, 1964, with the highlight of eighteen-year-old Gerry Lindgren's win in the 10,000 m. The London–Moscow match carried extra tension because the Eastern Bloc athletes had been so dominant six weeks earlier in the European Championships in Bern, winning twenty-seven gold medals. Then, on October 5, in a supposed friendly football match between English and Russian teams, the London club Arsenal was humiliated five goals to nil in Moscow by Moscow Dynamo. The Dynamo team's earlier tour of Britain had created such fervid ill will that it prompted George Orwell to write his derogatory essay about international sport, "The Sporting Spirit" (first published in the *Tribune* in 1945, accessible now in his 1971 *Collected Essays*).

Western culture, and certainly the West's dominance in sports, seemed under threat from the USSR's remorseless winning machine. A few weeks later, on December 12, 1954, all of Britain was horrified by the live television dramatization of Orwell's *Nineteen Eighty-Four*, with its bleak vision of a future under totalitarian Communism. Like thousands of anxious people, I bought the Penguin paperback of the novel on Monday morning.

In that fraught context, 45,000 people packed the White City, there was huge newspaper and newsreel coverage, and an unprecedented live audience of twelve million watched on that new but compelling thing called television. Sports events in those postwar years touched our impoverished, battered, hardworking society more deeply than today's mega-scale, packaged entertainment. They brought color, drama, and communal unison into lives that were constrained and surroundings that were dirty and bleak. They did that so well (better than the movies or the circus) because, as Arthur Conan Doyle (1899, 1922) wrote in a story about boxing, "the love of sport is one of the great agencies which make for the happiness of our people. It lies very deeply in the springs of our nature." Footracing especially lies deep in our nature; it is pure human movement and the essence of human contest.

To those of us in that patriotic crowd on October 13, 1954, the 5,000 m that ended the evening seemed like an extra chapter added to the World War II blitz. I'm not exaggerating. This sporting night had turned into another desperate battle for British survival against ruthless odds. It was less than ten years since Hitler's flying bombs were falling on London (and very nearly on me). You still passed frequent bombsites alongside the road to the White City. There were rumors that Churchill had been ready to rearm the German army in 1945 against the new enemy from the East. In 1954 London, war was a daily possibility.

That night we saw a track and field version of the brutal power we would face. The "Moscow" team at White City included nine world record holders from all over the Soviet Union, and they won almost every event. Many nominally served in the Soviet military. Their dominance in the field events was as embarrassing as Arsenal's five-goal thrashing in Moscow. The last chance of redemption, at the end of the evening, was the 5,000 m.

We all knew that race was going to be a duel between the remorseless, crushing might of Vladimir Kuts and the debonair, courageous élan of Chris Chataway. Forgive me if that sounds like a boy's heroic sports story—I was a boy, and I was watching a heroic sports story. The runners perfectly fit those images. Kuts was stocky, powerful, military, and sternly middle-aged in appearance; Chataway was boyishly handsome, dressed in all white with flying red hair. The whole crowd saw the race in those archetypal terms: our dashing hero against the scowling Cold War warrior.

In the darkness of that chill October night, wartime searchlight beams mounted in the high stands sought to follow the two frontrunners. As they ran, they flickered in and out of the shadowy, wavering pool of light. This was well before modern floodlights became standard, at a time when we were enduring frequent power cuts in London. I still remember the night, well after the war, when the streetlamps first came back on. We were used to inadequate light.

In the European Championships six weeks earlier, Kuts had raced equally relentlessly, and his repeated surges broke the field and the championship record, with Chataway twelve seconds back, outsprinting Zátopek for second place. In London, Chataway's tactics were simple. He had no choice. Stick to Kuts, whatever happens. Just hang on.

It was hard for us to believe that he could do it. Kuts went straight to the front, barrel chested, pugnacious, powerful, looking more like a boxer than a distance runner, but with a quick, pulsing, urgent stride. After four laps, only Chataway was there with him.

Kuts surged. Chataway stuck by him. Kuts surged, and surged again, lap after lap, elbows pumping. Each time, he gained a yard or two, and each time Chataway clawed it back. In the flickering floodlights, Chataway looked like Kuts's pale shadow.

Sometimes the two runners escaped from the unreliable moving pool of light into complete blackness. Then we could only catch glimpses of Chataway enduring smash after smash from the series of mechanical attacks by Kuts. It was like a grinding tank against a knight on horseback.

Still, Chataway stuck. Approaching the bell, the Soviet thrashed himself to one more assault, and it looked all over. A gap. Eight yards. Three strides. We watched in anxious despair. But somehow, one more time, Chataway was closing the gap. On the back straight he was there again, and they were racing for their lives, Chataway still on Kuts's heels, clinging by sheer will. Was that how it would finish? It looked inevitable.

"This man seems unbeatable," cried the television commentator as Kuts powered around the final bend (you can watch footage of the last lap on YouTube).

Chataway yet clung, matching Kuts's stride. Both seemed at top speed. After the bend, slowly, unbelievably, Chataway was drawing almost level—almost. And then! From some depth, miraculously, thrillingly, as we jumped and screamed and waved our arms in ecstatic disbelief, he was moving ahead, finding a brief, perfectly timed flourish of a sprint that won him the race by half a second, and the world record (13:51.6) by five seconds.

After the tape, as Chataway staggered to a halt in the shimmering pool of the searchlight, Roger Bannister himself appeared out of the darkness, caught his friend in his arms, and kissed him—in England, in 1954! That's how emotional it was.

That race is still regarded by now-elderly track fans in Britain as the most compelling ever run on a British track, including Mo Farah's Olympic and World Championship victories in 2012 and 2017. Bannister's subfour is more legendary, but that was a meticulously scripted and paced time trial, memorable only once the time was announced. Chataway versus Kuts was a race, pure and simple; a classic duel.

Chataway, who died in 2015 at age eighty-two (forty years after Kuts), was an appropriate British hero for that moment in history. Attractive and charming, he seemed to run for the sheer sporting fun of it, yet possessed a daring competitiveness that played a key role in some of the mid-twentieth century's most historic races.

Chataway was only twenty-one and still an Oxford University student when he made the Olympic 5,000 m final in Helsinki in 1952 and came close to upsetting Emil Zátopek and Alain Mimoun. He led the early laps, attacked adventurously with two hundred meters to go, and was still in front around the final bend, until he tied up, stumbled against the curb, and fell. He got up and finished fifth.

In his peak year—the year of miracles, 1954—he contributed to two epoch-making, 1 mi. world records. On May 6, he led with perfect pace the crucial third lap that enabled Bannister to be the first to break 4:00. Then, the next month, in Turku, Finland, he pursued John Landy so ardently and stubbornly that the front-running Australian was forced to lift the pace on his last lap, gaining new world records at 1,500 m and 1 mi., and beating Bannister's newly historic time by 1.4 seconds.

"When they rang the bell, Chataway was still there," was Landy's understated Aussie explanation for his world record time.

Chataway took his place as a hero of history in his own right later in that golden year. In August, at the British Empire and Commonwealth

Games in Vancouver, he commandingly won the 3 mi. gold medal. That race would be remembered as historic if it had not been overshadowed by Bannister's momentous defeat of Landy in the 1 mi., both sub-four, and less than one hour later by the horrendous sight of the marathon world record holder, Jim Peters, reeling and collapsing in heat-exhausted delirium. Later that month, in the European Championships 5,000 m in Bern, Chataway again went close to greatness, chasing Kuts and beating Zátopek.

Then came October 13, 1954, the night Chataway dashed past the Soviet iron man in that unforgettable Cold War combat.

Half a century later, I urged Chataway, now Sir Christopher and a former government cabinet member, to write his own account of that race. We'd been talking at dinner about whether writing about running could aspire to be literature, and his coach Franz Stampfl's belief that to run a great race was as much an act of artistic creation as to paint the Mona Lisa. For a whole generation of teenagers like me, I told Chris, his victory over Kuts was as indelible as art and was hugely influential, not only on those of us who became runners.

"For those who were there at White City, or watched it live on TV," I exhorted him, warming to the theme, "it was epic! An epic moment in history—epic in the true sense, meaning that one individual's heroism and achievement epitomized and inspired the whole nation!"

But Chataway was a man of genuine modesty, who always preferred to turn a compliment into a joke.

"No wonder it had such a big television audience, because there was only one channel in those days, so they had no choice," he said, with his disarming smile.

We were enjoying an overnight stop during a two-day relay along the length of the River Thames, a running memorial by the Thames Hare and Hounds and Ranelagh Harriers clubs for Chris Brasher, the other pacer in Bannister's historic mile, who had recently died. (The baton was a small flask of Brasher's favorite whiskey.) Passing through Oxford, with Chataway carrying the single malt, the relay diverted from the river to cover four laps of Oxford University's Iffley Road track, now renamed the Roger Bannister Athletic Track. I was appointed to represent Cambridge,

Brasher's university and mine, in the small group that accompanied Chat-away on that resonant section of the commemoration. Bannister was wait-ing at a riverside pub to buy the beers.

All was geniality and nostalgia as we jogged the laps, four elderly run-ning friends pretending to be happy that we could still run a mile. But as we came into the finishing straight on the fourth lap, Chataway said, almost under his breath and with a quiet chuckle, "This time, I'll win."

That trivial moment was true to the man. Kindly, good humored, often joking about his light twenty-five-miles-per-week training and his relish for fine wine, always delightful company, and genuinely charming and generous, Chataway also had a deep resolute desire to achieve.

"He had lots of persistence, very determined," was the first thing Cha-taway's Oxford and Great Britain teammate, Ian Boyd, said when I called him with the news of the death of his old friend. The three of us once had dinner together when Chataway's business brought him to Wellington, New Zealand, where Ian and I both lived. Persistence and determination are not the first things you expect to hear about the smiling, easygoing, red-haired hero, but they were the essence of Chataway.

3

September 2, 1960,
Olympic Stadium, Rome

New Zealand's Finest Hour

In the afternoon of September 2, 1960, Peter Snell and Murray Halberg won Olympic gold medals for 800 m and 5,000 m within forty minutes. For New Zealand Olympic history, this was the finest hour. Its impact went beyond the Olympic stadium. It helped shape New Zealand's sense of identity as an independent nation. Although the British anthem was still played, Snell and Halberg wore the defiant all black of New Zealand. Their loyalty was to their Auckland coach, Arthur Lydiard, not the Queen of England.

There was a bigger historical picture, of course. This was at the height of the era when colonies and protectorates were gaining independence. Kenya held its first open elections in 1957 and became independent in 1963. Morocco had emerged from French and Spanish control in 1956. War was raging in Algeria, which became independent from France two years after the Rome Olympics. Hungary had risen unsuccessfully against Russian imperial power in 1956, and Czechoslovakia would make the same attempt in 1968, with the support of Emil Zátopek. The process was less fraught for former colonies where settlers were in the majority, like Australia, Canada, and New Zealand, but their identities also were undergoing fundamental change. Canada symbolically adopted its maple leaf flag in 1965. Sport was playing a major role for New Zealand in this transition, as it still does. My modest proposal is that no single event did more than this one hour in Rome to make New Zealanders join the global postcolonial process of thinking of themselves as belonging to a successful independent nation.

The two gold medalists on September 2 have shared their memories: Snell in *No Bugles, No Drums* (1965) and *Peter Snell: From Olympian to Scientist* (2007), and Halberg in *A Clean Pair of Heels* (1963; all coauthored by Garth Gilmour). My recollections of the finest hour come from the sidelines. They are the impressions of a student from England, an enthusiastic but undistinguished distance runner who had scraped together enough lira to get himself into the cheapest seats of the Stadio Olimpico in Rome that September afternoon. This is an eyewitness account, though written from long-range memory. I haven't tried to be wise after the event. I had no idea in 1960 that eight years later I would become a New Zealander. Before that day I had never heard of Arthur Lydiard. The only document I consulted for these recollections was my copy of the day's program. Each day had a different-colored cover; orange for day 3. I deciphered some of the results and odd notes that I scribbled on it at the time. I did no other research. Authenticity is guaranteed, but not accuracy.

Olympics Day 3

2:30

Hotter than ever. The drink sellers did well, prowling the sun-blasted terraces with their call of "Coca-Cola! Gelati! Coca-Cola!" They sang it as they climbed the stadium steps, mellifluously as an operatic love aria. "Gelah-tiii! Gelah-tiii!" We were uncomfortably close to the block-seating of the German youth group, who were even noisier after Armin Hary's win yesterday. The leader was already rehearsing them in their chants, ready for today's victories. He called out, "Ticka-tacka, ticka-tacka," and they all responded in unison, "Ha-Ha-Ha!" "Ticka-tacka, ticka-tacka! Ha-Ha-Ha!" It resounded. It had been good to see their boy scout pleasure at Hary's success, especially from my place near the 100 m start, with a close view of Hary's explosive speed from the blocks. But I wished they would take a little interest in the events without a German.

3:00

Women's 100 m semifinals. A tall African American, Wilma Rudolph, won the first by 0.3 seconds, and it was no surprise to hear she had equaled the world record. Commanding and graceful, she was the finest-looking woman athlete I had ever seen.

3:20

Men's 200 m quarterfinals. We got a dramatic view from our high seats as they rounded the bend. Peter Radford boosted British morale. (He later became a versatile scholar and author of one of the great works of running history, *The Celebrated Captain Barclay.*) The last heat had Livio Berruti, who brought the Italians in the crowd exuberantly to their feet as he won in style with his seductive sunglasses and Latin fluidity. The drink sellers were instantly singing out "Coca-Cola Berruti! Gelati Berruti!" When he won the gold medal later in the week, the crowd set fire to newspapers and sent them blazing to drift up into the late-evening dusk, one of the most memorable sights I've seen at a running track.

4:00

Glenn Davis retained his title in the 400 m hurdles, not an event I much relate to, and the Americans swept the medals. We got another comedic interlude as the Italian band, with their pompous little conductor, played yet again their unique quickstep pom-ti-ti-pom rendering of "The Star-Spangled Banner."

4:20

Wilma Rudolph was sublime in the final. How often has an Olympic 100 m been won by 0.3 seconds?

4:30

The 20 km road walk set off, the field of nearly forty waggling out through the tunnel.

4:40

The women's shot began right under our section of the stands. The dominant figures were the Russian world record holder, Tamara Press, who was built like a bear, and a bespectacled African American called Mrs. Earlene Brown, whose histrionic and high-decibel squeaky grunt made her a great favorite with our section of the crowd. She was honored always as "Mrs." One of the finalists was relatively lean among the giantesses; her name was Sloper and she wore all black.

4:45

At last, the real action began for me with the distance running, the 800 m. The Germans had two in the final, so the orchestrated frenzy behind me was mounting, and the chants of "Mat-u-schew-ski" and "Ticka-tacka, ticka-tacka, Schmidt-Schmidt-Schmidt!" reverberated around the stadium.

 The British runners had all been eliminated, so I fixed my loyalty to the West Indian George Kerr. I had seen him run in England and admired his zestful energy. He had won his semifinal the previous day in an Olympic record of 1:47.1. The world record holder, Roger Moens, had also run faster than the old Olympic best, but he had cruised behind a big novice from New Zealand, Snell. They lined up Matuschewski, Moens, the Swiss Waegli, Kerr, Schmidt, and Snell—only six.

 Waegli led the first lap at a pace fast enough to drop Matuschewski, but the rest held close together. Even with the Germans chanting "Schmidt! Schmidt! Schmidt! Schmidt!" I could hear the spikes rasping in the cinders as they came around the bend just below me for the first time. Into the second lap, Waegli still led, Moens poised, Kerr watched

Moens, and Snell, prominently broad-chested and looking cumbersome, was on the pole line behind.

Then, with perfect judgment just before the bend, Moens moved to Waegli's shoulder, with Schmidt tracking Moens. I watched in sheer frustration as Kerr, clawing to get past, went wider and wider as they fanned around the top of the bend and past where I was standing, sweeping into the straight. They seemed like a swooping wing, Waegli, Moens, Schmidt, and Kerr, and Snell wedged at the back, looking heavy (I thought as I dismissed him). Moens knew Kerr's sprint was the danger and began to steer over to the right. Kerr at last got past Waegli and Schmidt, but he had given away too much on the bend. Moens, edging outward, had it won—the expected outcome.

Suddenly, a gap opened between the tiring Waegli and Schmidt, and the big man in black instantly pounded through it. Even from behind and fifty meters away, it looked as if he had strayed out of the two hundred meters, for he was moving with a power and pace totally different from the others. Pulsating like a locomotive through the gap, he charged

7. Peter Snell and Roger Moens at the finish line of the Olympic 800 m, 1960.

inside Kerr, and in a last-second flurry I saw Moens, now in lane three or four, fling a glance of utter despair to his left as they dived for the tape. They were several yards apart across the track, yet inseparable in the only dimension that mattered.

The photos reveal it all. The winner, youthful, burly, dressed all in black, thrusting forward to the tape; the other, white, lean, frail, older, with receding hair and a face of anguish from a Flemish painting. From where I stood it was impossible to split them. But Moens's hunched misery as they walked away said it all. The unknown Snell had won.

5:10

There was barely time to get up to date on the shot put. Press had a yawning lead, and Mrs. Brown the American and Sloper the long-haired New Zealander in black were next, as the top six went into the final three rounds.

Finally, the event I had come to Rome most of all to see, the 5,000 m, was on the track. It would not be quite the race I had hoped, as my friend Bruce Tulloh and the two other British runners, Gordon Pirie and Frank Salvat, were out. Pirie's demise in the heats on the first day was the shock of the games so far.

There were three Germans in the twelve-man final: "Jan-ke!" "Flosbach!" and "Ticka-tacka, ticka-tacka, Gro-dot-ski!" as my neighbors' pre-race chants informed me. The Australians Power and Thomas and the New Zealander Halberg had all done well at the Empire Games in 1958, though I was hazy about details. I'd seen Zimny the sturdy Pole and Bernard the sallow Frenchman race at White City. Conti of Italy, Artynjuk of USSR, and Nyandika of Kenya were unknown to me. I hoped the tall Hungarian Iharos would do well. I'd seen him set a 2 mi. world record in London, and I felt strongly about the exclusion of his equally great but exiled countryman Tabori, who had taken asylum in America and so was without a nation. The Olympics should not be about passports.

I confess that I can't remember who led the first nine and a half laps. Power, Thomas, and Bernard were up there, probably. The pack was whittled down a little. Iharos was dropped quite early, I think. Nyandika hung on. He would finish sixth, one place better and a half minute faster than he did in the 1956 Olympics. We should remember that Maiyoro Nyandika was the precursive world-class East African athlete, before Abebe Bikila or Kipchoge Keino. I'm pleased that I saw him run: another bit of history.

There was a lot of shuffling as the laps went down but no real initiatives. As they moved into the last mile, they seemed to settle, waiting for the bell. All this is blurred for me by time. What ensued remains as vivid as if it happened yesterday.

5:20

In my copy of the program (p. 30), beneath the list of names for the 5,000 m, I wrote "opened up lead of 20 yards at 3 laps to go." Only that one moment really mattered. A thin, scraggy-looking man in black, who had been obscured in the pack until now, edged outward along the straight, settled for a moment in second place, and, with exactly three laps to go, flung himself into the lead. The effect was like an electric jolt to the whole stadium. We jumped to our feet and yelled wordlessly. The field behind him thrashed and jostled and panicked around the first bend until Grodotski emerged at the head of the hunters.

The crowd went wild, some in shock and despair as they urged their own heroes in pursuit; others, like me, inspired by the sheer tactical daring of Halberg's move. From that moment, I wanted only for him to hang on and succeed. At first it looked beyond doubt. His stride was quick and fluid for all his unprepossessing upper body and clenched left arm, and he kept his precious twenty meters secure the first time around.

Then it all became less certain. He began to look strained and unsure, twisting his upper body in his urgency. He glanced anxiously over his shoulder several times along the back straight. Grodotski, a bigger man, blond and powerful, seemed to be edging closer, and the Germans were throwing all their vocal weight behind him: "Gro-dot-ski! Gro-dot-ski! Gro-dot-ski!" Indignantly, I squeaked "Halberg!" in forlorn response, feeling as desperate as he looked as he dragged himself around my bend and into the straight with a lap to go. The race seemed interminable. Yet still he led. Perhaps it was only fifteen meters now, or twelve, but Grodotski was barely closing it.

The last lap lives in my memory with the intensity of a slow-motion dream. It seemed to take ten minutes. Halberg, frail, vulnerable, yet still heroic, seemed to be driving himself along on a mixture of deep determination and sheer terror. He writhed as he ran, turning his head to fling looks over his skinny shoulder every few strides, as if each glance at his pursuers fueled his courage for a few strides more. Yet his legs were still moving at high racing rhythm. Grodotski showed the effort equally now, yet there was power in his stride, and at any moment he might be transformed into a sprinting blond Übermensch and trample down the puny and twisted Halberg. The rest chased in a ragged line. The chant, "Grodot-ski! Gro-dot-ski!" rose to Wagnerian crescendo. The rest of the crowd were screeching in the hope we could somehow lend a little willpower to this undaunted but fallible-looking man.

At last the two propelled themselves around the last bend, both apparently running on sheer guts. As they passed close beneath me, Halberg's

Athletic immortality for two gallant New Zealand runners

8. Murray Halberg wins the Olympic 5,000 m, 1960.

face showed that he knew he might be caught yet desperately did not want to be. Grodotski's face showed that he knew he was beaten yet desperately did not want to be. The gap was perhaps ten meters. I believed that Halberg would do it. The straight was like the final minutes of a soccer match when your team is leading by one goal—interminable. Wearily, they each quickened their stride, yet in a strange way it was as if they were not really moving, since only relative distance was significant. Zimny was closing, but that was an unnoticed triviality. After a lingering infinity of seconds, Halberg lunged, clutched the tape, stumbled three steps, and slumped down onto the grass inside the track. He was stretched prone, face up, with the white tape draped across his black singlet. Photos show that he was smiling slightly, but I was too far away to see.

5:30

When I calmed down it was possible to pick up the pieces on the women's shot. Sloper had been in second place, a performance as outrageous as Halberg's against the drug-boosted East European brawn of most of her opposition. But the last round ended less happily. The German Luttge moved past, the New Zealander failed to improve, and with the last put of the contest, Mrs. Brown squealed and heaved ahead of Sloper for the bronze by a mere three centimeters. New Zealand should never forget how near Valerie Sloper Young came to putting a third silver fern on the dais that same hour: three centimeters.

6:00

The ceremonies allowed us to pay a more relaxed tribute to the two New Zealand winners and to hear "God Save the Queen" played at the Stadio Olimpico for the first time. Even then, it seemed less than appropriate for two New Zealanders. I didn't feel as if I'd seen two British victories.

Then the 20 km walkers elbowed their way back into the arena: a big, smiling Russian, Golubnichiy, first, and another of these surprising New Zealanders, Read, in fifth. We noticed the all-black uniform now.

6:20

The sun was dropping and the Coca-Cola men were tired and grimy. It had been a heady afternoon. "Nova-Zelanda," the people were saying as we shuffled away toward the buses, ready to leave the gladiators behind for a while and head home to Rome's suburbs. In my case it was a bus back to the nunnery, to sleep on my penitential bunk bed. "Cheap student accommodation" is how the English travel agency described it, without advising that it was a girls' school run by nuns in full habits.

Postscript

September 2, 1960, stands high in New Zealand's historical consciousness. A tiny nation doesn't get many high-profile international triumphs. It had been seven years since Ed Hillary climbed Mount Everest, and he was part of a British team. Jack Lovelock's Olympic gold for the 1,500 m in 1936 was also claimed partially by Great Britain, where he was then living and competing within the Oxford/Cambridge athletics fraternity. New Zealand's only previous Olympic champions were Yvette Williams (1952) and Norman Read, who had immigrated from Britain less than a year before he won the 50 km walk in Melbourne in 1956. The double victory in Rome in one hour by men who had grown up, lived, and learned to run wholly as New Zealanders was unprecedented as a national achievement.

Peter Snell's victory was so unexpected that we were not aware that an awesome demigod of the track had just been revealed. For me, that realization came at White City in London a few weeks later, when he blasted an 800 m relay leg in something under the official world record. For New Zealanders, the full revelation came in January and February 1962, when Snell in two now-legendary races on grass New Zealand tracks broke the world records for the 1 mi. and 800 m and 880 yd. I was privileged to be part of the fiftieth jubilee commemorations as track announcer in 2012.

Halberg was an Ed Hillary kind of New Zealand hero—understated, impeccably prepared, daring, and capable of going in his quiet, pragmatic way where no man had gone before.

I need to add a personal note. If Snell's godlike power filled me with awe, Halberg had me out there sharing his black shorts and thrashing my own skinny body around the track. Whenever I am asked about the greatest race I have ever seen, even now, almost sixty years later, I say without hesitation, "Halberg's 5,000 at Rome." As a runner born with no fast-twitch fibers, who would never win any race on the finishing sprint, I was watching a man win in a way that might perhaps be my way, if I could ever make

H. 17,10		313	METRI 5.000 - Finale UOMINI	
	5.000 METRES - Finale HOMMES		5.000 METRES - Finai MEN	
R. M.:	13'35"0	V. KUTS	(URS)	1957
R. O.:	13'39"6	V. KUTS	(URS)	1956
MELBOURNE 1956:		V. KUTS	(URS)	13'39"6
1	276 F. Janke (GER)	4	13:46·8	
2	523 K. Zimny (POL)	3	13:44·8	
3	277 H. Grodotzki (GER)	2.	13:44·6	
4	13 D. Power (AUS)	5	13:51·8	
5	12 A. Thomas (AUS)			
6	602 L. Conti (ITA)			
7	196 S. Iharos (UNG)			
8	698 M. Nyandika (KEN)	6	13:52·8	
9	471 M. Bernard (FRA)			
10	84 M. Halberg (NZE)	1	13:43·4	
11	275 H. Flosbach (GER)			
12	556 A. Artynjuk (URS)			

9. Olympic Games daily program, 1960.

myself strong enough in lung and leg and will. My best track victories in the 1960s and 1970s were won Halberg's way, breaking away with two or three laps to go. Surprise them. Steal the gap. Give every drop to keep it.

When I think of Murray Halberg, I am still the admiring student in the cheap section of the stand, hoarsely shouting his name as he won, one hot afternoon in Rome in 1960.

4

September 10, 1960, Appian Way, Rome

Africa Arrives

I saw the moment. I stood beside the Appian Way that dark, hot Rome night in 1960, about two miles from the Olympic marathon finish. (We opted out of our nunnery dinner that evening.) The crowd stood two or three deep, chattering expectantly in a hundred languages. The course was lit by oil flares held on long poles by Italian soldiers, and we peered into the pools of flickering light, waiting for the runners.

Suddenly they came, minutes sooner than we expected, emerging almost mystically out of the night, glimmering in the torchlight. We knew the field and were looking for the world record holder, Sergey Popov, or Aurele Vandendriessche of Belgium, and we were hoping for the English. Arthur Keily had been with the leaders early on, someone had heard.

Now they came—but who were they? At first, we could only glimpse them, seeming to glide through the patchy yellow gleam from the flaring torches: two tall, lean, dark-skinned men, shimmering closer between the splashes of light, seeming to emerge magically out of the darkness. They were well clear, running with astonishing pace and smoothness for that late point in a grueling hot marathon.

A half century later, we know who they were and what it meant. This was the race when two Africans broke away from the best marathon runners in the world, which history interprets as the moment when Africa arose as a marathon force. Looking back, it all seems clear, but at the time it was a mystery in shadowy half-light. Some in our group of young runners from England who had raced European cross-country recognized the one behind as Rhadi ben Abdesselem of Morocco, simply called "Rhadi," who

10. Abebe Bikila and Rhadi ben Abdesselem on the Appian Way, 1960. Associated Press.

previously ran for France. But the other—the one leading, so skeletally thin, his face composed, in green and red, skimming with such astonishing serenity in and out of the pools of light—he was unknown. As he ran past, we saw with even more amazement that he was barefoot.

I truly did see the moment, so I will always believe. As they passed us, at that moment, the barefoot leader seemed to stretch his stride, and a small gap opened. I can't say for sure this was the crucial move, as I was only a peering spectator as they flew by on a dark night. I know now that Rhadi stayed only a few yards back for another mile, and the final decisive break didn't come until after twenty-five miles. But I still think I saw the actual surge when Abebe Bikila of Ethiopia took command of the race, when he picked up the pace for the few strides that can be so decisive in a marathon, when he seized his personal destiny as one of the greatest and most adored runners in history and moved high-altitude eastern Africa to the front of virtually every marathon race for the foreseeable future.

That's all. One split second. One impression on the eye. Marathon spectators are the world's most patient and tolerant sports fans, standing for hours for a fleeting glimpse of something that moves so fast they hardly see it and have little idea what it means. I may be the only writer ever to devote a book chapter (in *Spirit of the Marathon*, 2014) and later an entire article ("New Year's Resolution: Support Our Spectators," Running Times website, December 26, 2011) to their virtues and sufferings and how poorly the sport treats them.

Anyway, I was there among the spectators that humid night. I was near one of the soldiers with his high-held flare. I believe to this day that I saw the moment when the race was decided.

That was one of the greatest of all marathons. It was staged with an Italian sense of drama. Modern Rome proudly displayed its ancient history. For Italy, this was its opportunity to put the Fascist 1930s and the disastrous Axis alliance behind it, and to reconnect with its own greater past and the democratic postwar world. That was important, though it didn't matter to us visitors as much as it mattered in Tokyo in 1964, or Munich in 1972. As I said in chapter 1, Italy was welcomed back into the Olympics as soon as the war was over. No one of my generation thought of Italy as a recently hostile nation, which inevitably is how we thought of Germany when I was hiking there with friends in 1957 and 1958. It was not Italian bombs that dropped on London, and Italians have never been caricatured as evil greatcoated militarists, which is how Germans have been treated for (surely) far longer than their present nation deserves. More on Germany in chapter 12.

For Italy, and for Rome, the Games were significant as a coming-out party and a welcome world party, and they conducted it with typical brio. The stadium band did its best to make every national anthem sound cheerful, the crowds were exuberant, and the Swiss guards outside St. Peter's Cathedral lingeringly tugged young women tourists' scarves and kerchiefs into better position to cover their shoulders. Even the nuns who served our breakfasts and evening meals, and their sisters selling Coca-Cola and postcards high up at the top of St. Peter's great dome, all seemed in welcoming high spirits.

The Italians have always known how to put on a spectacle, from the Roman Coliseum to the production of *Aida* at the Baths of Caracalla as evening entertainment during the Games. As night fell on the last day of the Games, the marathon offered a triumphal tour of the grandeur that was Rome. For the first time in Olympic history, the course started and finished outside the stadium. It began in sunshine, ran into the very blazing heart of the sunset, plunged into darkness, and ended in golden floodlights.

Sixty-nine runners, the best the world had ever known, started from the foot of Michelangelo's swooping staircase to the capitol. The statues of Marcus Aurelius and Julius Caesar looked down on the runners as they surged across the forums of Trajan and Augustus, along Mussolini's arrow-straight imperial way to pass under the wall of the Coliseum, then by the Baths of Caracalla and out to the Appian Way and the city gates.

Beyond the city, the late afternoon was turning to twilight. Four runners broke away, and as they ran west to approach the turnaround they headed into a fireball sunset. Seen from behind on the camera truck, the runners moving through increasing dusk toward that huge flaming orb made a perfect pictorial symbol for the last spectacular act of those Games.

The return journey created some of the most unforgettable images in the history of the marathon, even in the history of Rome. Darkness fell. Two hardened marathoners, Arthur Keily (Great Britain) and Aurele Vandendriessche (Belgium), had led almost to halfway, but now the race was controlled by Rhadi and Bikila. Behind them the prerace favorite and world record holder, Sergey Popov (USSR), was struggling to hold off Barry Magee (New Zealand) and the closing Konstantin Vorobiev (USSR). Heading back to the city, the leading runners were lit by floodlamps from the chasing camera vehicle. There was no other lighting. Behind them, the darkness and silence made it a weirdly surreal Olympic experience.

"No spectators were allowed on many sections of the course. Not for security reasons, but because the Italian organizers feared there might be some swapping of runners in the darkness. It made it strangely surreal, running alone in the dark. I never knew where I was in the race until the finish," recalled bronze medalist Barry Magee in 2015.

Running through that surreal darkness, with seven miles (twelve kilometers) to go, at last they saw patches of light ahead. They turned now onto the Appian Way, the ancient road from southern Italy to Rome, constructed 2,300 years ago to be the source of Rome's military and commercial power. The night was hot and humid.

Flash back to nearly two hours earlier, before the race started: while the runners were shuffling into position, the team of three New Zealanders noticed a figure quietly taking his place alongside them. He was an unknown African with a frail, almost emaciated body, and no shoes. They nudged each other, looking at his bare feet. "Well, that's one we can beat, anyway," said Ray Puckett to Barry Magee.

That ill-fated remark has become urban legend. David Maraniss's (2008) book on the Rome Games wrongly attributed it to the American team. Magee confirmed the actual anecdote for me in 2016.

Now the skeletal Bikila's bare feet were flicking over the hot surface of the Appian Way in the lead of the Olympic marathon. He watched the glowing red taillight of the lead motorcycle. He saw the shimmering fluctuation of the soldiers' flares dotted along the road ahead. He heard Rhadi's breathing and footfall, but he never once glanced aside. He sensed, as every good runner can, that Rhadi was only clinging, and could be broken, when the moment came. Still he waited.

Together the two ran in and out of the quivering pools of light, from light to dark to light to dark along the Appian Way. Approaching the gates of Rome, where there was a rise, Bikila surged slightly, and/or he felt Rhadi drift. Contact was broken. That was the moment that I believe I saw. For Rhadi, it was that quintessential marathon crisis, the moment when your legs simply can't quite continue to answer the message from your brain. For good television coverage, that's the moment you must capture, and for good television commentary, that's the hidden psychic drama you must make evident to viewers who have never experienced it.

Bikila saved his real surge for the place he had agreed upon with his Swedish coach, Onni Niskanen, at forty-one kilometers, just after the last turn on the course. There stood the high stone needle of the Obelisk of Axum, a treasure of the ancient history of Ethiopia. It had been looted and taken to Rome when Mussolini's Fascist Italy invaded and occupied Ethiopia (then Abyssinia) in 1937. Italy, ambitious to be a new imperial power, plundered that great symbolic stone from where it had fallen. (It was repatriated in 2008.)

Whether a protest was intended, it was as they passed the obelisk that Bikila unmistakably lifted his pace. Yard by yard, he began to slide away from Rhadi. Only twenty-three years after Mussolini's big moment, an Ethiopian soldier was conquering Rome. Running was making more history.

Soon Bikila could see the soaring Arch of Constantine, its antique stone glowing rich gold in the floodlights, and behind it the walls of the Coliseum in silvery light. Along the finishing straight, 12,000 cheering spectators sat on special bleachers. Bikila, as serene as he had been from the start, his head steady, his arms scarcely moving, making no acknowledgment of the acclamation, ran calmly between the ecstatic crowds. He seemed focused inward, not looking out at the applause. There was no arm gesture of victory. There was no tape. The finish line was illuminated from above in deep red.

Bikila passed it, slowed, and immediately began a series of loosening callisthenic exercises. The footage is well known of Bikila after his second Olympic victory in Tokyo, on his back in the infield doing bicycle pedaling. Mere mortal marathoners gasp in awe. But he did the same in Rome, mostly hidden by the Arch of Constantine. It wasn't done for the crowds, who couldn't see, or the cameras, which were in front of the arch, but because his coach had told him to do it. You might find the authentic footage on YouTube. I chanced upon it in an obscure Italian movie called *Un Ragazzo di Calabria* (*A Boy of Calabria*), the story of a boy runner in a hill town in the rural south who is inspired by watching Bikila's victory on television. It's a fictional story, but a nice irony that an Italian boy adopts an Ethiopian (Abyssinian) as his hero.

Many were inspired by Bikila. He is widely regarded as the greatest marathoner of all time, even though others have now run minutes faster. Bikila is the Zátopek of the marathon, though a very different personality; he was always composed and private, "the king of silence," as one journalist dubbed him. He won that Rome Olympic marathon in soggy humid heat, barefoot on a course that was partly cobblestones, in a world record 2:15:16.2.

Bikila's later story is marathon legend. He won twelve marathons, failing only once, when he was fifth in cold weather at Boston in 1963. In 1964, despite appendix surgery only forty days before the race, he dominated the Olympic marathon in Tokyo, retaining his title by four minutes in a world record 2:12:11.2. That is often called one of the most perfect marathons ever run, and happily it was immortalized by Kon Ichikawa's superb film coverage in *Tokyo Olympiad* (1965). Injuries finally slowed Bikila, and at the Mexico Games in 1968 a stress fracture forced him to drop out. A worse, bitterly cruel fate intervened in 1969, when an automobile crash left him a paraplegic. He fought back to compete in archery and table tennis from his wheelchair, and in 1972 he was a guest of honor at the Olympics in Munich. After the marathon, winner Frank Shorter went over to where Bikila sat in his wheelchair and respectfully shook his hand. Bikila's early death of cerebral hemorrhage in 1973 brought a national day of mourning in Ethiopia, and his state funeral was attended by an estimated 65,000 people. Haile Gebrselassie always acknowledges him as the father of Ethiopia's great tradition. For most of us who remember 1960, he is the paragon. He remains there for me because he was a runner of such amazing grace, a consummate competitor, a racer, not a beneficiary of paced time trials, and because I can feel certain that what he achieved was done without drugs.

His win in Rome was also the dramatic beginning of an unprecedented phenomenon: the total dominance of modern running by Africa. I needn't linger over it, as it's woven through this book, especially in chapter 10. Bikila wasn't in fact the first African to win the Olympic marathon, since Boughera El Ouafi had won in 1928 and Alain Mimoun in 1956, both Algerian by birth and ethnicity, though at that time representing France. Rhadi ben Abdesselem had previously run for France, but as he dueled with Bikila in Rome it was in the red and green colors of newly independent Morocco.

So much history. It's a lot to build on the perspective of a tired young student peering into patchily illuminated darkness, a glimpse that lasted only a second or two. But Bikila's victory that dark night is worth a chapter in any book on races that made history. It was worthy of a triumphal arch as its finish line. It became part of the long, old history of Rome, and it began something new in the history of modern Africa and modern running.

I saw the moment.

5

June 15, 1963, Chiswick Stadium, London

Pioneer American

In the late 1950s and early 1960s, everyone in Europe and America lived under the dark shadow of history. Long-range missiles and nuclear warheads meant that the Cold War now threatened instant destruction, rather than the army conflict that seemed possible in 1954. In places like southern England in those years, we felt we were teetering on the edge of doom. I was aware every waking moment that Britain's early warning radar station in the Yorkshire moors was calculated to give London four minutes' notice of nuclear missile attack from Eastern Europe.

Can running intersect with such an unseen threat of doom? My friend Mike Turner and I sometimes ran from his parents' weekend cottage at Goathland in Yorkshire, passing after four miles across the moors right by the Fylingdales early warning radar station, a set of gigantic white golf balls high on the wild hills. And on the day of the Cuban Missile Crisis in October 1962, while I was teaching at Frensham, Surrey, and the world was teetering on the brink, I went for a run on Frensham Common after classes in the autumn sun, pointlessly watching the skies as I ran.

An encounter with less ominous history came in the Hog's Back Road Race from Farnham to Guildford in December 1962, when I finished not far behind sixth place, which was taken by an American, Buddy Edelen. England was the running powerhouse in those days, and every race had a deep elite field. That was why Edelen had moved there—to learn from us, race against us, be one of us. He became prominent and popular in our intensely competitive but friendly running scene. He was a nice, amiable man, a good schoolteacher, and he was happily obsessed with running,

11. Buddy Edelen breaks the world marathon record, 1963. Mark Shearman–Athletics Images.

like many runners at that time. If his teaching colleagues found him a bit of an oddball, he fit right into the oddball community of cross-country and road runners. Our Yank, we called him. He was the first American distance runner since Clarence DeMar to train with English or Zátope-kian intensity.

Six months later, on June 15, 1963, I watched Buddy Edelen break the tape to set a new world record for the marathon. World record! Knowing his quality and dedication, we were not exactly incredulous, but it was an unthought-of achievement for an American. Japanese, Russian, Belgian,

Ethiopian, New Zealander—that wouldn't have surprised us. But our Yank? He was good, but in the English competitive cauldron, he wasn't often a winner. That sixth place in a 9.5 mi. road race was typical. Now he was the first American to break the marathon world record since 1925. No native-born American man has done it since. It was historic for America, as well as for marathon running.

In some ways, the great American running boom, and the even greater world running boom, began at that pioneering moment. Maybe that's an outsider's view, since America barely noticed it at the time. It was Billy Mills and Bob Schul who fired the imagination of American boys with their distance running gold medals in Tokyo in 1964, and Frank Shorter who showed them the magic allure of the marathon in 1972. But Edelen's world record was earlier. He is entitled to the credit of being at least a major precursor. For me, he was the pioneer, because like every true pioneer, he staked his whole life on leaving the security of home and pushing his personal limits in an unknown place to explore unknown territory against unknown challenges. He took risks and committed follies, and he paid dearly for them. He went where no man had been before.

My view on the origins of the American-led running boom has always been affected by a conversation in 1965 or 1966, when an American runner called Vic Zwolak visited me while I was working on my PhD thesis. He was a US Olympic steeplechaser in 1964, and he was visiting Cambridge, looking for someone to run with and talk running with. I've remembered three things for fifty years. One, what a friendly and intelligent man he was. (In 2011, the Internet tells me, Zwolak was still setting age-group records.) Two, I was so unfamiliar with the American accent that I spent some weeks trying to find the racing spikes he recommended, futilely looking for "Medias" when what Vic said was "Meteors." And three, he told me memorably that "every kid in the US wants to be a runner since Billy Mills and Bob Schul won their gold medals in Tokyo."

Vic was a track runner, so like American kids and almost every other American, he overlooked the groundbreaking American in that obscure and unfashionable event called the marathon. That omission became part of Buddy Edelen's tragedy. I would like to do a little to remedy that imbalance of history. Here is Buddy Edelen's story, and my own brief encounters with it.

In late 1960, after the Rome Olympics, while Abebe Bikila was being paraded in gold medal triumph through Addis Ababa, Leonard "Buddy" Edelen was living alone in Finland, managing to survive by giving private English lessons. He had been ill with anemia at the American Olympic trials and did not make the team.

At age twenty-two, Edelen, originally from Sioux Falls, South Dakota, had just graduated from the University of Minnesota and was now in Finland to learn how the Europeans trained, but mainly in the vain hope of finding a fast 10,000 m race. No American had run the Olympic qualifying time of 29:40. Edelen had the US record at 29:58.9, the first American to break thirty minutes, when the world record was a minute and a half faster. That's how far behind the world US distance running was—more than a lap of the track. But with Edelen falling short in the trials, Max Truex got the only Olympic spot.

Guided via mail by the knowledgeable Fred Wilt, who was curious about training methods outside America, Edelen began a European training regime that no American had ever attempted: running twice a day, mixing repeats and fartlek with long runs. Wilt had studied the great runners for his seminal books *How They Train* (1959) and *Run, Run, Run* (1964), and he learned that in England Jim Peters, who transformed the marathon with his 2:17:39, did it on two race-pace workouts a day. The Brits, unlike the Finns, also ran cross-country through the winter. So in November 1960, Edelen moved to England. He would teach school, live austerely, train twice a day, join Chelmsford Athletic Club in Essex, east of London, and become a national-class cross-country, road, and track runner.

Running perhaps filled an emotional gap in his life. His mother was institutionalized when he was six, and his father went through two more marriages. One stepmother encouraged him to try sport when she learned the teenager was being jeered at as "Butterball Bud." He found that he "could jog forever," doubled the training his coach prescribed, and became an undefeated high school miler. After college, Wilt urged him to break the American mold and keep running. In those strictly amateur days, it was a big decision.

Edelen loved the English running scene. It was a heady mix of competitiveness and friendship, intense individualism plus profound loyalty to your club team. We had all come to maturity in the bleak postwar years, and in long-distance running we found an outlet for aspiration and a way for sheer hard work to give us an achievement that felt significant. We also bonded, especially in the vitally important team competition, in much the way our fathers' generation did in war service. I still have friends made in that era.

I was a scholarship student at Cambridge University and could have chosen an exclusively literary or scholarly direction, but I look back on my running time in those years as a life of commitment. My life verged on hardship in the English winter; I trained and raced in all weathers, often at night after study or after work, for absolutely no monetary reward, in an era when hot showers were rare and road-running shoes not yet invented.

Buddy and I met again years later, at the 1992 Tulsa Run in Oklahoma, where he was living. That time I was the elite runner; he was a perky but unprepossessing figure in the corner of a room, little known, and to me unrecognizable as the crewcut racer of 1963. But it really was Buddy. He followed up with a letter: "Roger, our conversation relative to running back in England in the early sixties stimulated the old neurons and brought back so many fond memories of the dear friends I had while competing over there. There's a song by Roger Whitaker about returning to England that I play again and again. I love reminiscing about athletics in an era when it was for the love of the sport, and not the financial carrot" (private correspondence, December 12, 1992).

We had been laughing over shared memories, like the day at the southern England cross-country championship when Edelen's contact lens popped out as he sprinted to the line in second place. Half the best runners in England had just spent forty-five minutes beating each other to exhaustion in the race, but we then spent a hilarious fifteen minutes crawling about together in wet grass to find Buddy's little lens.

He was always high in the mix of the take-no-prisoners' world of English running, even winning the national 10 mi. track title in 1962, in 48:31.8, an American record by two minutes. In the tabloids he became "The Killer Yank." Invitations began to arrive for races in Europe, all expenses paid. "Trips," we called them, and they were the perk of top-level running in those amateur days, when we were not permitted to accept money and few could afford a European vacation. We all aspired to get trips. Trips would be the undoing of Buddy Edelen.

In June 1962, he tried a marathon, the famed "Polytechnic" from Windsor to Chiswick. That year, the young Queen Elizabeth greeted the line of runners on Windsor Castle grounds. In her polished tones, she enunciated a special greeting to the American with a knotted handkerchief on his head. "Hi, Queen," he replied breezily. The Brits in the line tried to suppress their giggles.

Having disregarded Wilt's persuasions to take enough rest before his marathon debut, Edelen suffered. He was ninth, in 2:31, well behind Ron Hill's first marathon victory. "Last 15 miles were sheer hell," he wrote in his diary. A month later, he tried another marathon, on top of three high-level track races. This one went better, a win in 2:22:33. Edelen was rising.

Now it was the big marathons that began to offer him trips. At the end of 1962, he placed second at Košice (Slovakia) and fourth at Fukuoka (Japan), where he became the first American to break 2:20, with 2:18:56.8. In early 1963, after floundering in the snow of the severest English winter on record, Edelen got a trip back home, to race indoors. So here was the schedule of this dedicated and overeager man: a marathon in Japan, a snowy 7 mi. cross-country in Essex, and two fast 2 mi. races on the indoor boards in New York and Kentucky—all within six weeks. Then back to Europe and another invitational cross-country in Belgium, where the town mayor's seventeen-year-old daughter (so the runner-gossip went) fell madly in love with him. It was a full life.

On Wilt's advice, Edelen added what we would now call a tempo run to his demanding weekly schedule: fifteen miles in darkness after the day's teaching, in 1:20. His weekly mileage rose to 135. He made no concession to races. After breaking his US 10 mi. track record with 48:28, he ran twenty-two miles in training the next morning in 2:10.

"Our objective is the Olympic marathon title," Wilt's letters pleaded. But Edelen was driven, obsessed, perhaps self-destructive. In May, having struggled to the airport after a bad flu, he ran 2:23:06 on the hilly Marathon to Athens course, taking the course record held by the 1960 Olympic champion and 1964 Olympic favorite, Abebe Bikila.

Four weeks later, June 15, 1963, was the Polytechnic Marathon, from Windsor to Chiswick. By Edelen standards, he went in fresh: no race for four weeks. His long runs and interval sessions were his best ever. It paid off. That day, three years of dedication came together to a perfect peak. Edelen gradually cranked up the pace, and by sixteen miles he was alone.

"I felt helpless as I watched Buddy go," said Ron Hill. The lead vehicle took Edelen briefly seventy yards off course, but he was unfazed.

Taking a day off from the club track season, I was in the small crowd that waited at Chiswick Stadium. Most were seated in its modest grandstand. I joined a restless cluster on the grass bank. Finally, we saw our friendly Yank from Chelmsford, Essex, run in strongly onto the rough cinders, with his upright, clipped, almost metronomic, pecking-chicken stride, crewcut hair, and plain white T-shirt with a handkerchief knotted around his neck.

It seemed too humble a setting for a world record—no cheering thousands, no banks of cameras, no floodlit Arch of Constantine. The time came as a total surprise: 2:14:28, 47.8 seconds under the world mark set by Toru Terasawa in February 1963, and 48 seconds faster than Bikila ran in Rome. Edelen became the first American to break 2:15 and the first American since Albert Michelson in 1925 to break the world marathon record.

"I never dreamed I'd win or run so fast," Edelen wrote in his training diary. Nor did any of us.

Edelen kept fervently racing. In July, he broke his own American 10,000 m track record, with 28:00.8. In August, he was on a USA team track and field tour, racing badly in Moscow and London. Then, after a six-week break from races, came Košice, and another superlative marathon. He beat Sergey Popov, a favorite for the Olympics, and two Ethiopians, who ran in a series of aggressive surges. Edelen's time was 2:15:09.6. European champion Brian Kilby had run 2:14:43 in July, so Edelen now had the fastest and the third fastest times in history.

He spent the English winter battling a series of seventeen hard races that his biographer Frank Murphy (1972) said "calls to mind a binge drinker who knows that he must stop soon." No race was easy in England in those days. I still have the report on one of them that I wrote for the local newspaper. (By now I was the regular, though unpaid, reporter as well as the writer of my club's monthly newsletter, a task that required hours of slaving at a temperamental printing gadget called a mimeograph, whose green or purple ink stained you for weeks.) This was when Buddy ran second in the Hog's Back Road Race, 9.5 mi., in December 1963. I too "had a good one" (as we used to say): only a minute behind winner Mel Batty in a new course record.

"Second was the American schoolteacher who holds the world record for the marathon. Edelen and north of England cross-country champion Mike Turner battled fiercely, and the American broke clear only on the final uphill half mile," says my *Guildford and Godalming Times* report. Turner, my friend and mentor, and England's cross-country captain, was famed for the rigor of his training, and he was never easily beaten. The other runners in the top ten were all British internationals.

To place second in that field took intense commitment. And that was only one race—in the big picture, an insignificant one—of the seventeen that Murphy counted that winter season. That's how hard Edelen was racing, week after week through that English winter, with the most important race of his life only ten months ahead. Buddy Edelen raced not wisely but too well.

Edelen began to pay for his lack of wisdom at the US selection trial in Yonkers, New York, on May 24, 1964. It was his eighth marathon in twenty months. The temperature at the start was 91°F (33°C) with high humidity, traffic on the course, and notoriously nasty hills. Of 128 starters, forty-one dropped out. But for Edelen, the momentum of his character knew no patience, nor contemplated half-measure. He ran hard all the way and won by twenty minutes, a margin of more than three miles, in 2:24:25.6.

It was probably his greatest race. It was brave. It was folly. It was the beginning of the end.

Back in England, he began to be racked with sciatic pain in the hips and lower back, then down the left leg to the shin. It was so bad that he took two weeks off running. In August, he forced himself into a modified training regime, and by September he was back on routine, though always hurting.

The Olympic marathon in Tokyo was on October 21, 1964. A few days before their race, Edelen and Bikila passed each other, running in opposite directions. There was no exchange of greeting.

Bikila's second Olympic gold medal run (see chapter 4) has become legendary; he beat the strongest field in history by four minutes and eight seconds, in a world record 2:12:11.2. Few now remember that, as they went into the Tokyo race, it was the American who had the faster marathon time.

Edelen had a schedule taped to his palm for 2:13:48, the pace he thought would win it. But he ran every step in pain, his usual upright stance tilting into a backward lean, as if trying to muffle the impact. After halfway, his legs thankfully went numb, and he could push harder through the field. He passed Ron Clarke, Kenji Kimihara, and Aurele Vandendriessche (who won Boston the year Bikila ran). Edelen finished sixth, the best American placing since Clarence DeMar in 1928, in 2:18:12.4. It was a performance of enormous courage. Yet a year earlier he could have done so much better. Basil Heatley and Brian Kilby, from his peer group in England, whom he had sometimes beaten over various distances and surfaces, placed second and fourth.

Benefiting from some rest, Edelen recovered to run one more great race. He placed third at the 1965 Polytechnic in 2:14:34, his second-best time, splitting the dominant Japanese trio. Morio Shigematsu won in another new world record (2:12:00). The English crowds, bigger this time, acclaimed their Yank as one of their own.

Later in 1965, Edelen left England. We all felt sad reading in *Athletics Weekly* his warm letter of thanks to his many friends. He moved to a graduate assistant post and began a master's degree in physiology at Adams

State College, Alamosa, Colorado. At 7,540 feet, it would be the perfect location to train for the 1968 Olympics in Mexico City.

But it was over.

He won one more marathon, Denver, in 2:51, but the pain had him contorted and shuffling as he ran. He helped Joe Vigil, coach at Adams, bring the 1968 Olympic trial marathon to Alamosa. He was a key figure in the organization, but he couldn't run it.

Edelen's story ends on a falling cadence. He married and had a son, but the marriage lasted only a few years. In 1971, his car was hit by a truck and his pelvis was broken in three places. He coped valiantly. He moved to Tulsa, where he seemed to his friends "indomitable, cheerful, full of blarney," according to Frank Murphy (in a private letter to me). But he was forgotten. It was Bikila, also seriously hurt in a car wreck, who was honored at the Munich Olympics and shook the hand of Edelen's American heir, Frank Shorter.

Edelen used to wryly sign his name as "Buddy Who?" When we met in 1992, he seemed a forlorn figure, ironic rather than embittered to be so neglected by the sport he loved. Murphy's excellent *A Cold, Clear Day* had just been published, and that recognition meant a lot to him. He was always a friendly and positive man—perhaps too positive, too passionately committed, too willing to give his all every week.

But he deserves better than to appear as he now does on the Internet, where he is castigated in every reference as an example of mindless over-training. He sought the best knowledge, and he had the courage and dedication to go where few had gone before—none in America. His pioneering example enabled many more Americans, including Shorter, to reach that level. He was, for one year, the best marathon runner in the world. How many of his critics can claim that?

Near the end, fate seemed briefly to relent, as if willing at last to give something back to Buddy Edelen. But not for long.

"He married a beautiful woman and was enjoying his work, when he got his cancer diagnosis. It seemed as if someone was taunting him. But he was optimistic and courageous. He was taking an experimental medicine from Canada. When I said, 'what is it?' he said, 'rocket fuel.' We do still miss him," Murphy told me.

When Buddy Edelen died in 1997, the running community scarcely noticed. I nominated him for the National Distance Running Hall of Fame in 2015, but he did not get the votes.

All big changes in the human mindset take more than one pioneer. Edelen went to England to build on Wilt's advice and absorb English running culture. At the same time, Bob Schul, Billy Mills, Gerry Lindgren, and Jim Beatty, in different places and in different ways, were climbing peaks in the same mountain range. A few years later, Frank Shorter followed them up to the very top. All took training to new levels, won important races, earned Olympic medals, and broke world records. They permanently changed America's attitude to distance running and the world's thinking about what American runners can do.

The one who did that first was Buddy Edelen, on June 15, 1963. On that day, all his dedication, or addiction, came together, and he found the one perfect race. Our Yank ran into scruffy old Chiswick Stadium in his white T-shirt to become the fastest marathoner there had ever been.

Footnote: As I was working on this book, Buddy Edelen was posthumously inducted into the USA Track and Field Hall of Fame. I talked with his son Brent, who accepted the award on his father's behalf in New York in November 2016. Brent confirmed that his father had been disappointed to be forgotten, but not embittered; he was deeply pleased by Frank Murphy's book and was always a lover of England and English wit. Brent said he was "everybody's friend," "gracious," "congenial," "a huge admirer of Bikila," and "never said a bad thing about any runner." He gave away most of his medals and trophies, Brent said, but kept the important ones, "in his Olympic suitcase. That's where we found them when he passed."

At last, Buddy Edelen's historic pioneering contribution has been recognized in his own country. And there may be another late bonus. His granddaughter Frances, Brent's daughter, also shows potential as a runner, Brent reported proudly. "And she reminds me so much of my dad—same upright style, arms high, same quick stride. It's unreal."

6

July 10, 1965, White City, London

The Day the Mountain Grew Higher

I never saw (or suffered) military action. My 1939 birth date meant that Britain's compulsory two-year national service ended before I finished university. Just as well. I had no interest in saving the last shreds of the British Empire, the mission that took some of my contemporaries to war zones in Kenya, Malaya, Cyprus, and Suez.

But my timing also meant that I became a young adult too early for the counterrevolution of the sixties. I missed out on being a soldier or a hippy. I didn't feel deprived. Postwar dinginess finally ended, and I was busy and happy being a student, a teacher, a scholar, a father, and a runner. It dawned on me later that I was pursuing peace, love, and a better world in my own way through a commitment to literary scholarship and to running. That's not as outlandish as it sounds. We were a small, insignificant sport then, too busy training our brains out to stop and analyze our social importance. But fifty years later, when running has become a beneficent, global social revolution that transforms many thousands of lives, it's worth considering whether perhaps we were the ones who got it right. When people ask where the Woodstock spirit went—huge crowds finding individual fulfilment in a context of community benevolence and harmony—my answer is, go and watch a marathon.

I put these ideas forward in an interview for the excellent documentary film *Free to Run* (2016), directed by the Swiss Pierre Morath, which looked at the running movement as a version of the counterculture. The film interprets running as a search for individual freedom and open access for all, importantly including women, and as a rejection of old-style rules,

51

12. Ron Clarke and Gerry Lindgren, world record 3 mi., 1965.
Mark Shearman–Athletics Images.

restrictive organizational structures, and commercial pressures. I don't think that's the whole story, but in the 1960s and 1970s, it was a significant undercurrent helping to drive the running tide. The film shows running becoming a microcosmic version of the liberal society the counterculture advocated for the world.

Still thinking of those late-colonial 1950s–60s conflicts where I and my generation might have found ourselves fighting, in Kenya for Britain, or North Africa for France, here's a thought: the grandsons and grand-daughters of some of the people who were rebelling against our governments are now global heroes and role models as runners. They inspire the world by their running, which is something that we value and they do better than we ever dreamed possible. It's a nice irony. In chapter 10 I discuss how we have responded to this reversal of fortune.

Back in the mid-1960s, I had one brief personal glimpse of history-book history, a private footnote moment. I was warming up to race a cross-country championship at Bracknell in Berkshire, England, on January 30, 1965. Part of the course was alongside the London-to-Oxford rail line, and I stopped my warm-up to stand and watch the train pass by that carried the body of Winston Churchill on his last journey. It was pulled by the Battle of Britain class steam locomotive "Winston Churchill." His wartime voice on the wireless, as we called it, was part of my very earliest consciousness. (So were steam locomotives.) He was worthy of some moments of quiet respect before I went to the start line.

My other historic highlight of 1965 came at London's White City Stadium on July 10. I sat in the high stand with three friends, all of us committed young runners. It was the English Amateur Athletic Association (AAA) Championships, and the race we were excitedly waiting for was the 3 mi. At last, at 4:40 p.m., twenty runners emerged from the tunnel and began their stride-outs down below us on the old black cinder track.

Instantly, we picked out the commanding figure of Ron Clarke, the new world record holder from Australia. It took longer among the cluster of runners to find the teenage American phenomenon Gerry Lindgren, and we stared in astonishment that such a frail-looking boy could have shared the world 6 mi. record with Billy Mills only two weeks before. We spotted European 5,000 m champion Bruce Tulloh, barefoot as usual, the blond Hungarian Lajos Mecsér, the lanky Irishman Derek Graham, and, yes, there, bigger than anyone in the field except Clarke, Londoner Mike Wiggs, who ten days ago replaced Tulloh as British record holder.

This was a world-class field, the best our generation had seen on a British track. In those days, overseas athletes were often invited to the AAA Championships to boost the crowd, even though it meant some margin-ally elite English runners (like me that year) were denied a start.

You got a good, though distant, view in that famed, faded old sta-dium. Built for the 1908 London Olympics, known then as The Great

White City, it used to hold 100,000 spectators. It even had its own mid-field Olympic swimming pool, where now the discus was in progress. In the 1950s, big crowds still came to meets like the London versus Moscow match described in chapter 2. In the 1960s, track crowds were declining, and the down-at-heel stadium's main livelihood was from greyhound racing. The wire-fenced dog track and surrounding space for bookmakers' booths made a big gap between the crowd and the track and field action.

We leaned forward, stopwatches poised, as they shuffled into line to have their names checked. Twenty runners and 12,000 spectators went still and silent.

"Set!"

As the runners leaned forward, I had mixed feelings. I should have been crouched and eager down there among them. In my best track season so far, I'd beaten several of the English runners and twice got under the time standard. I felt aggrieved about missing the selectors' cut for the straight-final championship. As things turned out, I was lucky. The race about to start would become a milestone in history, a defining drama best witnessed from the fervor of the stands, not struggling unhappily at the back of the field.

"First lap 62—North." I can still read the notes I made on the now-yellowing page of the championship program. That was Geoff North who led the first lap, not his brother Gerry, who had narrowly beaten me for the Surrey Championship 3 mi. two months earlier. I timed every lap. Stopwatches in 1965 were metal hemispheres that filled your palm, a black hand sweeping around the circular face. You wound the spring by a beveled knob on top, pressing the same knob with your thumb to start and stop. We carried them everywhere, as young runners now carry their cell phones.

"Lap 2, 2:7, Lindgren, Cl[arke], Wiggs. Lap 3, 3:11, Clarke. Lap 4, 4:15.4, Lindgren." So says my long-treasured program. We expected it to be fast, but this was fantasy—eight seconds under world record pace! No Olympic 5,000 m final had come close to this speed. And it showed. As Lindgren and Clarke alternated in the lead, it took them less than four laps to turn that talent-loaded field of champions into a line of desolate stragglers. Wiggs tried to stay in contact, but by the end of the first mile even he was gone.

"Lap 5, 5:20.4, Clarke. Lap 6, 6:26, Clarke." Now it was Clarke in command: powerful, dignified, majestic. Lindgren was his shadow. Clarke's official world record stood at 13:07.6, and he had a recent unratified 13:00.4. Today, we calculated with disbelief, he was on pace for well under thirteen minutes. Out there on the black cinders, it was a new reality, even for champions.

"After running 4:18 for the first mile, and going though halfway inside my PR [personal record] pace at 6:33, I was burned off—as was everybody else. Even then, we knew this was completely changing the landscape," reflected Tulloh fifty years later.

Clarke was not as engrossed in lap times as we were, with our over-heating stopwatches. "I didn't hear any of the lap calls. I knew it was fast but I was not thinking about the world record, just about winning. At first, I thought it was great to have Lindgren helping to press the pace. Usually everyone else sat back and left me to dictate. But I started to think I would not be able to get rid of him," Clarke told me in 2015, only two months before his unexpected death.

Lindgren was in unknown territory for a nineteen-year-old not long out of high school. "In high school, the gun goes off, you go. So I led much of the first laps," Lindgren emailed me. "When Clarke raced around me, he really pushed hard, and most of those first ten laps I wondered how long I could keep going. But I tried to match his stride."

At halfway, Clarke began racing. He towed Lindgren through two miles in 8:36, only three seconds outside the British record. On the ninth lap, the stubborn little American edged cheekily in front. Clarke watched him for a while, like a tiger looking at a mouse, then began to put in surges, raising the overall tempo to a destructive tenth lap in 63 seconds.

"Not many observers discerned the surges, but there were three or four, each fifty to ninety meters, and they broke Lindgren's rhythm," Clarke recalled. Lindgren confirms that the first surge was critical. "On the ninth lap, Clarke eased up just a bit, which I welcomed," Lindgren says. "I was so tired. But then, going into a bend, he took off with a gust and before I could get my weary legs to go, he was several steps ahead. But

I learned a good race strategy from him that day, as I used it to slow down many times in my racing career."

At last, Clarke was on his own, how he liked it best. Clarke was sublime when he got free. In later eras, Dave Bedford and John Ngugi were his heirs in that lonely mastery. At twenty-eight years old, Clarke ran with mature power, upright, rhythmic, and with an upper-body composure that set him apart from his greatest predecessors. Zátopek, Kuts, and Halberg all ran tormented with effort, twisted and striving. Clarke's close-cropped head never bobbed and his arms never flailed. Calm, controlled, imperturbable—that's how he looked as we watched in awe from the stands. Against skinny young Lindgren, he appeared like a sedate demigod brushing away an impertinent schoolboy.

But inner human reality may be different from appearances. Clarke nearly missed that race. Two days earlier, he told me, he heard that his wife's mother was dying. "I had three races to go. [My wife] Helen talked me out of flying back to Australia with her, saying there was nothing I could do except support her, and she knew how well I had peaked. Frankly, I just wanted to get the run out of the way, compete in Oslo and Paris, and get back home to comfort Helen."

No man goes into no man's land without paying a price. Though every writer called Clarke "relaxed," that's not how it felt to him. "Believe me, I was hurting. All my races felt hard. Whereas Zátopek for instance used to grimace as if each step was agony, I tried to develop a stoic appearance, so my opponents had little idea how tough I was finding it," Clarke said.

While Clarke looked serene, the spectators were going out of our minds. As he disposed of lap after lap, as the world record became an astonishing certainty, each sector of the crowd began spontaneously to rise to their feet when he went royally past. It was a sort of adoring Mexican wave fifteen years before they were invented.

Then, in some unspoken way, we all felt the need to get closer to this great work of humankind. As if responding to the urgings of a charismatic prophet, we were drawn out of our seats and forward, down the aisles. Through the last three laps, 12,000 people were clustered around the perimeter dog-track fence. The high tiers of seating we had paid for were left empty.

We must have been whooping, but mostly I remember simply stand-ing there, watching every stride in a sort of stunned awe.

Clarke remembers the crowd's reaction. "I began to think it must be fast when I saw many other athletes running across the dog track in excite-ment, and the crowd noise was deafening, so I knew I must be running something special. It added to my own excitement and helped me forget the pain. Adrenalin and pain are a heady mixture."

The last two laps belonged wholly to Clarke. Alone, he went striding into a new world. Alone, he kicked to a 60.1-second last lap, at last showing the effort. I clicked my windup stopwatch. The official time was 12:52.4.

Why were we so awestruck? Partly it was the sheer scale of the break-through. Roger Bannister in those days used to speak about records being broken by ever-diminishing fractions, yet here was a man hacking eight seconds off a tough record. He ran eighteen seconds faster—the length of the straight—than the old world mark from only eight months before. Ban-nister's sub-four mile was the climax to years of effort and debate. Clarke put the figure "12" in the book before anyone even thought of it as possible.

Partly it was Clarke himself that compelled our admiration. At that date, he had not yet been condemned to go down in history as the man who couldn't win, because he did win, often and well, as he did on this day. Lindgren ran 13:04, one of his best races and six seconds faster than anyone ever, except Clarke. Mecsér in third ran a tactically impeccable 13:07.6 to become the third fastest man in history. But both were confi-dently and skillfully beaten.

Clarke did it all by relentless training and fearless racing. He never dodged any opponent. In 1965, he raced forty-six times, plus local club races in Melbourne. Tragically for him, the 1966 Commonwealth Games were to be in the heat of Jamaica, and the 1968 Olympics in the high altitude of Mexico City, where he nearly died, was given emergency oxygen on the track, and paid the price in his long-term health and perhaps his early death.

When Clarke later visited Emil Zátopek in Prague, his host quietly gave him a wrapped package as they said goodbye. It proved to be one of Zátopek's own Olympic gold medals, making a silent statement that Clarke had fully deserved one.

In 1965, the disappointments for Clarke still lay ahead. We knew only that Clarke was making that post-Olympic year a time of heady excitement. In ten months, he broke eleven world records at eight distances, from 2 mi. to one hour. He didn't just break those records, he transformed them. Only four days after he impelled us down to the fence at White City, Clarke electrified a different crowd, of 25,000, at Bislett Stadium, Oslo, with a 27:39.4 10,000 m world record. That hacked 34.6 seconds off the world record he had set only a month earlier. He passed six miles in 26:47, breaking the Lindgren/Mills mark by 24.6 seconds. That's seventy seconds in total off world records in four days. There has never been a one-man rampage like it. Even Paavo Nurmi and Haile Gebrselassie rank behind Clarke for the sheer scale and range of record-breaking.

We four friends went to a runners' party in London that evening. We felt tipsy before we even left White City. Clarke's run intoxicated us, but we understood what it meant. The sport we loved and labored at was never going to be the same. Every runner at that party, and every runner in the world, would have to rethink our commitment to running, and either give it away or raise our sights. No more half measures or half effort, no relaxed loping like the graceful distance runners on Greek vases. Instead, hammer past halfway a few seconds outside your best and then kick the last mile faster. Get strong enough to absorb extra distance with only minimal loss of pace. That was what we had to train for now. And we would have to train, train, train. Dave Bedford, Lasse Viren, Haile Gebrselassie, Paula Radcliffe, Eliud Kipchoge, every great Kenyan marathoner—all have run in the manner Clarke made obligatory fifty years ago.

"We were blown away, physically and mentally. Everyone had to change their ideas about what was a good time," is how Tulloh remembers it.

That wasn't a comforting message for those of modest talent. By 1965, I had cut my 3 mi. PR to within forty seconds of the world record—close enough to dream. Suddenly, in twelve minutes on July 10, I watched Clarke move the top level of the sport beyond my imaginable grasp.

Oh well, get over it, I thought. You didn't become a runner because it's easy. "A man's reach should exceed his grasp," is how Browning put it. Ron Clarke made the very effort seem more worthwhile. It wasn't only that at full stride he looked like such an imposing physical specimen. It wasn't only that he ran such a total race: full effort, gun to tape, not merely a last-lap dazzle. He showed us that great running can be a thing of wonder, a perfect fusion of body, mind, and spirit—something, the Greeks believed, that can put mere humans closer to the gods.

Was this a day when running made "history?" Or was it only another world track record, made to be broken, now forgotten? To us it felt like more, and in this book, I am trying to convey how history felt at the time. We were all reaching beyond our grasp in the 1960s. We knew that grasp had limits—you couldn't grow up in Europe in the 1940s–50s and have heroic delusions. But free education, opportunity, access beyond the dreams of earlier generations, and the widespread ideal of creating a meritocracy made it a time when you could pretty much choose your own challenge, if you were willing to do the work it would take. Never before could someone from my economic origins have advanced to a Cambridge PhD. Never was the top level of a major sport filled with runners from such diverse places in society.

In *Run Strong, Stay Hungry*, a 2017 book about the motivation of lifelong runners, Jonathan Beverly concludes that the defining characteristic of those who compete rewardingly for many years is "hope," which he defines as "not a naive wish that things might be better," but a willingness to achieve improvement by committing "our own efforts," and "a refusal to quit in response to adversity" (194).

That's what our postwar generation had, more than any generation in Western culture since: the willingness to work to improve. We didn't seek fame or absolute victory, but only aspired to get better at the things we chose to do. Watching Clarke as a runner was for me like listening to C. S. Lewis as a lecturer on literature at Cambridge a few years earlier—he set a standard I could never attain, but one that made the aspiration more meaningful. In England in 1965 there was none of the sense of being privileged or entitled that seems prevalent now, nor do I recall that we felt competitive with each other. We never talked about "goals." We simply knew we had to strive. Twenty years earlier the World War II flying bombs were dropping on us and we were hungry. We were still lacking many material things that today are taken for granted. I know things were different in America, and American generosity helped to reshape the world. But Gerry Lindgren was a striver if ever there was one, and so were Buddy Edelen, Bob Schul, and Billy Mills.

Sometimes in my later years, as I discuss in the context of aging in chapter 21, I've been criticized for trying too hard in races. "Why don't you just have fun?" they ask. Well, for me, the effort is its own reward. Is that so weird? My lifetime of trying to run as well as I can has been utterly fascinating and significant (and thus fun); yes, often frustrating, sometimes bitterly disappointing, loading my memory with failures, regrets, and self-reproach, yet at other times bringing the exultation of improvement and success that has redefined my sense of self. The perfect race, the rare season when the results matched the trying, the breakthrough to a higher competitive level, the knowledge that I had fully developed the limited physical talents I was born with—few things have matched those satisfactions.

On July 10, 1965, the running mountain suddenly got higher, but more worth trying to climb. That was what Ron Clarke's run meant for me and my generation that night, and for more than fifty years it has never ceased to be true.

On a personal note, when I watched Ron Clarke's world record in July 1965, it was with runner friends from Cambridge University, where I was working on my PhD and tutoring for several colleges. I have lifelong gratitude to the system of publicly funded graduate scholarships. My thesis was on social themes in the novels of Henry Fielding, who was also a magistrate and journalist. I've always sought to link literature to life.

I loved the literary work and my running, and I shared that in common with a strong group of runners at Cambridge, especially Mike Turner. I invented a new word, "turnered," to describe the depleted state his training often induced. A Scottish graduate student, Mel Edwards, became another close friend, bringing a Highland fervor for ferocious interval training.

In 1966, at age twenty-six, I made the England cross-country team, won the British Universities cross-country title, and broke Gordon Pirie's Surrey Championship 3 mi. record, with 13:41. As always, I also wrote about running, now mostly for the daily *Cambridge News*. With my thesis done, I took a position at the University of Leeds for a rewarding year, but I had already agreed to accept a lectureship at the University of Canterbury, New Zealand, where I was looking for opportunity away from England's big cities. On the six-week sea voyage (my last, I vowed), I ran laps round and round the promenade deck, and I worked on lectures. I gave my first, on Shakespeare, the day we landed, September 4, 1968. I won the Canterbury Road Championship over 10 mi. a few weeks later.

In New Zealand, I found a running world similar to that of England, though more local because of the distance between population centers. Standards were high, with many runners following Arthur Lydiard's high-mileage training. Interclub team competition was important, far more so than it has ever been in America. As in England, but not yet America, women's running was fully accepted though only small in numbers and with shorter racing distances than men. (See chapter 9 for more about women's running.) I was warmly welcomed and accepted in Christchurch. Being a runner is always a passport to a community of friends. The first years weren't easy, but I managed to combine university work with running, sometimes working as administrator or official.

And so, a little more than five years after arriving from England, it happened that on January 24, 1974, the first day of track and field athletics at the Tenth British Commonwealth Games, the voice on the public address around Queen Elizabeth 2 Stadium, Christchurch, New Zealand, was mine.

7

January 24–February 2, 1974, Christchurch, New Zealand

A City's Identity Remade

On day one of the Tenth British Commonwealth Games, the 10,000 m, the first track final, was a spectacle from the start. Three Kenyans blocked and jostled the world record holder, Dave Bedford, as he sought the space he loved. If you let Bedford get away, let him run as he ran every day at home on Hampstead Heath, alone, zestful, relishing the miles, that long, springing stride, free and confident, he was supreme. Harass and crowd him, instill doubt, confine his flowing stride and flying spirit, and he could be beaten, as he had been in the 1972 Olympics. It was psychological and it was physical out there in the lead group: elbows and spikes more than once making contact, a touch of the old Roman Coliseum on the new red track of Queen Elizabeth 2 Stadium (QE2).

But, for the Christchurch crowd, combat turned to delighted disbelief as Dick Tayler of South Canterbury began to claw back the gap from the leaders.

As stadium announcer, I had to ensure the crowd could identify the leading runners: "Just over four laps to go, Black of England leads from Juma of Kenya, Bedford, and then back to Tayler of New Zealand in fourth."

While announcing at major track and field events like the Commonwealth Games, you need to provide basic information such as names and lap times, and if possible enhance the drama, but always without being descriptive or partisan. You can't say, as you could on television, "Wow! Look at Tayler, only twenty yards back now, he's closing and he's looking

13. Filbert Bayi holds off John Walker in the greatest 1,500 m Commonwealth Games, 1974. Mark Shearman–Athletics Images.

great!" That could be construed as partisan or "giving assistance." (This was before the giant stadium screen that athletes quickly learned to use for tactical information.) Knowing the runners can also make it hard to stay objective.

It was a world-class field. Bedford was the world record holder, Lachie Stewart was Commonwealth champion, Ian Stewart had been third in the 1972 Olympic 5,000 m (beating Steve Prefontaine), and the Kenyans were the new powerhouse. I'd been an observer in the announcers' box for Bedford's world record 10,000 m in London six months earlier, so when he arrived several weeks early in Christchurch, I offered to show him the best runs. We began a friendship, driving often in my twenty-five-year-old Ford Zephyr (same age as Dave was) out to the beach, where we ran many miles together on the sand and in the shady pine forest. I enjoyed his sharp mind and roguish London wit. Once the teams arrived, a group of British distance runners sometimes joined us out there, and we splashed in the sea after a hot run. I'd known Tony Simmons as a rising teenager in my last years in England, and I'd raced all three of the Kiwis, Kevin Ryan,

Phillip Watson (a Christchurch local), and Dick Tayler. When Tayler at age twenty-two won his first New Zealand championship, the road 15K in 1970, I was in the chasing pack as we all tacked behind Dick into the Dunedin wind.

Fortunately for me on that first day of the Commonwealth Games, as Bedford tensed and lost his flow, and Tayler closed, the crowd took over. With four laps to go, Tayler's potent all-black singlet and shorts were right there, in the front group. No information from me was needed. "Black! Black! Black! Black!" chanted the crowd of 34,000—the old rampant All Blacks rugby incantation.

With less than three laps to go, the pace rose a notch. Bedford slipped back. The race now was between Tayler, Richard Juma of Kenya, and David Black of England.

"Black! Black! Black! Black!" roared the crowd, united for Tayler. "Black! Black! Black!" until it began to dawn on them that one of Tayler's two stubborn rivals had the surname Black, and the other was black. You could hear their chant fade into uncertainty, like singers who have forgotten the words.

Now Tayler positioned himself threateningly on Dave Black's shoulder. "Tay-ler! Tay-ler!" someone started up, a lone voice to the rescue, and in relief the 34,000 voices joined in and rose to ecstatic crescendo. "Tay-ler! Tay-ler! Tay-ler!" They must have heard it on the sheep stations of the Canterbury Plains and in the foothills of the Southern Alps. For South Canterbury, this moment of epic spectacle stands unmatched by anything in *Lord of the Rings*. The dream day one script was enacted. Tayler from Timaru (one hundred miles south of Christchurch, still in Canterbury province and now on the daily minibus tour of Middle Earth) won the first track gold medal of the Games and cavorted like a gleeful kid on the finish line.

Christchurch itself was gleeful that week. The joke used to go, "Ladies and gentlemen, we are now landing in Christchurch. Please put your watches back twenty years." A little provincial cathedral city at the remotest edge of the world, famous only for sheep and choral music, it had always been known for being safe, placid, conventional, colonial, comfortingly retro English, and locked in its own inward-looking "first four ships" settler history. It was a place where every one-story house in every suburb was proud of its clipped lawn and tidy rose garden; a "great place to bring up kids" and drive twenty-five-year-old cars.

Now Christchurch was smartly hosting a major international sports festival, and a crowd of 34,000 in a cutting-edge new stadium was going crazy as a boy from just down the road beat the world's best.

In 2005, I was invited to chair a session at a conference called "New Zealand in the 1970s." My session was on film and television. I took my place at the lectern wearing my 1974 Commonwealth Games official's blazer—flashy bright scarlet, square cut, with padded Carnaby Street shoulders like Steed in "The Avengers."

"I'm dressed like this as a protest," I began, as I rose to my feet in that outfit, luridly inappropriate for an aging senior professor among all the academic faded-black T-shirts and carefully frayed jeans. "This conference is supposed to be about New Zealand in the 1970s, but its program completely omits the most significant thing the nation did in that decade: hosting the Christchurch Commonwealth Games," I said. "And since this session is about film and television," I went on, warming red like my jacket, "it's surely relevant that the 1974 Games were the first major sports event in the world to be designed from the start for color television, right down to the officials' jackets. Those Games led the world in design for the media era."

It was all a brand image: the red running track around the sharp green infield, the orange ventilation tubes above the blue of the swimming pool, the startling scarlet of those officials' jackets, and the red, white, and blue zigzags of the ubiquitous Games logo. That striking logo summed it up. It still alluded to the British Union Jack, yet brilliantly incorporated an edgy, modern version of "NZ" with the Roman X for the Tenth Games.

With bright primary colors, modern design values, and a savvy but friendly image, it was all a surprising self-affirmation by a city traditionally regarded as cautious and complacent. Looking back, it's as if Christchurch,

14. Tenth Commonwealth Games logo, 1974.

and arguably all New Zealand, was rebranded that week in the summer of 1974, transformed from monochrome to full color.

And there was another matter of image that was also one of substance. At the opening ceremonies of all Olympic and Commonwealth Games, it is always a closely guarded secret who will be the runner to carry the torch, or in this case the Games baton, on the last lap of its long relay from Sandringham Castle in England into the hands of the Duke of Edinburgh in front of a mass television audience. But we all knew it had to be Peter Snell. Who could displace the nation's only triple Olympic gold medalist? His national standing is godlike. But we were wrong. When the honored athlete appeared, it was the frail figure of Sylvia Potts, who at the previous Games in Edinburgh had stumbled and fallen just short of the line while leading the 880 yd. final. It was a courageous choice, a conscious remaking of identity, and a redefining of the values of sport (see chapter 9).

Without a doubt, the Commonwealth Games should be prominent in any historical account of New Zealand in the 1970s or any discussion of the interaction between such sports festivals and the communities that host them (a major subject for sports and social history). There certainly were precedents, which I touched on in chapter 3 with reference to Rome. Perhaps the most striking community leap forward was when Vancouver, tucked away on the outer edge of western Canada, hosted what were then quaintly called the British Empire and Commonwealth Games in 1954. A fine book, *The Miracle Mile: Stories of the 1954 British Empire and*

Commonwealth Games by Jason Beck (2016), documents how important those Games were in giving Vancouver a stronger sense of community, a multicultural self-image, and a more confident place in the world.

In 1974, Christchurch was as remote a backwater as Vancouver had been in the 1950s. When I took up my post at University of Canterbury in 1968, the journey was six weeks by sea from Britain. Phone calls to my parents could cost most of a day's salary. An airfare was four months' salary. Remoteness is the very essence of Canterbury, as the satirist Samuel Butler had identified a hundred years earlier. In anticipation of the Internet, he fantasized about a time when a Canterbury farmer would be able to put his sheep up for auction in London without leaving his shepherd's hut in the Southern Alps.

Christchurch in 1974, like Vancouver in 1954, and Melbourne in 1956, was ready to be less remote, to move on from its British colonial provincialism. An international Games enabled that to happen. No one quite understood at the time what was happening, because nothing like it had ever happened there before.

I became part of the Games because I got glandular fever. Those years at University of Canterbury were busy and demanding, with big lecture classes to win over to the English novel, Shakespeare, and Chaucer, huge grading loads, the commitment to research and publish, involvement in administration, transporting one or other of my two small sons to kindergarten on the crossbar of my old 28-in.-wheel bike into the Canterbury Plains wind (they were the envy of all the other kids who arrived boringly by car), a salary that could not always buy shoes for their growing feet, and somehow trying to keep my running firing. In the summer of 1972–73, it all caught up with me. "The young man's illness," the doctor called it: glandular fever or mononucleosis.

Unable to race, I stood in half-willingly as temporary announcer some Saturday afternoons at Christchurch's old track and field venue, Rugby Park, with its bumpy grass track, antique wooden grandstand, local kids building sandcastles in the long jump pit, and occasional vagrant suburban dog loose on the midfield. In the high front row of the stand, the announcer, working with a crackly public-address system, had to haul up the lane draws and results from the grass field on handwritten pages clamped in a bulldog paper clip at the end of a length of string.

That's how big of a technological leap Christchurch made: we used closed-circuit television in a state-of-the-art stadium for the Games in 1974. From that grassroots beginning in Rugby Park, I was unexpectedly asked to apply for the position of stadium announcer for the 1974 Games. It opened a new volunteer career that had never even occurred to me. I suppose I brought a mix of professional skills as a university lecturer, public speaker, and occasional radio broadcaster, to the pooling of volunteer talent that made those Games so successful.

So, despite an accent still largely English, I became announcer for track and field at the most international sports event ever held in New Zealand. This time I was not only witness to history. I was its public voice.

My fellow officials were good Kiwis, not inclined to let me get carried away by any idea of my own importance. Crusty old Ted Lunn, the track referee, used to greet me every morning with a low, tobacco-stained growl: "'ullo, Golden Voice."

Track and field announcing done well is no ego trip, by the way. It's a high-pressure job, demanding a complex range of expert and up-to-date knowledge (which changes by the day), intense concentration, and mental agility. You can't put a word wrong or mistime any statement in a sequence of long, hot days of nonstop multiple action. I brought to it scrupulous preparation that enabled me to introduce each event in a way that helped crowds of 34,000 enjoy what for most was their first track meet since school.

You also must remember that all the competitors hear everything you say. There may be four or five events going on at a time. Each may be life-shaping for some of the athletes. Even if someone's running a world record, the shot put is equally important, especially for the shot putters.

I eventually did forty-five years at the announcing job: every regular Saturday meet as well as high-profile championships and international tours. It's unremitting hard work. But there's a fun side, too. I enjoyed giving voice to the drama, especially in events like the shot put where drama is not obvious. More than anything, I enjoyed meeting the athletes, because

I always tried to locate them beforehand to ask about their names. At what might be the most public moment of their entire life, they are entitled to have their name announced right. I had the Nigerians rolling on the grass kicking their legs in the air with hilarity as I stumblingly practiced their polysyllables. I learned that the "B" in Fijian is "Mb" (the greeting "Bula!" is pronounced "Mbula!" and the name "Rabuka" was "Rambuka"). A university colleague who had worked in East Africa was helpful. He taught me painstakingly that "Ayoo" (a Ugandan hurdler, I think) is pronounced "Ay-oh-oh." For years afterward, when we passed on campus, we would greet each other with "Ay-oh-oh, Cassells." "Ay-oh-oh, Roger."

So that's how I came to be driving through the Christchurch suburbs of St. Alban's, Mairehau, and Burwood in January 1974, on my way to be stadium announcer at the first day of the Commonwealth Games.

As I drove east through those modest flatland suburbs of one-story houses, the Games stadium rose like a clean, linear symbol of the future out of sandy marshlands. It "rose like an exhalation," as Milton says in *Paradise Lost*. It was deeply saddening to go back after the 2011 earthquake and find drab, flat open space again, dust, debris, and dirty liquefaction. In its own way and era, QE2 meant as much to Christchurch as the central city's iconic Victorian neo-Gothic cathedral. Both buildings embodied what a small, obscure community can achieve when they put their minds to it.

Arriving at the stadium that day in 1974, we were suddenly in the urgent present. The people of Christchurch knew how important this event was, and they were ready.

"I could see the crowd queuing to get into QE2. It was amazing—eight in the morning, thousands of eager people. That's the moment I realized I was part of a huge historic event, in a full stadium—and only three miles from my family home," recalled pentathlete Barbara Beable.

Those ten summer days in 1974 were a communal achievement of lasting effect. The colorful rebranding of Christchurch was founded on the community's long-established strengths, modest though those may seem. The most important unknown statistic of the whole festival is that among the thousands of citizens who contributed on dozens of committees to the months of preparation, not one dropped out, other than for reason of relocation or death. Chairman Sir Ron Scott's official report also affirmed, "There was not one instance of failure to perform." Impeccable committee work is not as newsworthy as Dick Tayler's last lap or Filbert Bayi's climactic world record, but it did just as much to make the Games a success.

That impeccable work reflected a tradition of Christchurch culture. The night after I arrived off the ship from Britain in 1968, after I had lectured on Shakespeare's *The Winter's Tale* that same afternoon (skipping the storm-at-sea scene), I sat in the motel room reading a little red-and-white brochure about Christchurch and its attractions that gave something like ten pages to listing the city's clubs and societies. From quilting to home wine-making, from wrestling to ludo, from choral singing to cat-breeding, people of shared interest had formed themselves into a club. That's how that remote little community created its own homemade culture, because when you were 12,000 miles from London in 1968 there was no point in waiting for the world's best to come calling. The people I knew all held themselves to high standards. Local theater and music were typical. You could not see a more powerful production of *Marat/Sade* or hear the choruses of "The Messiah" sung better anywhere in the world.

If you live in New York or London, that's not how things work. But in Christchurch, when the need came to organize a huge, multifaceted international Games, the local community possessed a deep pool of skill and experience in reliable and accountable management, all volunteer.

Volunteers ran the Games. That's something scholars now write theses about, so it is worth putting on record here. The Canterbury Rugby Supporters Club affixed the numbers to 34,000 seats. The New Zealand swimming squad did the same job for the pool. Car-parking was controlled by the Lions Club, Girl Guides were ushers, Scouts sold programs. Officials received no expenses and paid part of the cost of our uniforms. Some staff were seconded by public service departments. And so on.

Counting all those committees and volunteers, and all those involved in roles like catering, police, journalism, the arts festival, and building the stadium, the percentage of the total adult Christchurch population of 250,000 who directly contributed must have been at least twenty-five percent. Christchurch had reason to feel ownership.

Ron Scott as Games CEO brought the vision of a public relations specialist, skilled in the art of rebranding, and provided the kind of ego-free leadership to which New Zealanders respond. Not long before his death in 2016, I asked him to reflect on the Games from forty years later.

"Christchurch provided hundreds of skilled and knowledgeable people, and the rest of New Zealand gave total support, including finance from every local authority but one. The organizing committee were mostly company CEOs and knew how to manage things better than I did. All the committees were incredibly productive. We were ready early and could devote the last year to what we called 'finesse,' in every area. And it was satisfying to make a profit!" Scott said.

Scott used to regale friends with stories of how the initial funds were raised: a woman baking scones and cakes and selling them from her front gate, a paraplegic swimmer raising sponsorship for lengths of a pool, a ninety-four-year-old widow knitting clothes and selling them from a stall, a ten-year-old girl with terminal cancer who gathered her toys and donated them to Scott. "It was Kiwi do-it-yourself from start to finish," Scott said.

All very Christchurch. But at a less apparent level, so was the ingenuity and openness to innovation: a computerized ticketing system, the design for color television, the rethought strategy for public address announcing. Christchurch has always used ingenuity to make do with limited resources. They bred sheep profitably in the Southern Alps when the farmers had to build their own huts and it took six months to get the sheep to England. They built a cathedral city with tools carried on sailing ships. They created a 400-acre midcity park before there was a city. They did much the same with the Games facilities. QE2 was a unique double, with the running track and swimming pool literally back to back. The pool met Olympic requirements but had a waterpark attached. The running track was designed for triple duty as a venue for soccer and greyhound racing. Around that complex later came tennis, golf, miniature golf, indoor sports, and other things that enabled the whole park to become a family play-ground. It served the city well for almost forty years, until the earthquake destroyed it.

It was as if the challenge of the Games enabled Christchurch to remake its identity in that inventive spirit of the first settlers, not the con-formity that seemed to have replaced it. (I once traced this same cultural duality in a literary study, comparing the various editions of a book called *Canterbury Rhymes*, which went from a comically inventive collection in 1866, debunking immigrant utopianism, to being pompous, conformist, and dutifully imperialist in 1900. Sports history can be at least as revealing as literary history of what the Marxist critic Raymond Williams used to call 'the structure of feeling' of a community or era.)

The Christchurch model remains influential. Since 1974, successful Olympic and Commonwealth Games like Sydney (2000), Manchester (2002), and London (2012) have followed the Christchurch mix of busi-ness management, creative presentation, and massive but spirited local volunteer involvement. The world's greatest road races, most of them essentially local nonprofit enterprises, are built on the same principles. When President Obama announced a program to create a volunteer cul-ture in the United States, he might have noted that running had already provided the model.

If the 1948 Olympics largely managed to avoid politics, not many big Games since then have had that luxury. Only some skilled diplomacy saved the Christchurch Games from the large-scale boycott that at one point looked inevitable. For months, the "new" Commonwealth nations were uncommitted, and near-disaster would have ensued if apartheid South Africa's rugby team had been permitted to tour New Zealand in 1973 as planned. In an atmosphere of political turmoil, New Zealand's Labour government reversed its previous policy and canceled the rugby tour. That enabled Scott to do some self-effacing diplomatic work, includ-ing a previously unreported visit to meet Jomo Kenyatta privately in Nai-robi, which brought the African and other nations on board. That was another way in which the 1974 Commonwealth Games made history, though sadly it didn't change the world.

Near the end of his life, Scott sometimes shared such stories with friends. One night before the Games, he was woken at 3 a.m. by a personal call from Idi Amin, tyrant ruler of Uganda, who let Scott know about the extensive retinue he planned to have around him in Christchurch and listed their demands for hospitality. "Oh, Mr. President, New Zealand is a very small and inferior country, and we don't have accommodation worthy of you and your retinue," Scott ad-libbed, his head full of the horror of having the monster of Africa hobnobbing with the Queen as an honored guest.

In the end, the new Commonwealth fully supported what were dubbed "the Friendly Games," and the crowds acclaimed their teams. The Caribbean was already familiar as a sprint force (and for West Indian cricket), but the East African sweep of the men's 800 m, 1,500 m, 5,000 m, and 3,000 m steeplechase gold medals was unprecedented. Africa won fifty-two medals, fifteen gold. It was the first time the continent achieved such a presence on any world sporting stage. In distance running, Kenya's successes at the 1966 Commonwealth Games and 1968 Olympics had been attributed to the heat of Jamaica and the altitude of Mexico City, and the more modest Kenyan results at Edinburgh in 1970 and Munich in 1972 seemed to confirm that. But Christchurch was neither hot nor high. Kenya had truly arrived. The first display of total African dominance in off-track running also happened in New Zealand (see chapter 10).

I wasn't involved in the diplomacy, other than being aware as announcer that I needed to be scrupulously fair, handle firmly and formally anything controversial—like a disqualification in the steeplechase after a clash between a Welsh and a Kenyan athlete—and provide leadership in matters like the pronunciation of all names. That kind of equal respect makes a political affirmation of its own.

The title "Friendly Games" not only refuted apartheid but alluded to the terrorist murders at Munich in 1972, which came near to destroying the whole Olympic movement. The threatened world we now live in began halfway through Christchurch's preparation. Security was increased, and all of us involved were coached in the risks, but it was done in a Kiwi way, and was never obtrusive.

I can claim a few successful firsts in my role as announcer. One came in the decathlon. Eleven men, ten events, two days. It was like reading a multiplot novel. We came to know the diverse characters: the Englishman, the Irishman, the Scotsman, the happy Tongan, two fierce Fijians, and everyone's favorite, the lovable Samoan-Kiwi, Mene Mene. We felt for them as their fortunes rose and fell, and we watched them build bonds of respect among themselves.

When it was time for the medal presentation, I suggested to the head of athletics, Barry Kerr, that all eleven should be invited out for the medal ceremony, not just the top three. The crowd loved it. It was such a harmonious and sporting moment that it has become standard practice.

The fervid job of announcer can implant things deep into your mind. Thirteen years later, I heard on radio news that the Fijian Parliament had been taken over in an army coup led by a Colonel Rabuka. "Sitiveni Rabuka," I said aloud, and then wondered how on earth I knew his full name. It had not been used on radio. Hours later, it came to me. He was in that 1974 decathlon (he finished last), as well as the shot and discus. I had carefully pronounced his name, "Siti-veni Ram-booka," dozens of times that arduous week. It stuck, deep in the sludge of my memory, to rise unbidden when I heard his surname spoken.

Rabuka and others at the back of the field got full and fair coverage. Our policy for the public-address announcing was scrupulous equity. No jingoism. No celebrity raving. As Scott wrote, many years later: "Roger's fair, distinct and informed approach was mentioned by several team managements, and was one of the defining hallmarks of the whole Games." Forgive the quote; announcers rarely receive praise.

The crowd was exuberantly partisan when it got the chance, but also generous to all competitors. They even cheered Australians. They reveled in races like the wonderful 800 m, where two tall, commanding Kenyans, John Kipkurgat and Mike Boit, in the striking all-white that Kenya wore at those Games (even down to their long, white socks flashing on their long, black legs), held out the emergent New Zealander John Walker, only a dot outside the world record.

Another announcing coup (not my idea) was brilliantly successful. The race starter was patched into the public address. When his stern command suddenly resonated to every seat in the stadium, "Take your marks!" the whole arena went rigid in silence, as if the headmaster had spoken.

A last personal note. During all those hot hours in the little announcers' room, keeping track of four or five events at once, my challenge was to find and precisely time the information that would help 34,000 people enjoy the mysteries of the hammer throw or the pentathlon (as it was then), as well as the more accessible drama of the middle-distance races. And I had to do all that without affecting the punctual flow of the varied events or ever interfering with the athletes. That's not easy when highly strung pole vaulters or high jumpers can take what seems forever while you are almost stifling yourself for the sake of their concentration.

I am especially proud of one innovation, something I believe I did better than even Britain's Peter Matthews or America's Bob Hersh, the two best announcers of that era. I figured out that in the bewildering six-ring circus of track and field, the announcer's greatest contribution is not to "commentate," or tell the crowd what is happening or has already happened ("She's over! What a great jump you just missed seeing!"), but to tell them what is going to happen ("Next at the high jump is Elizabeth Bennet, for her third and final attempt at a height that would keep her in medal contention"). Sticking to this principle that I invented, a moment came during the first heat of the women's 1,500 m, when the crowd was going patriotically berserk for New Zealand runner Anne Garrett (later Audain), and I turned up the volume and interrupted.

"At the discus," I said, quickly, but firmly over the crowd's roaring, "next to throw, in the third round, is Tait of New Zealand, currently in third place."

And that is how 34,000 Kiwis (I like to think) took their eyes off Garrett long enough to witness the second of New Zealand's two gold medals. They're telling their grandchildren to this day that they saw Robin Tait make the winning throw, whether they did or not. Alone, I did it. My job, as I reinvented it, was to tell them what to watch and where to look, not rave about what they were watching anyway.

Tait popped the big one, and for the rest of the contest the big man strutted about like a prize rooster, declining any more throws, however much the crowd pleaded.

To get back to my main theme, these Games were essentially the expression of a community's whole culture at a moment of transition. I won't use the cliché "transformative," because I'm arguing that the inventive, innovatory Christchurch had always been there, though not dominant for 150 years, and that more conformist strengths like committee work were also key. There had long been a socially broad community that supported rugby, but that was almost wholly male. In 1974, the Games drew in everyone, to work on committees or contribute to the arts festival or sit in the stands and cheer, and sometimes it went to their very doors.

The marathon (only men's, in those benighted times), started at 5 p.m., a public relations masterstroke. It is always the marathon that brings sport to the people—that is one source of its huge social impact. With an out-and-back course that passed hundreds of homes, after work, so that everyone could see the race go by at least twice, it's not much of an exaggeration to say the whole city came out to watch. They saw the almost unknown Ian Thompson of England run away from a field that included such famous names as Ron Hill and Derek Clayton. They saw the forty-one-year-old New Zealander Jack Foster rewrite the world's notions of aging with 2:11.19 in second place, which stood as the world's best over-forty time for sixteen years. For many, this was their Games.

The track races are legendary. The men's 800 m, 1,500 m, 5,000 m, and marathon were faster than at any Olympics to that date. Raelene Boyle of Australia, who won both women's sprints, had been silver medalist at Munich in 1972.

The greatest race of all came on the last day, the men's 1,500 m. It was the grand climax and most stunning surprise of a superb week. We'd seen Ben Jipcho win the 5,000 m by 0.2 seconds from Brendan Foster and then dominate the 3,000 m steeplechase, and Mike Boit and John Walker finish second and third in the near world record 800 m. Rod Dixon was Olympic 1,500 m bronze medalist from 1972. The 1,500 m would surely lie between those five.

A less obvious possible medalist was Filbert Bayi from Tanzania. He had placed fourth in the 800 m, overshadowed by the fervent race between the two great Kenyans and the youthful brilliance of Walker, who flew past Bayi on the final straight. Introducing the 1,500 m field, I gave Bayi's credentials—fourth in the 800 m and African Games 1,500 m champion in 1973, beating Kipchoge Keino. But it was Walker, Dixon, Jipcho, and Foster the crowd rose for. For almost the last time, the starter's voice boomed out over the public address: "Take your marks!"

It was as if Bayi was shot out from the gun. By the end of the first straight he was three meters ahead. Tiny, with a quick bouncy stride, he pushed relentlessly away from the surging, shifting pack. Boit led the chase, then Jipcho. Dixon and Walker loomed, long hair flying, looking huge by comparison with the lone figure of Bayi. Foster and Australia's Graeme Crouch were always in the mix, and a mix it was, except for the solitary, separated leader. At 800 m, 1:51.8, Bayi was on pace to break Jim Ryun's world record; he was an astonishing twenty meters clear. On the public address I was groping for precedents. Not since John Landy against Bannister in Vancouver in 1954 had anyone led a big championship four-lapper so uncompromisingly. Not since Nurmi in 1924 had such audacity ended in victory.

Bayi couldn't hold on, surely—so riskily fast, so alone, so tiny and vulnerable. After 800 m, he would have to ease, forced by sheer pressure to slow, as did Landy and Nurmi. He did, but only to 58.6. No one before had ever reached 1,200 m in 2:50.4.

At the bell, Bayi had looked doomed. But now, at 1,200 m, with two thirds of a lap to go, from behind the hammer cage as I saw it, miraculously, he surged again. Suddenly his lead was back to twenty meters over the chase pack. It was tactical brilliance. And were they chasing! This wasn't a watchful, waiting pack; it was a frantic, urgent, incredulous one, desperate to close down a lead that broke every rule, ravening like hounds after the fox. As they rounded the last bend, it was Walker who seized destiny and charged around Jipcho into second. Now the final hunt was on, and the gap closed. His blond hair flying like an avenging Nordic thunder-god, Walker hurtled in pursuit. Yes, the gap kept closing. Along the straight, with only fifty meters to go, it looked all over. Walker had closed the gap to a fragile three meters, and he was pulsating with power. Time for the kill. But this undaunted little Tanzanian was not for killing. Perfectly poised and assured, looking as if he wasn't hurrying, Bayi found yet one more gear.

"World record! World record!" I cried above the wildly roaring crowd as he crossed the line. We had a policy of no announcing during the last two hundred meters of any race (the crowd doesn't need you then), but this was a finish for the ages. It broke all precedents and policies.

Bayi later revealed how in control he was: "On the last bend, I saw people coming. I waited. And then John Walker came about three meters at fifty meters to go, and then I just accelerated." I like his word "just." It was pure running genius.

That race stands as the greatest 1,500 m in history, with the world record and five national records for Tanzania, New Zealand, Kenya (Jipcho), Australia (Crouch), and Great Britain (Foster). Announcing that list, I added that we had just seen an Australian, in fifth place, break the Australian record that had been Herb Elliott's gold medal world record at the Rome Olympics in 1960. Privately, I reflected that Elliott's was the greatest 1,500 m I'd ever seen in person, till this one.

After the race, the athletes clustered outside my ground-level announcer's room, so I opened the side window and asked Brendan Foster how it felt to break the British record and finish only seventh. His reply melted the wiring.

It's hard to imagine a grander climax to any Games. Bikila's marathon in 1960 is the only one I've witnessed to match it. But the announcer's job doesn't stop. The women's high jump went on (and on and on, it seemed, as the winner relished her moment and the Queen polished her fingernails outside). One last victory ceremony and at last I could lie back and let the closing ceremony end the Games with what became a frolicsome, unscripted celebration. Even the Queen unbent slightly.

But even after the royals finally processed out of the stadium, with multiethnic athletes jogging mischievously alongside the Queen's car and clambering all over Princess Anne's, it wasn't over. The people of Christchurch didn't want it to be over. I was one of the last to leave, as always. I drove home along the route the athletes took every night to return to the Games village. Along those ordinary suburban streets of Mairehau and St. Alban's, people were still standing at their gates, applauding every car that looked as if it held Games athletes or officials as we drove past.

They wanted, I suppose, a last chance to be part of the extraordinary human happening that their community had created. Perhaps they were impelled to show once more their pride that their modest, do-it-yourself little provincial city had created one of the superlative sports festivals of the modern world. Perhaps they wanted the new image and spirit of their community to be sealed as permanent. Perhaps it was. Four decades later, it helped them endure the trauma that afflicted them after 2010.

Whatever the reason, in Mairehau and St. Alban's they were still out on their doorsteps, lingering on the grass verges, peering over trim front hedges, leaning over their gates, looking one last time for someone from the Games to clap for, even if it was only a very weary stadium announcer driving home in a twenty-five-year-old car.

8

June 1–September 19, 1980, Fountain Valley, Kansas City, Lynchburg

The Boom!

A year after the 1974 Commonwealth Games, I was appointed full professor of English at Victoria University of Wellington, New Zealand, a surprise early promotion that I expected would reduce or even end my involvement with running. But Wellington's windblown hills proved good for my health and fitness, I ran well enough to place fifth and second in national championships, and at age thirty-seven I was (proudly and incredulously) selected for New Zealand at the 1977 World Cross-Country. I was also pressed into weekly service as Wellington's track announcer, did some coaching, and continued to write running journalism. At one point, I wrote as "Gayle Fawce, Wellington correspondent," a name that punned on Wellington's notorious windiness.

In 1980, with the unnerving prospect of being made dean at age forty-one, I got away for some research leave. I wanted to see America, which had great libraries and had apparently discovered running. I thought that maybe I could sample the increasingly big road races I'd read about, with fields in the thousands, I'd heard, disbelievingly. I had read about a new phenomenon, the New York City Marathon, which in the American bicentennial year of 1976 had gone out of Central Park into the city streets and almost immediately exploded to become the biggest footrace of all time. I wish I'd been there to run that historic day, to include it in this book, but in October 1976 I was more than fully occupied with university work and getting my best national championship result: second (to Jack Foster) in the New Zealand road championships.

15. "America invented the concept of a road race as a party." Utica Boilermaker postrace party, 2017. Courtesy of Bill Keeler.

When the research leave came in 1980, my problem was money. The New Zealand dollar was cripplingly low, so I wrote some letters in those pre-email days and I received kind advice and an invitation from the leading American runner-writer Hal Higdon. I booked sixteen-day Amtrak passes and, with my tolerant first wife and two teenage sons, landed in Los Angeles ready to travel coast to coast via rail and road race, saving on accommodation in return for running some races.

June 1, 1980: Fountain Valley, California

Two days later, a warm Sunday morning in June 1980, I won the Huntington Beach Elks 10K in Fountain Valley and was enthusiastically greeted at the finish by the race committee, all large, friendly men, all in bright canary-yellow jackets, all drinking beer. I had stumbled innocent and unknowing into the American running boom at its true grass roots. When I made the arrangements, I had no clue how far Fountain Valley, Los Angeles, is from Los Angeles Airport (about 35 miles), nor how inadequate public transport is in the Los Angeles region, nor what Elks are, nor how many excited and expensively shod American runners would show up for a seemingly obscure race on a sleepy Sunday morning in a commuter township.

We'd spent the previous day at Disneyland, and that Sunday I wondered at times if I was still there. If this was reality, it was different from any I'd known. "Trophies and medals were presented by Exalted Ruler Earl G. Roach. After the ceremonies, a delightful breakfast was served by the Cinderellas," reported the Elks' own journal, *The Derrick* (July 1980).

Races like this were sprouting up all over America in 1980. By the thousand is no exaggeration. Some took root and became part of the culture of running and of their host locality. Some came, conquered, and went, like the Huntington Beach Elks 10K. All provided incentive that drew more and more Americans into running for its health benefits, its communal spirit, and its sheer fun. With little existing structure for post-collegiate running in the United States, many races were put on by people like the Huntington Beach Elks Lodge, who had sparse knowledge of running but saw a demand and a way of raising money for the good causes they support, and who were willing to give their weekend time to organize an event for several hundred race-hungry runners, mostly new to the sport.

What I saw that Sunday I later recognized as a uniquely American combination of efficiency, generosity, local pride, party-spirits, and show-biz. I'm serious—it was America that invented the concept of a road race as a party. The sociable lingering around laden tables that is such a pleasure of the sport was unknown before America thought of it in the 1970s.

For me, still competitive at forty-one, the race was like any race. Some of my competitors went out too fast on the mostly flat course; I ran watchfully, nursed my jet lag, moved through, judged my moment, broke away at halfway, and won without stress in 30:45. But nothing else was like any race I'd known, not the huge field, nor the balloons and flags and music, nor the heaped plates of breakfast, nor the infectious generous zest of the spectators and volunteers, nor the yellow jackets of the supervising Elks, nor their early morning beer, nor the sense that it all supported good causes outside running.

All I'd hoped for at Fountain Valley was a warm-up race in return for a night's accommodation and being dropped off later at the Santa Ana train station to start our long coast-to-coast journey. Looking back, I also gained the bonus of being again, in a small but authentic way, a witness to history, glimpsing in this preliminary grassroots encounter three of the essentials that went into creating the running boom, and still sustain it today: local initiative, a welcoming festive spirit, and raising money for charities.

There's an extraordinary binary chemistry in modern running, an interweaving of local and global. Running is a worldwide community, but that global community is sustained by the separate efforts of innumerable disparate local communities. Runners everywhere feel we belong together, yet there is no formal federation except for track and field. Big race directors are like regional warlords. Little race directors work independently of each other. Fountain Valley was an early and very minor contributor, but their absorption in the race operations and their pride in communal accomplishment made it all the more typical. That's how the American running boom happened.

June 7, 1980: Kansas City, Missouri

The next stop showed me how big, sophisticated, high-powered, well-connected, and affluent the American running boom had already become. I had never set foot in a hotel as grand as the Crowne Plaza in Kansas City. I'd never been given a free room, free meals, or a race shirt. I'd never seen race officials and volunteers all in matching outfits. I'd never been at a race where the results would be processed by computer ("hopefully, complete results will be available and in the mail within two weeks"). I'd never sat in on a cutting-edge sports medicine conference. I'd often been a speaker for running seminars in New Zealand, but never part of a forum like the star-studded lineup that entertained and educated eager audiences at the Hospital Hill Run Half-Marathon. Hal Higdon had trustingly secured a speaker spot for me.

I'd never raced a half-marathon. Until the running boom, they barely existed. To explain why, and to set the context in which the running boom happened, I'll offer a little history.

Back in the years immediately after the 1908 Olympics, when "marathon mania" swept the world, and marathons, especially indoors, became big business on the east coast of the United States, most long races (anything from six miles up) called themselves "marathons," while some confessed to being "modified marathons." The earliest I know of went from the Bronx to New York's city hall in 1911, when the *New York Times* colorfully reported how noisy, half-clad runners dashing about city hall caused panic among a group of women teachers also using the hall's facilities. In the 1930s to 1950s, several half-marathons were held in South and Central America, and the Victorian Marathon Club in Australia held one in 1953. In the United States, the earliest were the Fontana Days Half-Marathon in 1956 and Operation Snowball, which was first hosted by the DC Road Runners in 1963. In England, I recently spotted an ad in a 1961 issue of *Athletics Weekly* for the Romford Half-Marathon in east London. The earliest half-marathons that still continue are probably the Route du Vin in Luxembourg (1961) and the Freckleton Half-Marathon in Lancashire, United Kingdom, where the first race over that quirky distance in 1964 was won by Ron Hill. Today, the ongoing running boom is in large part a boom in half-marathons, which are especially attractive to the growing community of women runners. There are thousands of half-marathons worldwide, the largest in Gothenburg, Sweden, with 60,000 runners. But the distance was an eccentricity in the 1960s.

Overall, road racing was minor and not nearly as significant as cross-country and track, except for the Olympic marathon and the very few major marathons: Boston, Polytechnic, Enschede, Košice, and Fukuoka. And while we had our sixes and tens and twenties, most road races were not over set distances at all, but a traditional loop or point-to-point route, often town to town like the original steeplechases (village steeple to village steeple). Britain's first was Morpeth to Newcastle, and another typical point to point was Darlington to Barnard Castle, about 16 mi. on a road across moorland, where in 1968 I suffered from one of northeast England's rare hot days. The distances were random, so each race had its unique identity. One of the oldest and greatest, the New Year's Eve São Silvestre in São Paulo, Brazil, founded in 1924, varied over the years and did not settle at 15K until 1991, a sign of our more regulated era.

Some of the earliest running boom races were similarly conceived to offer a race of unique character rather than a regulation distance. The Falmouth Road Race in Cape Cod was created in 1973 by bartender and runner Tommy Leonard; it was a run between two bars, the Captain Kidd in Woods Hole to the Brothers Four in Falmouth, 7.3 mi., though no one cared much in those days about the exact measurement. Leonard was inspired by watching Frank Shorter's Olympic marathon victory on television in the Brothers Four bar, and he wanted a race combined with a festive party. As I said above, that combination was a component of the fuel that powered the American boom. Another of the best was Springbank in London, Ontario (Canada was often important in the story), where runners as good as Amby Burfoot, Jerome Drayton, Ron Hill, Kenny Moore, and Frank Shorter came to win over 18.6 km and later 18.5 km (11.55 mi.). That, too, eventually became a certified half-marathon.

Or, adding further to each race having its unique identity, the course took in some natural feature of the terrain, like North America's oldest, the Around the Bay Road Race in Hamilton, Ontario (founded 1895, still going strong), or southern England's Hog's Back Road Race (Farnham to Guildford, up and along the ridge, about 9.6 mi.), where I'd chased Buddy Edelen in 1962 and 1963.

Now, about the mid-1970s, all that began to change. The new generation of runners had their imaginations caught in new ways. The very idea of half a marathon really makes a statement about the new magic of the word "marathon." However obscure and local, a modern half-marathon by its very name acquires a little of the glamor and significance of Athens, Boston, New York, or (after 1981) London. Names were important in the early running boom, as I discuss in the next section of this chapter. "Marathon" was the big one. It became universal currency. Before 1980, in England or New Zealand, whenever I met another runner, the key question to start the acquaintance was always, "what's your best national?" (i.e., placing in the national cross-country championship). In running's new American world, that question had become, "what's your best marathon [time]?" Frank Shorter's gold medal inspired that change, plus the magnetic allure of the New York City Marathon post-1976.

Marathons and then half-marathons sprang up (see appendix A). By 1980, the United States was leading the world in creating great half-marathon races and fast runners. Four American women and five men set world records on American courses (Michiko Gorman 1978, Ellison Goodall 1979, Patti Catalano 1979, and Joan Benoit, who broke the record four times, her fastest 68:34 in 1984; and Kirk Pfeffer 1979, Stan Mavis 1980, Herb Lindsay 1981, Paul Cummings 1983, and Mark Curp, 60:55, 1985). Curp tuned up for his world-record Philadelphia Distance Classic performance with a 63:48 course record on his notoriously hot and hilly home turf of the Hospital Hill Run.

I didn't know all that history until many years after I stepped off the train in Kansas City in 1980, but that was the context I stepped into: a sport on the cusp of historic change, in the middle of a creative five-year period when the new running boom was making that earlier era obsolete. Mingling with runners, listening to the speakers at the Symposium on Physical Fitness, and soaking up this vigorous new running culture, I began to feel inadequate because I'd never run a marathon. It was as if I was traveling without a passport. A half-marathon seemed a good way to start.

It's hard to communicate how new and full of creative energy it all seemed. Having a medical symposium in conjunction with a road race was stimulating; it was an important connection between running and the health profession, and it recognized the intellectual significance that I have always believed is part of running. That symposium was when I first heard of the anaerobic threshold and amenorrhea, and I realized that elite runners can be important subjects for studying the human body under extreme stress. I saw a new attitude, the beginnings of a view of exercise as natural and necessary, and a kind of sports medicine that above all fosters the health benefits of exercise rather than only healing injuries.

Throughout the whole weekend there was a palpable vibrancy, a feeling that we were all breaking new ground, a zestful joining together, and a sharing of information, ideas, and stories. This was not just another race of the kind I knew. No loneliness for these long-distance runners; this seemed to be a bustling, brave new community of welcoming and positive people. I would see more, perhaps understand more, at other races. I'm trying now to recapture how it felt at the time. Future historians will be better placed to interpret it all.

Also new, for a sport that used to be rough around the edges, was the sense that things were being done at high quality. Not only the high-level commitment of runners, great and less great, but the whole culture and its settings and operations had moved into a new world that made my scruffy old running look prehistoric. There was no football whistle to summon runners to the start, no wavering chalk line to stand behind, no heaps of tracksuits, no traffic to fight or pedestrians to weave through, no fading chalk arrows as the only marking of the course, no scrambling sidewalk finish zone or cloakroom tickets on a spike to record your place. Here, we were mingling in the Crowne Plaza. The speaker forum was held in a state-of-the-art conference room.

The speaker list tells a lot about where the running boom was in 1980 and the elements that had gone into its making. There were the sports medicine experts, who were already using running to break new ground. Derek Clayton was world record holder for the marathon and also worked for *Runner's World*. A running magazine that could employ people! Never before had I met a top runner making a good living from something so essentially related to running. There was talk of things like shoe contracts, the Frank Shorter apparel line, stores devoted to running shoes and clothes, camps where runners went to get intensive coaching, and a famous speaker called George Sheehan (not there that year) . . . all new. I was listening hard, learning as I went, and glimpsing the beginnings of what we now confidently call the running industry. From hindsight, I have set out some of the key initiatives and their dates in appendix A.

Gayle Barron, the voice of another key initiative, spoke about winning the Boston Marathon in 1978 and about a race in her home state called Peachtree, which was only ten years old but already huge. Barron also spoke about women as partners in the running boom and how they would become equal partners in the near future.

Hal Higdon told skillfully funny stories aimed at helping every runner feel significant. As a writer, Higdon was the pioneer, followed quickly by Joe Henderson, George Sheehan, and Don Kardong, and later by Jonathan Beverly, Bart Yasso, and John Bingham, in a new kind of running writing: neither the life stories of great champions nor coaching how-to, but personal reflections on what running means, and especially what it means to the not necessarily talented individual runner. Surveying this new field in my book *Running in Literature* (2003, 238), I wrote that these writers "have given rich expression to the activity they love . . . [in] books that remind me that running is universal and raises important issues." Higdon also terrified me that day in 1980 by repeatedly warning that if you race hard in such hot, humid weather, "your kidneys will shut down." I didn't know they could. Dr. Jack Scaff of the Honolulu Marathon assured us that regular running gives us protection from heart problems. He also (I think I remember) insisted that we drink a lot of beer.

Not all of these were new ideas to me, although never before had I raced for 13.1 mi. worrying about when my kidneys would shut down. But the sheer scale was new, as was the conference-like sense of absorbing yourself in running as a subject and learning from a variety of expert practitioners. That Saturday afternoon was a microcosm of the way the whole 1970s/1980s running movement built an expanding culture around the explosion of new races.

The Hospital Hill Run was one of the first races to grow to boom proportions. Four thousand ran that day in 1980, by far the biggest race I had ever run or witnessed. It began in 1974 as a 6.8 miler, which was typical of the earlier era. The story tells a lot about the sources of the boom. Dr. E. Grey Diamond, head of the University of Missouri–Kansas City School of Medicine, planned a symposium on physical fitness and had the idea of including a run. Dr. Ken Cooper's *Aerobics* (first published in 1968) had swept America, preaching the health value of exercise, especially running. Its appearance in the mass-market *Readers' Digest* was a seminal event in the running boom. Health-conscious Americans began to run for reasons other than to commit to the competitive sport. In Kansas City, another physician who was a runner, Dr. Ralph Hall, supported the proposal to start a new race, and they went to a recently formed running group, the Missouri Valley Masters Track and Field Association, for operations help.

Wellness, aerobics, masters, new organizations for runners—four of the boom basics went into making the Hospital Hill Run. Another essential component soon emerged: visionary and super-competent race directors, Russ Niemi and Rich Ayers.

They added the longer distance in 1976 and in my year, 1980, it became an officially certified half-marathon. Part of the success of running was the way it raised its standards of management, including course measurement. The new name worked. Numbers soared, course records tumbled down (though the masters record I set in 1980 lasted thirty years), and the international stars came to race over the next few years: Priscilla Welch (Great Britain), Greg Meyer (USA), Richard Kaitany (Kenya), and Domingo Tibaduiza (Colombia). Crowds flocked to hear the forum speakers. Everyone was learning.

Hospital Hill is a great race if you're like me and more interested in a tactically tough course and challenging conditions than a fast time. Leaving the hotel at 6 a.m. was like stepping into a Turkish bath. I'd never experienced such oppressive humidity. "Go out slow, go out slow!" I recited, like a boring parrot on my own shoulder. At three miles I caught Hal Higdon, eight years older but secretly hopeful (he confessed years later) that he could put this intruder in his place. Hal had helped and welcomed me warmly, but among elite runners such kindnesses only last till the gun fires. After a boyhood of cowboy movies, I'd woken at 3 a.m. on the train journey across Kansas to put my head out of the window and see Dodge City, venue of so many real and imagined gunfights. Racing Hal had some of that feel.

Though the heat and humidity were new, I had no fear of the big hills. Wellington served me well. I worked carefully through the field, surging over each crest in the way I used to coach younger runners to do, and I ran the last two miles battling for second place overall, finishing three seconds back, in third place at 1:10:28.

The most memorable moment came at about eight miles. By that time, the runners in front were getting sparse, Hal was behind, and I thought I should be winning the masters. Up ahead was a guy with thinning hair who might be my age. In New Zealand at that time, the term for the over-forties was "veterans" or "vets." As I drew alongside him, I turned and asked, in my polite foreign accent, "Are you a vet?"

He looked puzzled. "No, I'm a computer salesman," he said.

I've always wondered if he thought I was going to ask for advice about my cat.

From Hospital Hill we continued the long coast-to-coast train journey across the states. We were hosted by runners in Washington, DC (despite

Amtrak arriving ten hours late), and I joined the Potomac Valley Seniors in a run on the Potomac towpath. I went briefly to New York and by cab to JFK airport, the driver enthusiastically telling me we were going in reverse on the course of the famous marathon. Then on to the United Kingdom for research in London, where I watched a memorable marathon (see chapter 9) and won the World Masters 10K Championship in Glasgow, Scotland, on the way to an academic conference. The growth of masters running was an important element of the boom (see chapter 21), but things in the United Kingdom were not yet up with American standards. That Glasgow course was extended by six hundred meters at the last moment because of road works, according to *Athletics Weekly*, though the runners were not even told. The extra distance detracted from one of the best races I ever ran, as my official 31:09 was for 10.6 km, so my 10 km must have been sub 29:30. But world champion! That's something I never dreamed of when I was watching Zátopek or Halberg.

Back in America as summer was ending, I found myself in the middle of a changing world.

September 19, 1980: Lynchburg, Virginia

Herb Lindsay is angry.

"We're as good as the best baseball players and footballers and golfers! We train twice a day! We bring in crowds, media, and sponsors! We give interviews! We have living costs, medical costs, equipment and travel costs! We've given up salaries to do this! We prepare like professionals, we perform like professionals, why can't we be paid like professionals?"

Eight or ten of the world's best runners are perched on chairs and lolling on sofas. Beer flows. It's warm in the basement of Rudy Straub's Lynchburg house, but the atmosphere is fervent. It's the night before the Virginia Ten Miler, another of the suddenly great new races on the American running circuit. It's September 1980, the last struggling, stupid days of the fusty old amateur rules, the days of dollars covertly passed in brown bags, the days when a race director had to say (as one did) "I can't pay you for racing but, look, I'm a betting man, and I bet you five hundred dollars you can't jump over that suitcase."

Great runners like Lindsay, Rod Dixon, Nick Rose, Craig Virgin, Rick Rojas, Paul Williams, Gary Fanelli, and Jacqueline Gareau are all (I think) in the basement that night. I'm going from memory and at the time I didn't have much clue who everyone was. There's no doubt, as Lindsay says, that they are superlative at what they do, celebrities to the media and the public, inspiring role models for the rising hordes of regular runners, and sought after by race directors. In addition, they are despised as troublesome upstarts by the committee men in their white officials' trousers who still try to manage the sport as if it hadn't changed for a hundred years.

I'm not a star or a rebel, but as an invited masters runner, I'm there in the basement, wide-eyed at the anger and agitation. I'm new to all this, but I'm also the oldest, and I've seen angry runners before. I was close to the UK International Athletes Club that challenged their fossilized officialdom in the 1960s, before Bob Schul and Steve Prefontaine did the same in America. I'd been on world championship cross-country teams for two countries, England and New Zealand, both struggling with the same financial constraints, and I'd shared the runners' resentment that we were somehow expected to feel guilty about the money spent on our fares and accommodation. The pot had been bubbling for a while.

I was also old enough to know how radically running had changed by 1980, as this chapter has described. The elite runners were a key part of the attraction for the mass fields (2,000 at the Virginia Ten Miler that year), the media, and public interest. It was obvious they were entitled to a share of the benefits.

They did what they did at a wholly professional level. They ran times for that hilly Lynchburg course that still haven't been surpassed, not even by East African full-time professionals. And when I was first there, the race was only six years old. That's how suddenly and spectacularly the running boom happened in America.

It's time for some more context. The running boom happened, and is still happening, because of an extraordinary surge of creative energy. Before 1970, in every country, racing opportunities were limited, controlled by local, regional, and then national federations (you can already imagine the layers of office-holders and committees). Major races were typically "championships" under tight federation control, weighted with rules about amateurism and eligibility. The federation officers were volunteers who were not evil and not usually mercenary, but they did have a vested interest in rules that justified their positions of importance. There was a rule in America, for instance, that an athlete had to apply for permission to compete out of their home region. It's hard to understand why. In the United Kingdom, if an elite athlete was invited overseas, a "manager" had to go with him (it was always "him" in those days). Why not send two athletes for the same money, we used to ask?

No doubt the officials who controlled the sport meant well, but it was reminiscent of wartime military in the way they imposed rules and ordered the athletes about. Such hierarchies and regimentation didn't fit 1970s America. The baby boomers grew up to be the running boomers. Their generation wanted a better kind of race: more inclusive, more welcoming, more glamorous, more significant, more fun. So, they invented them. Some gave their races names that evoked the romance magic of this new sport: Peachtree, Falmouth, Cascade Run Off, Lilac Bloomsday, Avenue of the Giants, Cherry Blossom, Crescent City Classic, Maggie Valley Moonlight, Gate River, or Sun Run. Others gave them quirky, memorable names that expressed the sense that the sport's appeal was idiosyncratic, maybe radical, and definitely not mainstream: Gasparilla (first race named after a pirate), Bobby Crim (ditto after a politician), Grandma's (ditto after a restaurant), the Boilermaker (a heavy metal factory), Bix, James Joyce Ramble, or Hospital Hill.

These energetic creators invented more than just races. They started new running-related businesses: race management, start/finish/timing operations, announcing, apparel, medical services, nutritional products, stores, travel, photography, and, most profitable of all, shoes. A whole new literature exploded into existence, with magazines, books, and a pantheon of writers. Speakers emerged and gained their followings, like George Sheehan, the charismatic preacher; Jeff Galloway, the inspiring pragmatic coach; Hal Higdon, the droll stand-up man; and Joe Henderson, the disarming guy next door. As an itinerant runner/speaker/writer, in return for some help with travel and accommodation, I too was doing something new.

The running boom was not imposed or imported, but grew from within. Every new race and every new business came from the creative ideas and energetic enterprise of local runners who were already giving many hours per week to their own training, motivated solely by love of their sport. In those severely amateur days, no one could yet officially make a cent from running itself.

"You pursued your passion first and somehow made a living to support your addiction." That one-liner from Thom Gilligan is a perfect summary of the way running was in the 1970s (Clerici 2013). Gilligan was one of those who took a further step and found a way to combine his living with his addiction, creating Marathon Tours and Travel, the first running travel business. That kind of passionate dedication went deep into the field.

In the basement with us that day was Rudy Straub, our host. He was probably serving the beer, but I forget the details. Six years earlier, he was a Lynchburg engineer and one of a bunch of running friends who dreamed up a new race called the Virginia Ten Miler. That was 1974, which was early in the timeline of the world-changing running boom. At the fortieth running in 2013, Straub and I were guests of the revamped race, and we ran together nostalgically over part of the course. (Hilly! Good grief! How did I run ten 5:18 miles at age forty-one with jet lag on those wicked hills? How did Rod Dixon run 46:50?) Running with Straub, both in our seventies, I learned more about the origins of the race than I did in his basement in 1980. Good-humored and sharp-minded, Rudy gave me a pithy version of why his race became so successful so fast. It makes a good ground-level snapshot of the running boom.

"I was vice president of the Lynchburg Area Track Club, but some of us were road runners and saw the need for a separate club. We met in the basement of my house, six or seven of us, because someone has to grab the horns. We named ourselves Lynchburg Road Runners. A club needs to put on a race, so I talked to George Stewart, CEO of First Colony Life Insurance. I showed him a budget of $450. George came in and added $100 to buy trophies. We had 225 starters, and Jon Vitale won, with Jeff Galloway and Marty Liquori in the field.

"The next year, 1975, George enabled me to offer Bill Rodgers and Frank Shorter $500 to come and race, and we got their legendary dead-heat, TV coverage, and nearly 500 runners. [The payment, of course, was against amateur rules but typical of that era.] From then on, the top runners wanted to come. I kept trying other ideas. We used the Lynchburg Amateur Radio Club from the beginning. I had bicycle riders with flags to show the leading woman and master. We staged block parties for the neighborhoods on the course. The volunteers along Rivermont Ave. have always been local residents, organized by the same family. In 1979, we had an international race, with teams from Australia, Finland, Great Britain, New Zealand, and USA. From the start we made women equal, and Grete Waitz set a world record. One time we had corporate teams. I had a trophy specially sculptured in the form of a road runner."

Straub prefers amiable self-mockery to any touch of boastfulness, so his favorite story is the time he handed out hundreds of pairs of white gloves to the crowd. "I imagined all these white hands pointing the course for the runners, but no one caught on to what I wanted. We had a lot of waving and we lost a lot of white gloves," Straub said, enjoying every moment of the story. "I also had the driver of the lead vehicle dressed up in a rabbit suit, because he was the pace bunny. Get it? The folks didn't. One year we were the road test for a new TV camera, on a runner's head."

His narrative shows vividly how the sport evolved—the love of great racing plus concern to provide for the slowest, the visionary initiatives, and the ideas that went wrong. Ever-growing numbers. And money. The race's budget doubled every year. Straub delivered such a cutting-edge event in terms of quality that in 1979 Brooks hired him to write *The Brooks Guide to Long-Distance Footrace Administration*, a classic management manual that ends its list of advice to race directors with the one-liner, "Pray!"

Reading between the lines, the secret of the Ten Miler's allure to the cream of elites in the late 1970s was simple: it slipped them some dollars. Five hundred dollars was a lot to Bill Rodgers in 1975, when he could scarcely afford a table to be paid under. "Bill drove down from Boston in his VW," Straub remembers. Fred Lebow built the New York City Marathon on the same evasion of the amateur rules, one that had been used for decades by European track meet promoters, as I'd witnessed when racing in Sweden in 1967.

But as this chapter shows over and over, running was changing fast. Those discontented elites at the 1980 Virginia Ten Miler, agitating to be treated with the respect due to professionals, were part of the transformation. They were weary of the hypocrisy, the bossy old hierarchies, and the very limited money that could trickle to them. We were all weary of the silly prejudices and injustices the rules created. Back in the late 1950s in England, I used to see "the Ghost Runner," as the newspapers loved to call him: the persistent John Tarrant, who gained a doubtful fame for running well in road and ultra races without an official entry number because he was a "professional" who once accepted a few pounds as a teenage boxer (see Jones 2011). I would have met the same fate as Tarrant at that time if I'd ever accepted money for writing about running.

The full story of the change to professionalism, as always, is more complex than the version that has become accepted, especially in America. The federations were in fact bestirring themselves. In 1981, the International Amateur Athletics Federation (IAAF) was awaiting its members' responses to a paper on "eligibility" and a proposal to delete the word "amateur" from the IAAF constitution. In New Zealand, for instance, "it was decided at the Council meeting in March 1981 that the Association should take steps to inform the IAAF that we were in favour of liberalising the amateur rules" (New Zealand Amateur Athletics Association 1981, 17). But while subcommittees around the world were considering the implications, the Cascade Run Off rebellion occurred in Portland, Oregon, in June 1981, when that Nike-supported race openly paid prize money to place-getters. That precipitated months of dispute and negotiation, short-term suspension of some athletes, eventually the first arrangements for prize money and sponsorships for elite runners, and a seismic shift in the sport's underlying power structure.

That power change also was for the better, at least in the short term. Nike was the biggest of all the enterprises that grew from running's creative energy, and as it gained influence, it contributed generously to the development of the running movement, race sponsorship, research, a magazine, and runners (not only top elites). I remain grateful for the shoes and airfares Nike gave me, a forty-two-year-old part-timer, in 1981. That support made the last part of this chapter possible.

The Cascade Run Off revolt spurred or perhaps only hastened a necessary change. My regret is that the new arrangements were not more carefully thought through, and that we lost the process of global debate that had begun. I gave a speech to New Zealand sports journalists early in 1982 in which I argued that professionalism should work as it does in music, or the sciences, or baseball, with a portion of available money dedicated to important support roles (like public-address announcers, I said, not lacking in self-interest) and to developing talent. In the system the elite runners forced into place after Cascade, the money all went to them, plus their agents and managers.

It was ironic, but not coincidental, that in 1981–82 we saw the first glimpses of the invasion of winning foreign talent who carried off most of the money and have done so ever since; at first to Mexico and Europe, then increasingly to North and East Africa (see chapter 10 for more on that phenomenon of running's history). The result was a long-lasting slump in standards in America and other first-world countries. Running is only now recovering, nearly forty years later, through (surprise!) investment in developing talent.

I'm only suggesting that it would have been wiser for the sport as a whole, when professionalism began, to do more forward thinking, some sharing, and some investment in development. Not for a moment am I detracting from the merits and entitlement of the elites. That night in Lynchburg, I witnessed firsthand their passionate commitment. The sheer supreme quality of what Dixon, Gareau, Lindsay, and Rose did in the hilly 10 mi. race the next day embodied excellence at as high a level as I have encountered in any field. Truly, they were leaders and creators. Or, shall I say, we were, given how my generation of over-forties in those years transformed masters running (see chapter 21).

It was an exciting evening for me in Rudy Straub's basement, jet lagged and bewildered, yet conscious of being witness to the frontier action, being inside a drama of history, and hearing the voices that would bring the obsolete wall of amateurism tumbling down and further energize the running boom.

Riding the Wave, 1980–1989

Those were my earliest encounters with the American running boom. Soon I was dashing across the Pacific every few months like a balding surfer riding the cresting wave of the running movement. The boom gave me new places, new friends, a whole new community, new ideas, a new sense of my own capability, a new love and marriage when I met and married Kathrine Switzer. We set new long-distance records in romantic commuting. Relevant to this book, the boom gave me a new sense of history as it happens and of contributing to a significant movement. It took commitment and time management to fit training, travel, and racing into a demanding academic life (I did two terms as dean from 1981 to 1986). In both fields, I was striving daily to push myself to the limit and beyond, making each race like a major lecture or piece of writing, an expression of the best I could do.

I ran many of the great boom races. The New York City Marathon was at that time the great throbbing dynamo, almost doubling its numbers year by year, bringing in elite fields of Olympic quality, and creating a wholly new kind of interaction between a sports event and its host community. I ran my debut marathon there (at forty-one) in 1980, winning the masters with 2:22; I placed second master in the horrible hot fog year of 1984, and I set an over-fifty record (2:28:01) in 1989. I got a Boston over-forty record on a cold, wet, mostly headwind day in 1984 (2:20:15) and a Vancouver masters record (2:18:44 in 1981) that still stands.

All these races are ineradicably part of my life narrative. I still feel the icy splash up the thigh from an inattentive step into one of Vancouver's puddles that teeming cold day, and the anguish of the downhill calf tear that cost me the win against Antonio Villanueva at the Cascade Run Off in 1983. The name Maggie Valley brings back the biggest and most luridly yellow full moon I've ever seen, floating huge over the course as we waited to start the Moonlight Run; Utica Boilermaker means the tactically important golf course hill at three miles and the cauldron uphill at ten kilometers that I had to survive to win the over-fifty. At the Tulsa Run, all along the fast, scenic riverside, you keep telling yourself to save something for the mile-long drag up the final hill into the city. There was Gasparilla (concrete), Bobby Crim in rain (wet bricks), Lilac Bloomsday (jet lag), Twin Cities (beat a lot of old rivals), Christchurch (frosty), Honolulu (steaming), Philadelphia Distance Classic (where at fifty I found myself right behind the whirling ponytails of the leading women), Fairfield (where the race slides seamlessly into a beach party), Parkersburg (homecoming parade and a paddle-steamer cruise), and many more.

Since I began living partly in the United States, I've run not only classics, but lots of local races where I simply show up and pay my fee, as I like to do. At seventy-eight years old, I keep finding new races, new courses, new experiences of the sport. I can claim to have studied the running boom from the inside for nearly forty years. Two more races illustrate how that boom has made history in different ways.

The Peachtree 10K Road Race was a regular for me for several years, because it fell during my university's midyear break, and because the race kindly gave me an elite entry and speaker role. It was one of the first of the new wave of races, founded in 1970 (see appendix A). It quickly became one of the biggest and best, and it has stayed that way. Support from the *Atlanta Journal-Constitution* newspaper was crucial. When I first ran it in 1983, the field was an unparalleled 30,000. Now it's 60,000. The race is an industry leader in managing the logistics those numbers demand. When I wrote an article about mass road race starts (in *Marathon & Beyond*), it was Peachtree that I went to for the technical information. Intensive use of the subway, parking, corrals, waves—in these and many other ways, Peachtree was a pioneer. Before that field of 30,000 at Peachtree in 1983, the biggest I'd ever seen had been 4,000 at Hospital Hill and 13,000 at New York, both in 1980. Running was growing that fast. It's hard to remember how big and innovative all this was, and it's even harder to realize that most runners today have known nothing else.

But Peachtree's special place in the movement's history comes in part from its date, the Fourth of July. To me, while experiencing Independence Day for the first time by racing Peachtree in 1983, the race seemed a rite, a postmodern festival of freedom for a nation that prioritizes the individual. What I mean is that each runner's solitary ten-kilometer journey seemed multiplied by 30,000, and all were thus combined into a mass celebration of individual endeavor. In that personal/communal paradox, Peachtree seemed to act as a living metaphor for a society that from its very founding documents has based its national endeavors on affirming the significance and inalienable rights of its individual citizens. More than thirty years later, I have met nothing that expresses that spirit of combined individual citizenship better than this annual participant carnival of people who choose to do something as hard as run ten kilometers in Georgia's mid-summer heat and humidity purely for the sense of personal accomplishment, and who gain extra meaning for their accomplishment by sharing it on such a scale. If you want to see what truly makes America great, the Peachtree 10K Road Race on July 4 would be a good place to start.

Historically, this celebratory dimension shows the running boom in some ways to be a later expression of the spirit of the sixties, as I've suggested; a variant on Woodstock—a big, benign, positive gathering of Americans asserting individual freedom. What had changed from the sixties was the emphasis: "In the '60s we marched; in the '70s we run. The political difference is profound. . . . The protestors sought to change society by the collective force of their morality. Runners . . . seek to change themselves, *by* themselves" (Vitiello 1979, 69).

Peachtree has become one of the races that define the sport. To run those hilly, humid ten kilometers under the fat golden peach of the southern sun is a rite of passage for residents of Atlanta. Men and women testify in their wills that they want to be buried in their Peachtree finisher's shirt. A complete year-by-year set of shirts collected by scientist/historian Dr. David Martin is one of the treasures of the Museum of the Marathon and Road Running in Berlin. (America has failed to create such a museum of its own, to its discredit. Running has been too busy creating its future to care properly yet for its past.)

With such a prominent place in community consciousness, Peachtree is also one of a select group of races that have become essential to the identity of their host city. The clearest example I know of that historic phenomenon is the Utica Boilermaker 15K Road Race.

The Boilermaker began in 1978 in the same way as most of those new boom races: a local runner, Earle C. Reed, wanted a better race and had the creative energy to invent one. In his case there was the extra dimension of wanting to contribute to the local community that supported the family business, which made radiators and boilers. The name Boilermaker also meant a whiskey/beer cocktail or chaser. Reed secured sponsorship from his father at Utica Radiator and from the F. X. Matt Brewery, with the *Observer-Dispatch* newspaper completing a potent triumvirate of support.

"It would be difficult now to think of Utica without the Boilermaker," reflected sportswriter John Pitarresi, who has covered the race for each of its forty years and wrote its definitive history after the first twenty-five years. "It was an unusual event in the beginning, and quickly became important to the community, the highlight of the summer. I like to say the race captured the imagination of the community, which is true, but an immense amount of hard work by the leadership and thousands of volunteers were part of the process," Pitarresi wrote in the 2017 Boilermaker program book.

The director of another major American road race, who works as announcer each year at the Boilermaker, is filled with envy. "The Boilermaker gets so much support from the community and the state and city authorities. Where I am, they scream, 'You want to do *what?*'" jocularly lamented Phil Stewart of the Credit Union Cherry Blossom Ten Miler in Washington, DC.

With those ground-level origins, the race has remained embedded in the community. The statistics say a lot. Almost all the 14,000 runners are local (typically 4,500+ from Oneida County) or regional (12,500+ from New York State). The 5,000 volunteers are local. Most of the estimated 30,000+ spectators only walk to the end of their street. An estimated 45,000 runners, volunteers, and others drink beer, cheer the music, and whoop when the US Air Force planes go overhead at the postrace party at F. X. Matt Saranac Brewing Company. Set those figures against the city of Utica's latest population count, 60,000, and the social impact is huge.

The seventy-five sponsors are almost all local. Utica media give the race saturation coverage and strive for quality, as I can testify after having done radio commentary for WIBX for twenty years. (My theory is they hire me for the exotic novelty of my accent.) Boilermaker Week, as it is affectionately known, is a fixture in the community's calendar. Utica people are happy to describe it as up there with Thanksgiving and Christmas and as a time for neighborhood, family, and volunteer parties, when family members who have moved away return to Utica to run or work the race and join reunions. The elite international field and visiting media add the extra buzz of making the locals feel like they are on the world's stage for the day. "It's like the Olympics in our town. We get to help the best in the world perform at their best," said longtime volunteer leader Jack Coughlin.

Most important, the race has astutely built a year-round presence that goes deep into local life and the self-image of a community trying to bounce back from its rust-belt decline. One early initiative was to adopt and revitalize Butler Park, a rundown patch of ground in the old city, and enhance it with Boilermaker Square, which features a walkway path in the shape of the race course that is made of engraved bricks donated by runners and supporters and was installed with materials and labor donated by local contractors. The race supports local charities, funds high school scholarships, gives awards to coaches, volunteers, and journalists, hosts huge parties for volunteers, encourages and rewards crowd support, sets aside a "Unity Mile" on the course as a place for immigrant and other minorities to identify and affirm themselves, and organizes year-round training programs and other races. It is starting a library, and it is a major provider of paid employment, as well as organizer of volunteer labor.

The latest initiative, now in process of construction, is a permanent interactive reality exhibit to be titled "The Boilermaker Experience." The concept is evidence that running is adapting with its usual creativity to new developments in technology and popular culture. It is also evidence, at a time when the race is seeking another home for the struggling National Distance Running Hall of Fame (founded by Earle Reed in 1998), that for major running events like the Boilermaker, their deepest commitment and most dynamic energy are essentially local.

And the Boilermaker does even more for its local community, by existing as a strongly identified community within it. Radio celebrity Bill Keeler captured what it has contributed to Utica's recovery and how essential it has become to wider community projects. "It's more than a world class race, it has been an inspiration to this rebounding community. When I wanted to collect supplies for hurricane victims in New York back in 2012, I teamed up with the Boilermaker. When we decided to collect water for Flint, Michigan, I teamed up with the Boilermaker. Now there are programs like charity bib, events in the schools, and the public market that are changing this area for the better," Keeler said when awarded the Les Diven Journalism Award (one I also won).

The Boilermaker Public Market he mentions is part of a four-point program that is taking the Boilermaker brand into community service. The Boilermaker Kids in Training, reminiscent of the New York Road Runners' successful scheme, is creating after-school running clubs. The other points have no direct connection to running, but they exhibit every connection between the event and its community. The market includes organic smoothies made from produce in the Boilermaker Urban Garden, a plot of land at race headquarters where local students learn to be urban farmers. Boilermaker Nation is a community outreach educational program. The philosophy is to create a year-round opportunity to change individual lives and enhance the whole community.

"The city government uses the Boilermaker as an example of community collaboration and achievement by the whole population," said race committee member Lauren Mattia.

A hundred years or so ago, the things this running race is now doing for its community would have been done by a church, a philanthropic charity, the government, or a regional saint. But I am not a deluded idealist. Every year I drive around the Boilermaker course, much of it shaded by fine trees, alongside grand homes, where the spirit on race day is one huge happy party, and every year I also drive across the inner city where the few trees are dirty, the homes are ramshackle, the stores and streets dingy, and the people loiter or shuffle with a kind of dismal hopelessness. This is still America. Much work is always to be done, but in this city, and others, running has begun doing it.

The improvement of a community like Utica's is one way that running can be said to have made history. How valid is that claim for the running boom in general? This book is not offered as a definitive analysis, but here are ten starter ideas.

1. Running has convincingly proven its capacity to transform a significant number of individual lives. At a time when many people lack the communal, religious, or ethical support structures of the past, and suffer from disorientation and anxiety, running provides individual purpose and discipline, a sense of accomplishment, and an incentive to make a difficult and character-strengthening commitment. Vitiello discussed that dimension in his 1979 article: "One of our national, perhaps global, problems

has been a failure of confidence, an unwillingness to chance anything, since we are all characters in the new literature of despair. In running a marathon we chance our stamina, our pride, our knowledge of what lurks beyond that 20th mile, known to marathoners as 'the wall.' Maybe that, in the end, is what marathoning is all about: a willingness to risk the wall that circumscribes our daily lives" (71).

2. As well as that reforming, barrier-breaking dimension for the individual, running offers an accessible and supportive community. Millions now find one of the greatest sources of meaning in their lives is their membership in the running community. Its appeal is partly that it is so inclusive and egalitarian. These days, "fan engagement" has become a buzz phrase, and team sports give (or sell) their fans a sense of connectedness with the star players. Running had that figured out forty years ago when Bill Rodgers first greeted every runner around him on the start line before the race. I know no activity outside running where the stars are so approachable.

There are countless examples of a local running community providing life-saving support for individual members or others. Bill Keeler's quote earlier in this chapter discussed the extent of the Boilermaker community's philanthropic outreach. One of the most dramatic and recent examples was the rescue network organized by Houston runner Calum Neff that evacuated an estimated 600 families during the Hurricane Harvey flood disaster of 2017. "Because of running we had our own army within the community," Neff revealingly told *Runner's World* ("Houston Runner Leads Rescue Efforts," *Runner's World,* September 5, 2017).

In the dual function of enriching the individual and creating a supportive community, running has similarities to a traditional church. Jokes about "born-again runners" and running as a form of religion have some underlying truth. Many runners feel a spiritual dimension. I dealt with the historical origins of that connection in the chapter "Ritual and Religion" in 26.2 *Marathon Stories* (Switzer and Robinson 2006).

3. The impulse among the majority of runners to run for a cause other than, or greater than, their own result has brought measurable enrichment of the work of many charities and thus society. Running has also generated many charitable projects, especially for medical research, for children, and in Africa.

4. The health benefits of running are now well researched and widely known, and its active contribution to society's wellness is proven, including its major contributions to the tasks of combating the obesity epidemic, alleviating substance addiction, and redefining many issues of aging.

5. Medical research into the condition and problems of runners has brought benefits to a much wider public in topics such as cardiology, respiratory science, the effects of altitude, muscle science, chiropody, knee replacement surgery and its aftereffects (that's one I contributed to), active aging (same), and obviously much more. None of that would have happened if there hadn't been so many runners pushing themselves to an extreme of physical effort that gives them rare value as research guinea pigs.

6. Running programs for children and teens, like the highly successful New York Road Runners Run for Kids (expanded in late 2017 into Rising New York Road Runners) or the Girls on the Run foundation, have achieved well-documented progress in providing incentives that improve health, academic results, self-esteem, family stability, and freedom from drugs and teen pregnancies.

7. Running has become an economic generator as a major industry in its own right and in the economic benefit many races bring to their host communities. Thousands of jobs nationwide and worldwide now depend on running. It's worth adding that these jobs contribute to something that is beneficial to consumers physically and morally, which is not true of all industries.

Another way that running may be pioneering a better world is the alliance between the commercial industry and the development and servicing of the running community. When they first emerged in the 1970s, running stores immediately took on a social and educational function, very often becoming the local running hub and a place to mingle, learn, and train, as well as buy. The shoe companies are major sponsors of the elite sport, not wholly altruistically, of course, but still indispensably. The most recent development is the multipurpose alliance of all these commercial and community interests in the phenomenon of mega running centers, usually associated with a major marathon, but also acting as an ambitious combination of race office (for collecting race bibs, etc.), training base, locker and shower room, coaching source, sports medicine clinic, retail outlet, café, even historical museum. Prague's Running Mall was the pioneer and major examples now include Boston's Adidas RunBase, Berlin's Adidas RunBase, and New York's New Balance Run Hub.

8. Running is a major leader in fostering volunteerism, an important direction for our increasingly leisured society. Volunteers develop their own strong community sense, drawing their main satisfaction from collaborating in something significant and beneficial for the community where they live. (I learned a lot from interviews when I wrote what may have been the first feature article about volunteers, originally published in *Canadian Running* magazine.)

9. Running is generating an increasingly artistic culture. This culture began with the books, magazine journalism, and speakers of the 1970s, like those I first encountered at the Hospital Hill Run. Some of its journalism has been outstanding in print, online, and in television and radio broadcasting. Some of its books compare well with any field of literature. Kenny Moore's (2006) *Bowerman and the Men of Oregon,* to pick only the best, is a biography worthy of a Pulitzer. A small literature of fiction, poetry, drama, and creative nonfiction has continued to grow since I documented it in *Running in Literature* (2003). Films like those of Jon Dunham (*Spirit of the Marathon* [2007], *Spirit of the Marathon 2* [2013], and *Boston* [2017]), or Pierre Morath's *Free to Run* (2016), are imaginative, supremely crafted, and deservedly award-winning as documentary features, despite the impossibility (it seems) of breaking beyond the running community for audiences. Running as a visual subject is beginning to produce significant artwork (see my introductory "Running in Art," *Running Times/Runner's World* website, December 21, 2014), some impressive public statuary, and a massive output of quality photography. The unprecedented spectacle of running's huge fields has inspired a new visual art genre: photographs, paintings, and film of massed runners early in a race, often moving through some memorable cityscape or landscape.

10. Running is a leader in environmental conservation and usage, which I discuss in chapter 17. Within urban areas, it has led the establishment of recreation trails and green necklaces, and in myriad ways it has joined or led the pushback against the dominant motorcar. All this in

addition to, once a year, famously transforming even our biggest cities into centers of supportive goodwill.

And negatives? Has running changed the world for the worse? It has some problems that go with its size, but it has moved commendably fast to clean up its act in the amount of waste produced by its big races (see chapter 17). The travel the sport stimulates by its alliance with destination tourism carries a cost in carbon footprint, but the payoff in health, international understanding, and individual opportunity more than balances that cost. The downside of becoming an industry is that corporate interests can become too powerful, as I believe happened with the damaging shoe-promotion stunt of the sub-two-hour marathon. Becoming a retail industry also means that an utterly simple and almost cost-free activity has been captured by the usual capitalist process of commodification. To my generation, all the clutter of special apparel, compression clothes, nutrition supplements, and high-tech watches is alien to our very being as runners—liberated, natural, innocent. But (I think, as I prepare to go for a run on a warm day wearing nothing but eight-year-old shorts and two-year-old shoes) you don't have to buy the stuff. In social demographic, as I argue in chapter 18, running has allowed itself to drift into the deepening divide that besets our society, but it can't in any sense be held responsible for it.

But think of it the other way around. If all major marathons and road races were compulsorily closed, wouldn't the world be changed very much for the worse? So, yes—I believe the running boom is historically important, has indeed changed the world, and is still changing it, and for the better, in those ten ways and more.

Appendix A records key points in the history of the running boom. More than anything in this chapter I have tried to convey how exciting it was to be part of that movement in the 1970s–80s, to witness and participate in something so intense and creative and beneficial. "Bliss was it in that dawn to be alive," enthused Wordsworth about being witness to the idealistic beginnings of the French Revolution, and that's how it seemed.

I wrote articles and *Heroes and Sparrows* (2011) as if shooting from a handheld camera from the thick of the action, sometimes scribbling on the plane back to New Zealand to meet a deadline, trying to capture the vividness, the energy, and the individual satisfaction of this extraordinary new sport; or, as I called it even then, in 1983, "a major social movement of our time." As early as 1978, I wrote about the social significance of "The Fun-Run Phenomenon" for a guest editorial in the mass-market weekly *New Zealand Listener*. I wasn't one of the great pioneers of the running boom, but I was often part of it. I won't go down in history, except perhaps as the first to understand and to write that important history was being made.

9

August 3, 1980, London; October 25, 1981, New York City

Women Rejoice and Conquer

I'd never seen a women's marathon. The first anywhere was in 1974, in Waldniel, Germany. There had been only five since. So, it was with some curiosity that I was running back and forth along the Victoria Embankment in London one Sunday morning in August 1980, logging a repetitive version of a long Sunday run as I waited for the women marathoners to come by.

I used to watch some wonderful women runners as a boy at Motspur Park, especially the hurdler Maureen Gardner, who was only narrowly beaten by Fanny Blankers-Koen in the 1948 Olympics. From the Rome Olympics, sprinters Wilma Rudolph and Dorothy Hyman still shine in my memory. Nor did it ever occur to me that it was inappropriate for women to run longer distances, although few did. My father had once race-walked for Birchfield Harriers in the English Midlands, so when Diane Leather (now Charles) of Birchfield became the first woman in the world to run a mile faster than five minutes (4:59.6 on May 29, 1954), it was as big in our household as Roger Bannister's sub-four three weeks earlier. It was a special pleasure to interview and write about Diane Charles when *Runner's World* recognized her as a legendary pioneer sixty years later.

The athletics club I joined at age eighteen, Guildford and Godalming, had a quite strong women's section, guided by coach Dennis Jordan and his wife, the recently retired, world-class middle-distance runner, Joy

16. Avon Women's Marathon runners prepare on Westminster Bridge, 1980. Courtesy of Yellowdog/Avon Running, Kathrine Switzer.

Jordan, who had placed sixth in the 1960 Olympics 800 m and set a world record at 880 yd. Good-humored and modest, Joy was the first international athlete I knew as a friend. Woman runners were always part of my consciousness.

Histories of women's running have been dominated by their breakthrough into the marathon, especially Boston. A few years later, I would be living in daily contact with that story, after marrying one of its most significant figures. But Boston is far from being the whole of women's running. By my own limited observation, women runners were active and accepted in England in the early 1960s, premarathon, although their numbers were small and their track distances usually limited to 800 m, with the occasional 1 mi. There were still those who thought it inappropriate for women to do anything that made them tired, or look less than elegant, or in any way (as some believed) risk their childbearing function. That age-old fear was much aired, for instance, in the 1890s, when women began to ride bicycles. A climate of heightened reproductive fear followed the catastrophic loss of young male life in World War I and produced the distorted reporting of the supposed (but wholly invented) mass collapse of women runners in the 1928 women's Olympic 800 m. But by the 1960s that was in the past. If there was some protective anxiety when women started to run marathons, it should be remembered that there was still plenty of supposedly informed medical opposition to men being allowed to run marathons. All runners at Boston had to pass a prerace medical examination.

Women raced on the track up to 1 mi.—Diane Charles's world record was done in an official championship race—but no further. The best opportunity for women to run any longer distance was in cross-country, where their courses were usually about 3 mi./5 km. Perhaps cross-country was tolerated because it takes place mostly out of public view, although the Dipsea race in Marin County, California, had to name its flourishing women's race a "hike" in the 1920s and eventually was pressured to drop it from the program. There were also women's road running championships and interclub road relays, increasingly after World War II, and in my day one or two women habitually entered men's road races, notably Dale Greig in Scotland in the 1960s and Leslie Watson in the south of England in the 1970s. Julia Chase and Sara Mae Berman would be American equivalents in the early to mid-1960s, when Millie Sampson was also competing in New Zealand. There were certainly others, not in great numbers, but many of them committed athletes who deserve to be acknowledged. Sometimes they met resistance from officials, but mostly not.

As far as I knew, there was no pressure yet from women to run the full marathon distance, but I remember no exclusion. That problem seems to have been in America. When Dale Greig showed up for the Isle of

Wight Marathon in 1964, she was allowed to run, but out of concern for her health (surely forgivable) was made to start ahead of the men, with an ambulance nearby. The same cautious officials cheered her as she completed what is now recognized as the first fully authentic women's world record, 3:27:45. Her run was positively reported in *Athletics Weekly*, the runner's bible. In New Zealand later that year, male runners in Auckland almost dragged Millie Sampson out of bed after a night's dancing (she merrily told me a few years ago), so eager were they for her to fulfil her promise to run their marathon. In good shape from track, and fueled on midrace chocolate, she broke Greig's world record.

Athletics Weekly in the United Kingdom covered women's running fully. There was a weekly section called "With the Ladies," and women were featured routinely in profiles, analyses of elites' training, rankings, and in-depth reporting of major championships. The magazine often put women athletes and teams on its green and yellow cover.

One problem in Britain was that the men's and women's federations were separate, holding their championships at different venues, and there were some separate women's clubs, like London Olympiades and Spartan Ladies. Those names surely indicate heroic aspiration, but because of this separation there were few chances for male runners to see the best women race. Among coed clubs like mine, they were treated equally, without any fuss that I recall, and in Guildford we all trained on the same night on the same scruffy grass public park.

By 1963, when I was twenty-three, I was the (unpaid) athletics/cross-country correspondent for the *Guildford and Godalming Times*. I wrote full weekly coverage of Valerie Tomlinson, Maureen Sargent, Sheila Bradbrook, and the other Guildford women whose names I've forgotten.

All this may seem trivial and personal, but it's a glimpse from the grassroots, and it is a history that has never been told and is in danger of becoming lost. There is also, as always, a much longer history, which I can only briefly skim.

Women ran competitively in ancient Greece, the surviving statues show, though separately from men, and in Atalanta the Greeks created one of the great myths of running and of love. In the Roman Empire, running appears as one of the sporting activities represented in the "bikini girls" tiles in Sicily, and in other images. For *Running in Literature* (2003), I found the earliest written record: a diary note by Samuel Pepys on April 14, 1667, about a family picnic, when two of their maids, Barker and Jane, "did run for wagers over the bowling green." "Smock races" between women were standard in rural sports days in the eighteenth century, and they are celebrated in a delightful body of mock-classical poems, as well as novels by Smollett and others. In the nineteenth century, Jane Austen, George Eliot, George Meredith, the Brontë sisters, William Morris, Algernon Swinburne, Kate Chopin, Elizabeth Barrett Browning, Thomas Hardy, Olive Schreiner, and Sarah Grand all praised energetic women who walked fast and, in many cases, ran (see Robinson 2003).

In real life, Part-Sky-Woman, a Chippewa who was famous in the mid-1800s for winning every race at the Hudson Bay Trading Company Sports Meet at Fort Francis in the Great Lakes, was probably the earliest documented woman to race more than a sprint across the green. Women had a full place in Native American running culture, with Navajo and Apache girls running long distances during rites for puberty (see Nabokov 1981). Women's first heyday, if we include fast competitive walking, was the era of the hugely popular ultra performers in the 1870s, documented in Harry Hall's (2014) *The Pedestriennes: America's Forgotten Superstars.*

One other early winner is worth recording in this chapter. When New Zealand's women were the world's first to be given the vote by law in 1893, the women of the town of Greymouth were so eager to exercise their new right that on polling day, November 28, 1893, they literally raced each other along the street. First at the booth was Mrs. McPherson (Charlotte McDonald, "Sprinting to the Polls," *Victoria News*, September 19, 2017).

With that tradition, it's not surprising that women runners were prominent when I emigrated to New Zealand in 1968. Marise Chamberlain had won the bronze medal in the 800 m at the 1964 Olympics in Tokyo, and Sylvia Potts reached the Olympic semifinals in 1968, a month after I arrived in Christchurch. In 1970, Potts lost first place in the Commonwealth Games 880 yd. in Edinburgh when she fell just before the finish. Four years later, as I recorded in chapter 7, it was Sylvia Potts, not Peter Snell, who was

given the honor of running the final leg of the Christchurch Commonwealth Games baton relay.

It's worth pausing on that decision, since my subject is when running
made history. Potts was the first woman to carry the final baton or torch
at any major Games, Olympic or Commonwealth. By selecting a woman,
sport and especially running took a leadership role in a gender breakthrough, a notably big one in the New Zealand South Island. Despite
New Zealand's legal egalitarianism, its settler culture was still based
largely on male values in male contexts—farming, rugby, beer, mateship
in war and sport, and the archetype of "man alone" in the backcountry
mountains. Less than ten years before the 1974 Games, New Zealand
was still a country where socializing was done in all-male beer barns or
at mixed parties where invitations would say "BYOG [Bring Your Own
Grog] Ladies a Plate." In that context, the choice to give the highest honor
of the nation's most important international sports event to a woman, and
one who didn't win, added whole new dimensions to the cultural redefini-
tion I discussed in chapter 7.

Historians like those at that conference on the 1970s in New Zealand
(see also chapter 7) have made a great deal of International Women's Year,
1975. Again, they would have done well to remember the 1974 Commonwealth Games, Sylvia Potts, and the Ghanaian, Kenyan, and Nigerian
women who won medals and became national figures at home, possibly
the first women ever to gain such heroic status in those cultures. We know
this to have been the case in the 1990s with Tegla Loroupe, whose story is
told later in this book; and with Japan's women marathoners, Naoko Taka-
hashi and Mizuki Noguchi, who won Olympic gold medals in 2000 and
2004. As early as 1974, and making such global impact, it is an important
addition to our understanding of how women's running made history.

In New Zealand, there was only one federation, so women's races and
field events formed part of every meet, local ones and national championships. Every cross-country event had a women's and often junior women's
race. As a runner, and as stadium announcer when that role began for
me, I was therefore witness to the emergence of the great generation of
Kiwi women distance runners as they moved up from their midteens:
Anne Audain, Allison Roe, Lorraine Moller, Diane Rodger, Heather

Thompson, Barbara Moore, Mary O'Connor, and Debbie Elsmore. (For clarity, I use the names by which they mainly became known.) In 1977, I was teammate with several of them when we represented New Zealand at the World Cross-Country Championships. No one who knew those runners could doubt women's capacity to train intensely and intelligently, and to race to the very limit of endurance. A tactical duel between Moller and Roe in the national road championships in 1979 is still vivid to me, and O'Connor's power through deep, slushy mud to win that year's national cross-country title was a phenomenon. Christchurch coach Bruce Milne had a big women's group all running more than one hundred miles a week in the 1970s, and they got results, with O'Connor's 2:28 marathon the best of them.

A little-known episode that illustrates how women's running overcame outmoded obstacles in those changing times came when I moved to Wellington in 1975. I joined Victoria University Harriers, a sociable running/drinking club that preferred not to take its sport overly seriously. Two or three wives or girlfriends ran with us on Saturday afternoons, without problem. But when (around 1976) the club put down the name of one of these women members to run in the C team in the big interclub road relay, the entry was rejected by officialdom. There was no separate women's race in those days, and no woman, it seemed, was permitted to run as far as six miles against men. Allison and Don always ran with their dog, named McGregor, who was one of those roguish, good-natured, tousled English sheepdog tykes, with hair straggling down over his eyes. The club revised the entry and registered the dog as D. (for dog) McGregor. With his race number tied around his shaggy midriff, and Allison running alongside, he cheerfully completed his lap. History needs to recognize that one fearless pioneer in women's running was a hairy male sheepdog called McGregor.

In Christchurch, I again found myself moonlighting from university duties to be the running correspondent (paid a bit this time) for the *Christchurch Star*, a daily evening paper that also put out a Saturday special sports edition, on yellow newsprint. Again, I took it for granted that I should give full coverage to the women, sometimes headlines, and the editors never questioned it.

One time, around 1970, I gave full coverage when an experienced local cross-country and road runner, Diane Dixey, applied for permission to run in the region's annual ultra run, the New Brighton 50 Miles. The usual debate happened among officialdom, and thanks to advocacy from an enlightened committee member named John Smart, Diane's entry was accepted. That was for a fifty-miler, when America hadn't yet permitted women to run marathons.

"NZ girls ready for marathon?" That was the headline the *Star* gave to another women's running story, on June 8, 1974. I'd read that in February 1974, in San Mateo, California, the United States held a national marathon championship for women—a world first. If America had been behind the world in women's running until the early 1970s, that initiative by the federation quickly put it ahead. Credit where credit is due. I thought the innovation was worth putting out to the wide general sports readership of the *Star*. I did more research and published an article that affirmed the new phenomenon of women running marathons as an important development. I included Judy Ikenberry's win in the inaugural championship, I told of Lyn Carman and Merry Lepper in 1963, and I pointed out that Michiko Gorman's recent 2:46:36 would have earned her a place on the Canterbury men's team. I referred to a cross-country 100 mi. race in England, where three women had finished. For local interest, I came back to Diane Dixey, who now ran the New Brighton 50 Miles every year, and to Millie Sampson's world marathon record.

All that early history is too often overlooked. The bigger and more familiar story started in 1980, when I again found myself close to history in the making: the day an international women's marathon was run on London's streets, only a mile from where I was staying.

I was in London for literary research and was renting a flat near Hyde Park so I could train for the world masters road 10K championship in Glasgow. I read about the Avon Cosmetics International Marathon

Championship for Women (as it was designated that year) and that Lorraine Moller, whom I knew quite well in New Zealand, was one of the favorites. So, I went out to watch, running back and forth along the Victoria Embankment until at last the police escort and official vehicles appeared.

High on an open-topped red London double-decker bus draped with Avon Running banners, I glimpsed (I'm now prepared to swear) the white jacket and flying hair of the dynamic American director of the Avon races, Kathrine Switzer, who would become my wife on closer acquaintance a few years later. Then Moller came through in second place and was looking good. Not long after, at mile twenty-one, she took the lead and won. I won't describe that race, as it's a key chapter in Switzer's (2007) book *Marathon Woman*, and I had only a brief spectator's view. But it was a big one for women's history.

That race was the first sports event to close downtown London, a prototype for the next year's inaugural London Marathon. It was the first to have endorsement from the lord mayor of London. It was the first marathon outside the Olympics to get extensive television coverage, including British, American, European, and South American. It was the race that swung the world's media, print as well as television, behind women's running, partly because it skillfully filled the gap left by the widespread boycott of the 1980 Olympics in Moscow. It was a breakthrough race in sheer quality: the first time five women ran under what was then the key barrier for their marathon, 2:40. It was the first women's marathon to include runners from five continents. With runners from twenty-seven nations, no women's race had ever been so international, and maybe no women's sports event of any kind. It thus crashed right through the International Olympic Association's criteria. It was positioned and promoted as a crucial step in the campaign to include the women's marathon in the 1984 Games. The race program carried an article by Switzer titled "Next Step Olympic Games?" in which she expressed confidence that the "enthusiastic response and measurable rewards . . . will strongly influence the governing bodies of athletics to push for acceptance of women's distance running in the Olympic Games." The campaign succeeded. Joan Benoit's win in the first women's Olympic marathon has become the iconic image, but it was Switzer's 1980 London Avon race where much of the ground-work was done that made that huge breakthrough possible.

By good fortune I was there, an unobtrusive onlooker, but also a committed runner and student of running taking the first opportunity to watch and acclaim a women's marathon.

In the fall of that year, I headed back to the United States to run the Virginia Ten Miler, Hal Higdon's Brooks Master Run series, and climactically my first marathon, in New York. A year later I was home in Wellington, wishing I could afford to fly to New York to defend my masters title. It was some consolation when TV New Zealand hired me for my first television role, an in-studio analyst for their first live New York City Marathon broadcast, taking the feed from the American ABC network coverage.

Our commentary used some of ABC's, though increasingly the director left it to Keith Quinn and me. I knew the course and several of the top runners, and I'd been at a press conference with Alberto Salazar before his debut win in 1980, so I brought that memory to analysis of his extraordinary winning surge at eighteen miles.

But that day was historic for much more than launching me on yet another career. The 1981 New York City Marathon was one of the most important events in the growth of the running boom because it was on television. The ABC broadcast was the first wire-to-wire live coverage of a city marathon, huge as a technical challenge and even more huge in its social impact. In two hours, a new set of iconic images burned themselves into the consciousness of the era: the massed field surging over the Verrazano-Narrows Bridge; the intense focus of the lead pack seen from a motorcycle camera alongside; the lead pack seen distantly from above by a helicopter camera, with those tiny dot heads and amazing giant, fast, raking strides; the close-ups on the leaders as they battled hills, wind, potholes, fatigue, and each other; New York's streets, bridges, and skyline; and, above all, the crowds. Such amazing crowds! Until that day marathon crowds had been minor extras on the edge of the photographs and rarely mentioned in race reports. Suddenly they were the biggest stars of all: their effervescent energy, their noise, their color, their omnipresence, their infinite variety, and, being New Yorkers, their idiosyncrasies. There were people with signs and costumes and bells and rattles and drums; church choirs in full religious regalia; live bands and booming ghetto blasters; coffee-bar yuppies all along First Avenue; kids leaning over the barriers, insatiable for hand-slaps; robed and poker-faced Hassidic Jews; exuberant black Harlemites; and the unique, funneled crescendo of acclamation that is the modern marathon finish area.

That day, and that crowd, also marked a huge breakthrough for women's running. A new heroine burst into prominence, for the crowds as well as on the television screen: New Zealander Allison Roe. Her win was a lucky bonus for me. At that time, the New York City Marathon was held at the end of October on a Sunday morning, which meant that in New Zealand it happened in the early morning of a Monday public holiday, Labour Day. So New Zealand woke, sleepily remembered it was a day off work, grabbed a coffee, turned on the television, and learned from me that Allison Roe was winning, why she was winning, who she was, what she was like as a Kiwi teammate at the world cross-country, what it would mean if she won, what happened to Grete Waitz (injured, did not finish), all about New Zealand's great tradition in the marathon (from Millie Sampson to Barry Magee), what was this huge, noisy, extraordinary happening called the New York City Marathon, and what it's like to run it. As Allison powered away to her mighty win, our viewing figures went through the hole in the ozone layer, and when she finished, moving smooth and strong like a Wonder Woman warrior goddess, the entire nation danced on their breakfast tables with joy.

In every camera shot, we could see the New York crowds going crazy with adoration of Allison. But further back in the field, something even more important was happening. Out in those crowds were women cheering for women. Everyone was especially cheering for women. How often in human history had that happened? They were cheering not only the women's winner, but women runners fast and slow, from every state in America and more than forty other countries of the world; 2,029 of the full record field of 14,496 runners were women. With that ratio, women were still special, and the whole phenomenon of women running marathons was new. Only ten years earlier there were four women in this race; the year before that, one.

The crowd in 1981 recognized that it still took a special kind of courage for a woman without Roe's talent to take on this rigorous, male-majority sport, to push herself to the edge of exhaustion, under the scrutiny of a watching public. The public's response was best experienced from inside the race. "The crowd's cheering goes berserk at the sight of every woman competitor," wrote English journalist John Bryant, who wrote personal coverage of the race for the *Daily Mail* from deep within the pack.

This was new. There was no such mass acclaim available for any preceding woman runner, except if she won on the track at a major Games. There were no crowds for routine track or cross-country, not for men or women. When I ran alongside Moller for a bit in the London Avon race in 1980, though there were crowds waiting at the finish, we were the only two people in sight on Victoria Embankment that early Sunday morning. This response in New York in 1981 was what the 1960s/1970s women's movement dreamed of and fought for: women gaining satisfaction and being acclaimed not for how they looked or how they gave faithful support to a husband or children, but for something they did, for who they were, for what they dared to aspire to, for what they were willing to risk.

Perhaps what the cheering New York crowds gave them more than anything was approval. For centuries in almost every society, women needed permission for many things. Here it came in the unprecedented form of two or so million New Yorkers enjoying a great new way of being noisy, and by going (in Bryant's word) "berserk," thus endorsing this new public endeavor by women. Whatever the truth of that, each of the 2,029 women in that race was doing something by her own choice and for her own personal sense of accomplishment, probably for the first time. For the women in the crowds, this was perhaps their first opportunity to acclaim other women in an act of public accomplishment. In all those ways, it was historic. And all the more so because it happened on network television and in every form of media coverage then available.

The eager, welcoming goodwill of American running that I described in chapter 8 becomes relevant here. All was positive. There was no resentment. These women were not gate-crashing into something designed for men, but were fully entitled to be there. The entire American sport had rethought its mission since the days when Lyn Carman, Merry Lepper, and Roberta Gibb had their entries rejected and Kathrine Switzer was assaulted by an official trying to rip off her bib number (and was then banned for, among other offences, running without a chaperone). And the best women runners since then—Maureen Wilton, Adrienne Beames, Cheryl Bridges Treworgy, Nina Kuscsik, Liane Winter, Jacqueline Hansen, Chantal Langlace, Christa Vahlensieck, Michiko Gorman, Joyce Smith, Gayle Barron, Grete Waitz, Patti Catalano, and Allison Roe—had in barely ten years proven their capability to do this arduous thing supremely well.

It's impossible to measure the impact of the New York crowds' public affirmation that day, but it was surely important. That 1981 New York City Marathon and other events around 1980 kicked off the unceasing upward trajectory of women's numbers into what quite soon became a majority.

Our culture tends to represent the story of women's running as a smooth progression, but it's a better story if we remember that running is arduous and challenging; by definition, rarely smooth or reliably a progression. Not all women cross the finish line looking like a warrior goddess. Accepting the responsibility of racing means also accepting the risks. The greatest of all women marathon runners, Paula Radcliffe (see chapter 15), was a fearless tactician who won eight major marathons, was world champion at marathon, half-marathon, and cross-country, and set a world record 2:15:25 that stands unchallenged after (so far) fifteen years. But she also must live with public fascination in her failures and fallibilities. She broke down in tears when she had to drop out of the Olympic marathon, had a marital spat on camera about track tactics, and is in danger of being mainly remembered for once squatting midrace with diarrhea. You can't redefine being feminine without redefining being feminine. Running has been a leader in allowing women to accept full responsibility, which meant they also accepted every risk.

That risk is part of the whole story, which is profoundly positive. At every race expo, I meet women (men, too, but far more often women) whose sense of self, health, and of living a fulfilling life has been transformed by running. There are millions of these stories, infinitely multifarious. In all of them, running, with its challenges and rewards, is close to the center of meaning in a woman's life. This social transformation is so vast, and goes so deep, that it's impossible to document, but everyone who has been near a running event will recognize its truth.

The story of Kenyan Tegla Loroupe is a particularly positive one. Overcoming resistance from her family and sports administrators, partly because she was so small, she became the first African woman to win a major city marathon. She won New York, London, Berlin, Rotterdam, and others, took three World Half-Marathon Championships, was honored by her own Pokot tribe by being the first woman ever to be declared a warrior, and by the United Nations for her work in creating her Peace Foundation and Peace Marathons. She has created a school, an orphanage, and a program for reducing armed violence among nomadic tribes along the borders of Kenya, Uganda, and Sudan. When some of her cattle were stolen while she was away racing a marathon, they were returned because of her sporting fame.

To go beyond the anecdotal, the US State Department in 2017 is supporting women's running in Brazil, China, and other places as the best available way of promoting the empowerment of women.

Appendix B, a timeline of women's running, 1896–2017, gives more detail of the historical process. The big picture is that the upsurge in women's running numbers happened so fast and in so many countries that it must have arisen from profound forces of culture or economy, not only from the inspiration of pioneers, however attractive that is as a story, and however compelling it was to media at the time. The wider women's movement itself was of course important as context. It was truly consciousness raising—forgive the cliché, but there is no better way of describing what was happening. Title IX (mandating gender equality in all educational, and therefore sports, programs) was passed into law in America in 1972. The other sporting expressions of the wider movement were the Women's Sports Foundation, founded in 1974, the same year as the magazine originally called *womenSport*, later *Women's Sports and Fitness*. Tennis stars like Billie Jean King and Martina Navratilova began to rival men in public recognition. King's highly publicized defeat of Bobby Riggs in 1973 changed many minds about women's capability. The example of pioneer runners like Merry Lepper, Lyn Carman, Julia Chase, and Roberta Gibb provided important role models, but more practical progress was achieved by those who went beyond their own running to devote time and energy to working for opportunities for other women, notably Kuscsik and Switzer in New York, Sara Mae Berman in Boston, and Jacqueline Hansen in California. Through hard-graft volunteer labor in administrative and committee roles, they advocated relentlessly and effectively for the expansion of opportunity in women's running.

This work is continued in 2017 by Switzer's international 261 Fearless Foundation (led by Austrian Edith Zuschmann) and by women who have created women's running organizations and events, from Australia's Running Divas to the Leading Ladies Marathon in Spearfish, South Dakota. This chapter ends with one typical story, but first I return to the history and the key developments in bringing women into running.

At the beginning in the 1970s, the essential contributions were those that gave women opportunity and approval. These contributions were of three main types, all of which were positioned outside the conventional sport.

1. *First came "run for fun" and the jogging movement, a major development in the 1970s.* These were not confined to women but had special appeal to them in being defined as noncompetitive, licensing anyone and everyone to get out and run for health, pleasure, or sociability with no pressure to run fast or even pretend to try hard. "Jogging" had grown fast from the 1960s initiatives of Arthur Lydiard, Bill Bowerman, and Ken Cooper (see appendixes). The world's first "joggers' club" was the one Lydiard created in Auckland in 1962. As events, San Francisco's Bay to Breakers and Sydney's City to Surf were important precursors, but those were still races, with awards and records, so the first and seminal noncompetitive fun run was Auckland's Round the Bays, which began in 1972 and by 1977 had grown to 20,000. At peak, it reached 80,000, one quarter of the city's population. Jogging clubs and marathon clinics developed, offering a noncompetitive and therefore nonthreatening alternative to conventional running clubs and their races. On January 7, 1978, I wrote the guest editorial that I referred to in chapter 8, "The Fun-Run Phenomenon," endorsing the

jogging movement for being so inclusive and for redefining sport by placing priority on being a participant, not a star or a spectator. Fun runs, I wrote, broke radically from "the Victorian attitude that sportsmen were either gifted gentlemen or dedicated professional players, uniformed 'representatives' of the rest of the population, who just placed their bets and watched."

For women, fun runs quite often provided the extra reassurance of being for women only. An experimental one in Auckland in 1978, for instance, attracted three hundred women, and one thousand a year later.

We don't now hear about jogging or fun running because the central sport of running adroitly redefined itself to absorb them. Most runners now are fun runners. *Runner's World* became a "jogging for health" magazine. The distinction between runners and joggers has blurred. As a culture, running is like a benevolent boa constrictor.

2. Races restricted to women provided similar reassurance. They enabled women, in simple terms, to feel secure from being judged in comparison with men, and from being overshadowed by men. They enable competitive woman runners to accept the responsibility and sometimes the loneliness of making tactical decisions without being paced, accompanied, or followed by men. They also provide a supportive sisterhood community that has proven crucial in attracting and retaining women in running. There had long been separate women's events on track, cross-country, and road, as I recorded from my young days in England. New Zealand, for instance, introduced a 4 km road championship for women in 1970. But all those early events required membership of a club, and were thus precursive to the boom story.

In 1972, Johnson's Wax went to Fred Lebow at the New York Road Runners Club with the idea of a women's marathon to promote a leg-shave gel called Crazylegs (it was men's shave gel colored pink, I am reliably informed). Lebow and two leading women runners and activists, Nina Kuscsik and Kathrine Switzer, who were then working in New York, persuaded the sponsor that a shorter race would be more appealing. Named the Crazylegs Mini-Marathon, it attracted a large field of seventy-eight (many men's races were smaller at that time) to race a 6 mi. loop of Central Park. It was the world's first "open" road race for women, and it is still held annually, most recently with a field of 8,481 (in 2017).

A change of sponsor in 1976 proved momentous. Switzer brought in Bonne Bell, an Ohio cosmetics firm with an ardent runner as CEO who aspired to start a whole series of women's races. Bonne Bell was sponsor of the Mini in 1976 and 1977, loved it, and decided "we're going to run these things all over the country" (CEO Jess Bell quoted in the *Chicago Tribune*, April 19, 1978). In 1978, Bonne Bell spent $250,000 on twenty women's races, with Gayle Barron as the winning celebrity, and the next year they expanded into Australia, Canada, and New Zealand. At the same time, Switzer had convinced Avon Cosmetics to accept her visionary proposal for a global women's running circuit, which began with the first Avon International Women's Marathon in Atlanta in 1978. Switzer's ongoing engagement is the part of the wider social movement that I have been able to observe most closely since 1983. She compellingly tells her own story in the two editions of *Marathon Woman* and innumerable speeches and interviews, so I won't repeat it. The key point is that, however enthralling the 1967 Boston Marathon episode is as a story, Switzer's significance is not in what happened to her that day. She was attacked by a man and defended by a man. What matters is what she did next—the active verb, not the passive. What should define Switzer's contribution to women is how she stepped out of the female stereotypical role of having to be compulsorily rescued, then outside the role of being another aspiring woman marathoner, to actively make her own decisions (to finish that traumatic race, first of all), rebuff the criticisms, build on the approval, correct the record, seek and handle publicity, affirm rights and aims, take initiatives, pressure the Amateur Athletics Union, organize, and work and work and work for change for women runners nationally and globally, thus shaping women's future. She has been doing that for fifty years, and I've been close witness to thirty of them.

Switzer's Avon series of women-only road races achieved many things. One, to put it simply, was to create a new international sport—women's road running. That didn't exist in 1975. It was a huge accomplishment. Avon's budget and Switzer's energy, diplomatic skills, celebrity image, and perfectionist insistence on the highest operational and promotional standards enabled those events to validate women's running as something to be taken seriously. They compelled the Amateur Athletics Union and the

International Amateur Athletic Federation to revise their thinking and in some cases their rules. Because she wanted women to have access via the Avon series to championships and eventually the Olympics, Switzer took a more diplomatic approach than the International Runners Committee's confrontational legal action, instead establishing good working relationships with many national federations and what might be called an uneasy truce with the US federation, which didn't take well to an alternative power center.

Women's running was now changing innumerable women's lives in many countries, including places where women were and still are second-class citizens. All were Avon markets, of course, but that still gave close to global coverage. No sports circuit had ever reached out to tens of thousands of underprivileged and often impoverished women in non-Western patriarchal cultures like Brazil, Japan, Malaysia, the Philippines, and Thailand. This was indeed running changing the world.

Nor has running at any other time had the benefit of such a structured and funded developmental program. Every local Avon race was preceded by an eleven-week series of welcoming introductory clinics, led by local running personalities and designed to make every woman, of whatever age, size, or weight, feel included. Once past that stage, the structure provided rewards and incentives to continue and, if desired, to improve.

A memorable but still typical story demonstrates how the funding worked at the top level. When Marianne Dickerson, age twenty-two, a straight-A student and track star at the University of Illinois, defied her coach and ran her first marathon at the Avon race in Missouri, she won it. Like every other Avon regional winner, she thus earned a full expense-paid trip to the 1983 Avon International Women's Marathon in Los Angeles, where she finished a surprise runner-up to Julie Brown. That won her a place on the USA marathon team in the inaugural World Track and Field Championships in Helsinki, where on an inspired day Dickerson fought past Europeans and Russians on the last miles to win the silver medal behind Grete Waitz. "There are Marianne Dickersons everywhere," she said, and one mission of the Avon program was to find and help them.

3. *The third major contributor to attracting women to running was the new phenomenon of runs for charity.* Again, these emerged outside

federation control and combined the appeal of being noncompetitive, often for women only, and with the extra incentive of doing good for others. It is often said that women have an innate compulsion to do things for others rather than themselves, and recent research suggests that the "guilty response" about committing time to something seemingly selfish is the greatest cause of women dropping out of running (Beverly 2017, 20–21). Running for a good cause eludes this guilt.

The most successful charity program for women was the Race for the Cure series initiated in 1983 in Dallas, Texas, which commemorates Susan G. Komen, who died of breast cancer in 1980. The series grew to unprecedented size and popularity, introducing many beginners to running. Now branded simply as "Komen," it is the largest breast cancer foundation in the United States; in 2010, 1.6 million donor-participants supported by 100,000 volunteers took part in more than 130 Race for the Cure events worldwide, enabling the foundation to report earnings of $400 million. Other highly successful charities provide training programs and team access to races, the biggest being the Leukemia and Lymphoma Society's Team in Training, founded in 1988, which has an extensive mentoring structure.

And so the women came, through fun runs, jogger groups, women-only races, charity runs, charity training programs, clubs, networks, causes, and running groups based at colleges, gyms, hospitals, or running stores. In Canada, the many branches of John Stanton's The Running Room are key to attracting and supporting great numbers of beginners, especially women. Or women simply stood on the sidelines watching other women run and thought, "maybe I can do that." Some were inspired by role models, stories, speeches, coaches, friends, or their kids, and once they summoned courage, they were welcomed by a community that never, ever said, "you're not good enough, you don't look like us, you don't belong." Millions of women have come to think of themselves as runners and to identify with a women's running community. And all that happened since 1972, the year when nine women were first accepted at the Boston Marathon, when all six women in the New York City Marathon sat down in protest at being compelled to start separately, and when the new Vancouver marathon simply accepted women—only two, that first year—and gave them equal status from the race's beginning.

It's an extraordinary story. Its driving impulse must lie deep in the consciousness of our age. I have been close to it since I met Kathrine Switzer in 1983, when the Avon series was at its height. I was forty-three, so I'm hoping in the movie to be played by a slightly graying Orlando Bloom or perhaps Tom Hiddleston. We met as premarathon speakers in the unlikely venue of Canberra, the conformist federal government center of Australia, and I can always get a laugh from Australian audiences by claiming we are the only people who think of Canberra as romantic.

Since then, for more than thirty years now, sometimes as speaker or announcer, most recently emcee for the 261 Fearless Foundation's events at the 2017 Boston Marathon, I have been frequently present at events at which thousands of happy and festive women join together and transform the modest old sport I have known since 1948 into what is surely one of the most positive social developments of the modern world. The demand seems to be always there, everywhere.

To give women runners the last word in their chapter, here is a typical story that I encountered one hot December afternoon beside my nephew's pool in North Sydney.

Di MacDonald ran Sydney's City to Surf race and the next year wanted to improve, so she asked her friend Jo Davidson to keep her company on some runs. Both had very busy modern urban woman schedules, but early Thursday suited, so they met at the Coogee Beach promenade at 5:45 a.m. After a few weeks, other women heard about their Thursday runs and asked if they could join them. Slowly, without anyone trying, the numbers grew. That was in 2009. Now there are more than 400 "Coogee Cougars," still meeting every Thursday morning but also running, racing, and socializing far beyond. Their low-key mission statement perfectly catches the spirit of modern women's running: "We meet once a week to run, to catch up and to check in with each other. Life is busy . . . we make sure we steal a piece of the day to run. It's a very simple philosophy . . . but it works for us. You are never too old to start running. No runner is ever too fast or too slow."

10

March 26, 1988, Auckland

The East Africa Phenomenon,
and How Running Responded

> First, Ngugi, Kenya! Second, Kipkoech, Kenya! Third, Koskei,
> Kenya! Then Merande, Kenya, looks like a dead-heat with Mekon-
> nen, Ethiopia! Sixth, Tanui, Kenya! Seventh, Kiptum, Rono, Muge,
> all Kenya, too close to call! Unbelievable! Almost a perfect sweep,
> eight Kenyans in the first nine. There's never been anything like it!
> You just saw the greatest display of team running in history!

Several events could signify the emergence of East Africa as a force in running. Bikila in Rome (chapter 4) was the harbinger. The Commonwealth
Games in Kingston, Jamaica, 1966, was the first occasion when Kenyans
won several international medals, followed two years later by their successes at the Mexico City Olympics (three golds, two silver, one bronze
in the four longest track races), plus Mamo Wolde's Ethiopian win in the
marathon. Christchurch 1974 (chapter 7) was important because Kenyans
triumphed with no advantage in heat or altitude. The timelines in the
appendixes identify the impact made on major marathons by Fatuma
Roba, Ibrahim Hussein, and Tegla Loroupe.

But the single day when Kenya's rising national strength was elevated
most dramatically into all but total world dominance was March 26, 1988,
the World Cross-Country Championships in Auckland, New Zealand. It
was the first time those championships had been held in the Southern
Hemisphere. I was there, this time on the television microphone, trying to
communicate to an international television audience how extraordinary
that moment of history was. "Eight Kenyans in the first nine!" I cried as

17. East African dominance: John Ngugi and Abebe Mekonnen lead the World Cross-Country Championships, 1988. Mark Shearman–Athletics Images.

they swept across the line. "There's never been anything like it! You just saw the greatest display of team running in history!" For a cross-country team runner, it was almost beyond belief.

That whole week was a memorable personal experience as well as a professional media one, because I was still a runner. Being a runner (this sounds naive but isn't) gives you direct and unfiltered access to all other runners. That's one thing that makes running so remarkable; it is an intensely competitive sport that is also an egalitarian community. Just put your shorts and shoes on and if you're fast enough, you can run with, befriend, and, if so inclined, interview the greatest celebrities on earth.

Going pretty well at age forty-eight (I had run a recent 10K race in thirty-two minutes), I could run every day in Cornwall Park in sight of, and sometimes with, the visiting athletes. I could assess them on the hills, check whether they preferred to train alone or in groups, join up with some, and note with amusement how almost all the members of one European team were propped against trees, simultaneously suffering nosebleeds (an effect of blood-boosting).

As a commentator or writer, I do my best to bring the runners to life as individuals. Running in Cornwall Park, and providing lifts there and back for a heap of Kenyans in the back seat of my modest little car, I got to know them a little, especially John Ngugi and Kip Koskei, and their genial manager/coach, Mike Kosgei, although I never mastered the complicated African handshake Mike tried to teach me. Back at the motel, I made another friend: a small, energetic, jet-black kitten that I presciently named "Ngugi."

One warm afternoon, I ran around a curve on Twin Oaks Drive and there they were, the whole Kenyan squad, lingering beneath a grove of trees, stretching, yawning, slowly jogging about, moving lithely in and out of the dappled sunlight. That memory stays with me thirty years later; the image helps me understand how movement on foot over the earth is so profoundly natural to these humans who have been runners on the high plains for thousands of generations.

Equally vivid is the image of how hard and skillfully they trained. I learned the details of their carefully shaped structure from Coach Kosgei, who initiated the famous and notoriously competitive national training camps. He told me about their three-times-a-day training regime, the hill repeats, the tempo runs, the sessions and trials to select the teams and at the same time build team chemistry.

The team member I got to know best, perhaps because he was nearest to me in age, was Kip Koskei, who may or may not have been over forty. He explained to me one day, after we'd pushed together up the steep, grassed volcanic crater to the top of One Tree Hill, that the uncertainty about his age was because he and other kids used to be taken out of school whenever times were hard on the family farm. They were always re-enrolled at the same academic level, although among mostly younger kids. He didn't recall how often it had happened. So, Koskei was probably, but not certainly, the only runner to win a World Cross-Country podium medal at over forty years of age when he followed Ngugi and Paul Kipkoech home that Saturday afternoon.

That finish is another vivid memory. On the television microphone, my co-commentator and I had to race through something like the opening lines of this chapter as the Kenyan squad poured across. For the record,

Kenya placed 1–2–3–4–6–7–8–9, for 23 points. That's only two points from the perfect 21 total points in six-to-score team racing. They were frustrated only by Ethiopian Abebe Mekonnen in fifth. Another Ethiopian, Haija Bulbula, was tenth, so the top ten were all East African.

It was, as I said on the microphone, the most superb team performance in the history of world-level running, more dominant in depth even than Finland at the 1924 Olympic cross-country. I needed a way of telling our viewers how astounding an accomplishment they were seeing: "In rugby, this would be winning the World Cup final by a hundred points to three!" I said.

Earlier, Kenya did almost the same in the junior men's race. They placed 1–2–4–5–6, and that was with the sixteen-year-old Cosmas Ndeti (later three-time winner of the Boston Marathon) being disqualified after placing second. The winner was Wilfred Ouanda Kirochi. He told me that he preferred his Kenyan name, Ouanda, to the Wilfred conferred on him by his Christian school, so that was how I announced him on television that day and again two years later in the Auckland stadium, when as Ouanda Kirochi he won the Commonwealth Games 1,500 m silver medal.

For a little perspective, in case anyone suspects the field was weak, here's a selection of other placings—names that glittered on other occasions, but were mere also-rans to Kenya this time: Domingos Castro 16, Steve Moneghetti 21, Pat Porter 28, John Halvorsen 59, Craig Virgin 102, Rod Dixon 117, John Treacy 127, Abel Anton 177, and Rob de Castella (who did not finish).

Mind-blown by such unprecedented supremacy and stunned with the sense I had just watched running move to a new level of perfection that I could not adequately define, I was staggering about outside after the commentary job ended when I bumped into Mike Kosgei.

"Your guys were incredible!" I gasped, resorting to feeble cliché.

"Thank you. And soon, we will do as well in the women's race," he said quietly, smiling. That's a man who knew what he was talking about.

A comic footnote: The Ethiopian teams arrived late, and an unwise Auckland official decided to re-allocate all the bib numbers, inserting the nine new names into the alphabetical team sequence. That folly meant every runner representing nations from Eth- onward wore a number different from the one on the list issued the previous day—and the media were not told. Unwise? I could use other adjectives. As Kenya's junior men swept irresistibly forward at the head of the first race of the afternoon, I heard a radio commentator behind me loudly proclaiming on air the utterly astounding performances by the young team from Gibraltar. I'm not unkind. I twisted back and quickly told him. "Not Gibraltar, mate, Kenya. That's why they're black, eh. Some dork changed the numbers."

That remarkable race heralded a total change in elite running, one that thirty years later shows no sign of abating. In my lifetime as a runner and a voice of running, three great changes in the sport have spilled over to contribute to change in the wider world—the sheer numbers seeking healthy exercise, the upsurge of women, and the domination of the elite sport by East Africa.

Is that change significant more widely than in sport? Well, sport no longer has a merely marginal place in the world. The emergence of Brazil as a football (soccer) power changed the world in ways significant for millions of people over most of a century, and it gave that diverse nation a more unified identity. And the East African phenomenon also goes beyond sport because it has elicited a response from the running community and beyond that may be historically important as a step in postcolonial thought and behavior, as I shall argue.

This is a book of fortunate eyewitness. I've been on the spot for many key moments in the rise and reign of East African runners, from watching Maiyoro Nyandika and Abebe Bikila at the Rome Olympics, to reporting on some of the greatest marathons by Ibrahim Hussein, Tegla Loroupe, Catherine Ndereba, Geoffrey Mutai, Haile Gebrselassie, Wilson Kipsang, Eliud Kipchoge, and more. What a privilege to see something that I love done so supremely well! To see running of such sheer beauty is to feel you are witness to the sublime.

My closest personal encounter with East African running was at the finish of the World Cross-Country Championships in Düsseldorf, Germany, in 1977. Struggling to the finish of a flat, fast race that did nothing to favor my hills-and-mud harrier skills, I collapsed in an exhausted, entangled heap with Omer Khalifa from Sudan, who crossed the line alongside. We were so entwined that my name didn't appear in the official results for thirty years.

As a reporter, I was also very close to Haile Gebrselassie when he made his heartbroken announcement of his retirement to the stunned New York Marathon media room; close enough to see that his tears were absolutely real.

The Kenya/Ethiopia phenomenon is almost beyond comprehension. We simply accept that they will fill almost all the top places in every major race. In any ranking of the world's fastest in any year, in the top three hundred, men and women, 290 will be from East and Northeast Africa, including Eritrea, Somalia, Tanzania, and Uganda, with increasing numbers of those with other national affiliations because of migration or sometimes sponsored change of citizenship. Year after year, they totally dominate the World Cross-Country, World Half-Marathon, Olympic and World Championship medals from 800 m up, and every professional marathon and road race. I just watched a World Championship 10,000 m final (2017) in which the first fifteen athletes were of East African ethnicity, though they represented Great Britain, Canada, USA, and Bahrain, as well as Ethiopia, Eritrea, Kenya, and Uganda. This dominance is normal.

But pause: it is unparalleled, unprecedented, abnormal. In no other field of human enterprise would such a monopoly be accepted as normal. Italians are good at singing and Brazilians are good at football, but they don't produce ninety-eight percent of the world's best singers and footballers. In distance running, one small geographical area, about one sixtieth of the geographical area of Africa and a minuscule fragment of the total globe, has become absolutely dominant. Running is not a niche sport. It's global, it's popular, and it's newsworthy. Never has any internationally practiced human activity been so monopolized at the elite level by such a small region.

This extraordinary state of affairs has come about in less than fifty years. In the 1964 Boston Marathon, the top ten men came from five nations on three continents: Belgium, Finland, Canada, USA, and Argentina. In that year's Olympic marathon, five continents were represented in the top ten finishers. No important race in the twenty-first century could conceivably see such a range in the top placings.

I'm not offering to explain why the East Africans are so good. That's a high-level question for biochemical and kinetic science. The genetic and environmental causes have been somewhat investigated. Altitude is clearly the key element, producing a high red blood cell count and other adaptations to maximize oxygen utilization. It's no coincidence that three centuries ago the most famous long-distance runners in Europe, often hired as running footmen (couriers), were the mountain-bred Basques. The first wave of winning runners in the new professional era after 1981 were Mexicans and Colombians. More work has to be done on the varied evolutionary processes of adaptation to altitude. Nepalese Sherpas, for instance, who are acclimatized to even higher altitudes than denizens of the high Rift Valley, are very different in body type, remarkable for their clambering and lifting ability, not running. Therefore, a high red corpuscle count does not alone make a marathon runner. Economic incentive clearly plays a major role, as do astute locally based mentors like the legendary teacher–coach Brother Colm O'Connell, the "godfather of Kenyan running." But responsible commentators are also careful to recognize the rigorous and scientifically based coaching cultures that help make these athletes so good.

All these points are familiar from many marathon television broadcasts; here, I want to ask a different question, an important one culturally and politically. How has running responded? How has the thriving, Western-based but global sport, industry, culture, community, or social phenomenon of running (choose whichever term you like best) reacted to this sweeping takeover of its most profitable sector? Because this book is in part a history of the running boom, I'm asking how that historic movement has responded to having its top tier transformed in this unforeseen way, by a ceaseless flood of talent that fifty years ago we didn't know existed. It's a question with significance beyond running, in a world that is increasingly globalized but still far from being free of racism or exploitation. The answer is profoundly to the credit of the running community. It gives us a sign of hope in the often-negative history of the early twenty-first century.

Here are the basic facts. Within running, generation after generation of Kenyans, and more recently Ethiopians and Eritreans, have been accepted entirely on their merits as people who do something that we (the running community) love—run fast for a long time. They have been welcomed, admired, celebrated, and rewarded. In more than forty years of running and working in elite-level running, I have rarely seen or heard any resentment or learned of any exclusion. The visiting elites are my main subject, but an important development is that many have made their homes in America or other nations, have become citizens, won races, and in increasing numbers are winning places in national teams. Twenty years ago, when this citizenship process first began, there was enough scattered muttering about "not real Americans" for editor Jonathan Beverly and I to confront the issue in a *Running Times* feature, "Foreign Born Americans" (January/February 2003). So soon after the 9/11 terrorist attacks, it was a courageous editorial decision. We advocated acceptance and welcome, and our readers were almost wholly supportive; one (a police officer) confessed in an email to being made to feel ashamed of his previous reservations. A decade later, Meb Keflezighi in the United States and Sir Mo Farah in the United Kingdom are the objects of national adoration. American track fans have warmly adopted Bernard Lagat, Paul Chelimo, and others.

In our specialist media, I've been impressed by the sincere effort to give African runners the attention they deserve. As senior writer for *Running Times*, I was proud that it frequently put elite Africans on its cover, as well as featured them in profiles and interviews, analyzing their training for us all to learn from, always striving to present them to readers as distinct human beings. That is one of many reasons why the closing of *Running Times* in 2016 was such a huge loss. Deeply informed television commentaries by Toni Reavis and Larry Rawson, notably, have also contributed to educating a wide public. If the very talk of African elites makes you switch off—and there are citizen runners who profess such lack of interest—well, that has not been the response of the sport as a whole.

Even ordinary people in ordinary cities have proved generous. On the streets of the Utica Boilermaker 15K Road Race every year, the spectator crowds chant "Africa! Africa!" (as reported by John Pitarresi in the *Observer-Dispatch*) to cheer on runners whose names they don't know and couldn't pronounce. You don't hear fans at other sports so eagerly encouraging visitors who are blitzing the home team 10–0. Once they have become familiar as individuals, they are fully embraced. Tegla Loroupe succeeded Grete Waitz as the marathon crowd favorite in New York City, Catherine Ndereba won the hearts of Maine, and Haile Gebrselassie's happy smile became world famous.

Then there is an aspect of the contemporary sport that no one seems to address openly. Look at results of prize-money races around the country on any day, and you'll find Kenyan and Ethiopian names on top of every list. This influx is not a few superstars. Hundreds of second- and third-tier East Africans now visit to compete for short periods, or they gain visas that allow longer residence and more competition. These runners live modestly, sometimes communally in facilities provided by their agents, and they make the most of whatever time they are allowed on their visa to find races with prize money. They cover many miles traveling to and from races, squeezed in a shared van that arrives late enough to minimize accommodation costs. A few become known and more lastingly successful, but most are almost anonymous, picking up a few hundred dollars at best every two or three weeks. It's not an easy or lucrative life. They must feel isolated and dependent. They survive on the obscure fringes, until race day, when they are acclaimed by the ordinary people of many a small town, crowned on a podium, and given a modest check. Few ever get into four figures for a race. That kind of money simply isn't there, and when it is, the real elites come in to collect it. Each has a story, as I have found interviewing them—a family at home to support, children who have been left in a grandmother's care, a partner who is also a near-elite racer, academic aspirations, or ambition to enter a long-term career in another field, since some are gaining qualifications. Inevitably, there are abuses. One East Coast agent was found to be administering performance-enhancing drugs, probably without the athletes' knowledge. Running has no overall system of controls or code of professional practice.

Races, media, and regular runners almost without exception welcome and celebrate the extra level of talent these out-of-town athletes bring to their event. A lot more could be done, especially by runners' agents, to provide the media and the public with information that enables them to recognize the East Africans as individuals; but the response generally has been inclusive and generous. Coaches like Owen Anderson in Lansing, Michigan, and Mike Barnow and Adrienne Wald in New York (and no doubt many I don't know of) have made it their mission to assist East African athletes to find homes, work, education; gain residence and even citizenship; and above all compete at their best. Such generosity reflects well on our culture and contributes to the necessary process of nurturing immigrants and helping them become good citizens. Their host running communities often become proud and fond of them. When Harbart Okuti from Uganda and some friends put on a race in 2016 to raise money to build libraries in his country, the running community of New Paltz, New York, gave full support, perhaps because he always gave such a friendly greeting when he flew past us on the rail trail at a running speed we could only dream of.

To be involved in elite running these days means getting an education in East African culture. That's what impresses me most. Among committed runners and people involved across the whole of running culture, including race organizers, coaches, agents, media, shoe and apparel companies, and the running-travel business, there has been a huge effort to climb the steep learning curve of knowledge about East Africa, its runners, their personalities, training, home environment, languages, customs, and cultures. Every major running writer and television analyst I can think of has made the not always comfortable journey through East Africa at least once. Some go often and have become deeply expert. Interviews and conversations in media centers now are of a different order from twenty years ago. Do all baseball commentators go on research visits to the Dominican Republic and pass on their findings on air to a mass audience, as Reavis and Rawson do? It's not quite a fair comparison, but it does say something about running's response as a culture to this source of talent.

All the effort to learn has preceded formal academic research, which is overdue but no doubt will follow. In this chapter, I can only begin the process. This new form of interaction between two cultures through the single elemental activity of running is a human subject well worth study.

Has there been exploitation of Kenya's running talent by outsiders? Yes, though it's hard to quantify. Wesley Korir, an elected member of Kenya's Parliament while still a world-class marathoner, made scathing comments about some agents to a small group of us journalists before the 2013 New York City Marathon: "It's modern day slavery. Agents and managers come in from overseas, recruit many young runners, put them away in training camps, and throw them out when they get injured. The majority are being taken advantage of. There are also drugs issues. We have to protect our athletes."

It was the most forceful statement about such issues I've ever heard from a current athlete. Here was a man who sees the situation of being encircled by international journalists as an opportunity to say something worthwhile, even challenging. His two identities as runner and politician are not kept separate.

Since then, doping revelations have reflected badly on the enclosed fortress-camps that some European agents have established. Some were deported in light of doping scandals, to the surprise of none of us who had followed their runners' results. At a distance, it's impossible to judge how widespread the exploitation is and how that balances against those agents who provide a necessary and honest service. I go a little further into this unsavory topic in the next chapter. But there's no doubt that, as in the colonial past, considerable profit is being made from African talent and African labor.

The situation is grave, but it is limited to the profitable elite sport. Overall, if running represents our Western culture in its response to the East African phenomenon, it does it largely with honor. Information has been shared. Books and many articles have been written, films made, social media discussions generated. Big tour groups go to African races, and by my observation a great deal of real learning occurs. Real friend-ships are commonplace, and marriages increasingly so. Some Western runners and coaches have become bonded with East Africa, including (for human nature is complex) some of those exploitative agents.

The earliest running-based charitable project was probably Shoes for Africa, started by runner and running writer Mike Sandrock in 1986 after a trip to race in Yaoundé, Cameroon. "Olympian locals in Boulder like Frank Shorter, Steve Jones, and Arturo Barrios donate gear, and we changed the name to One World Running, to reflect the work we do in non-African countries. All volunteer, we are still running strong!" Sandrock said in 2017.

New Yorker Toby Tanser's Shoes4Africa similarly moved on from shipping used running shoes to building an entire new children's cancer hospital. The Gathimba Edwards Foundation helps Kenyan children get medical care, education, and housing. Sandrock, Tanser, and Myles Edwards all ran and lived in Africa, gaining awareness that impelled them to help.

People in the running community have collaboratively created events as important as the Great Ethiopian Run, which was founded by Ethiopians and Europeans in 2001 and is now one of the world's great race festivals with more than 40,000 runners. The festival expanded into an event promotion enterprise that puts on more than a hundred races a year in Ethiopia. In chapter 17, I discuss another one of these events, the Safaricom Marathon at the Lewa Wildlife Conservancy in Kenya.

The Rift Valley Marathon in Mosoriot, Kenya, was founded by three self-described "crazy but idealistic" Canadian runners calling themselves RunforLife, in collaboration with the equally philanthropic Kenyan Olympian Laban Rotich. The race funds microprojects by Kenyan women, such as a poultry operation or construction of a chemical cattle dip that protects cows from deadly insect bites.

A world-class running track in Iten, Kenya, was donated and maintained by the London Marathon, which also funds an endurance training program. A collaborative venture, this program enables Western runners to train with and learn from the world's best. The visitors test and extend themselves in the Kenyan environment, alongside Kenyan runners like the girls who attend the Lornah Kiplagat Sports Academy, many from underprivileged backgrounds. The initiative comes not from any government or aid charity, but from running, financed from a marathon's budget.

"If you can't beat 'em, join 'em," goes the old adage, and a good many Western runners have been doing just that. Best known are the twin brothers Jake and Zane Robertson, who virtually ran away from home when they graduated from high school in suburban New Zealand in 2007, lived and trained in poverty in Iten, and became world-class runners. Scottish 1,500 m champion Myles Edwards goes regularly for extended periods in Kenya, and he established the Gathimba Edwards Foundation with Kenyan ex-star Gideon Gathimba. "In the high season, there can be up to fifty serious Western athletes at any time in Iten, plus some recreational runners," Edwards told me. "About ten of us live in simple rental houses. You have to train, eat, and sleep like the Kenyans. It's not just the environment and lifestyle, it's the work ethic. At the end of each trip, I thought I couldn't have worked harder, but the Kenyan attitude is you have to keep pushing new limits. You never stop learning."

Learning, that's the key word. Another educational project was when top Ethiopian coach Sentayehu Eshetu was "coach in residence" at Shrewsbury School, England. Shrewsbury is not only an elite private school; it is historic as the birthplace of cross-country as an organized sport almost two hundred years ago (see Robinson 2013). Twelve young Shrewsbury runners, members of the school club that is still called the "Royal Shrewsbury School Hunt," familiarly the "Hounds," then went to Ethiopia in 2013 to train in Iten and Bekoji. What a perfect conjunction of the past and present of running! The historian in me went into rapture.

The full dominance of East Africa's runners began that newsworthy day in 1988 when ten crossed the finish line at the head of a world championship that had thirty-five nations represented from six continents. As the dominance became the extraordinary norm, the running community responded, not with resentment or exclusion, but with admiration and, to use an old word, humility. Admiringly and humbly, student runners from a privileged English high school go to Bekoji. Fifty mixed Scots, Kiwis, Americans, and others live admiringly and humbly, train ferociously, and study the local running stars in Iten. Canadians dig wells and create a race in Mosoriot. All go to learn. And that's not counting the hundreds of American and European runners who travel there to run in events that bring incalculable benefit to the local people and the environment they live in, and send the tourists home better informed and more sympathetic.

Learning is why they are there. Learning and, in wanting to become better and more knowledgeable as runners, self-improvement. That makes them unlike most visitors from the first world to the third, because they are not there to exploit or to patronize or to even bring home trophy selfies, but to observe and imitate. They take away no natural resource, they misuse no cheap labor, and they impose no Western technology, value system, or religious belief. The local people are enabled to benefit from a unique indigenous asset: their innate running ability. In the relationship between running and East Africa, despite the exploitation that Korir identified, the old imperialism has been reversed. Isn't that a way of making history?

11

September 24, 1988, Seoul

Dirty Running

Silence. Tension. Expectancy. The eight best sprinters in the world wait to go to their marks. This is the race of the Games, the much-hyped Seoul Showdown that will settle the acrimonious rivalry between Ben Johnson and Carl Lewis. Quite possibly, it is going to be the greatest 100 m of all time. Quite possibly, the winner will become the fastest human of all time. More than possibly, it will be the race most tainted of all time by illegal performance drugs.

The stadium crowd below me holds its breath. The world's media, high in the stand, are poised over their laptops and microphones. Millions watch on television. As television commentator, what do you say at such a moment? On impulse, I choose something that provides historical context and carries some ironic implication.

"If they ever make a *Chariots of Fire* movie about this Olympic 100 m," I say in the hush before the call to their marks, "who will be the hero, and who will be the villain?"

That's the nearest I can legally go on air to saying how deeply anticipation of this race is subverted by suspicion. The 1981 film *Chariots of Fire*, hugely popular and still familiar, reimagined the 1924 Olympic 100 m final through clouds of heroic glory and inspiring romance. I want to suggest for my viewers, without being sued, that the 1988 version has little to do with heroism, or even decent behavior.

The full story of the 1988 race has been told many times, best by Richard Moore (2012) in *The Dirtiest Race in History*, a book that was

18. Ben Johnson leaves a tainted trail, Olympic 100 m, Seoul, 1988. Mark Shearman–Athletics Images.

less sensationalist than its title, a careful professional piece of investigation, and extremely depressing. It showed that of the eight finalists, only Calvin Smith (USA, third) and Robson Da Silva (Brazil, sixth) never had a doping charge against them. Carl Lewis's only infringement was when he tested positive at the 1988 USA Trials for three stimulants, at two to six parts per million, but he and other American sprinters were excused the three-month ban on grounds of "inadvertent use." The documents did not come to light until 2003, fifteen years later. By then, it must be said, the permissible level of those stimulants had been raised to ten parts per million, so Lewis would have not have been questioned.

My job as commentator gave me a personal peephole into the history, good and bad, that was being made in Seoul in 1988, mainly because my media pass provided access to the athletes' training track. A year later, I was setting over-fifty age-group world records, so I was fast enough to run laps there without looking too incongruous. It was a great way of meeting athletes and coaches and gathering impressions and information. Not about drugs. No one talks about those.

This is how I recorded it at the time in my training diary: "No racing in Seoul, but some memorable training runs, notably at the training track with Mike Turner [an old friend who was the Great Britain team manager]; and at various times with John Ngugi, Douglas Wakiihuri, and Paula Ivan. Occasional company included Annette Sergent, Vicky Huber, Lisa Martin, Hans Koelman, and Kenya's coach Mike Kosgei. And they all chatted openly and convivially, so it was better than being an inactive groupie or depending on press conferences."

Sometimes I would run a few laps with them during their warm-up or warm-down, and I began to get a real sense of them as people; as runners, anyway. I'd befriended several of the Kenyans at the World Cross-Country in Auckland earlier that year (chapter 10), so I was able to build on that in conversations on the run with John Ngugi and others, which gave me priceless material for my analyst job.

At other times, the training track was a less pleasant experience. The first time I saw Ben Johnson, it was a shock. From behind, shirtless, his shoulders, neck, and back looked grotesquely over-muscled, and his inner thighs were so bulging he couldn't walk properly. Truly—his thighs rubbed together. Face to face, when we talked for a few moments, he was all yellow, swollen eyeballs. No *Chariots of Fire* idealism could survive that encounter.

There were decent people and honest competitors at that training track, like most of those I named above. But the daily scene there, with its elongated high jumpers, super-muscled shot putters, swollen sprinters, and deep-voiced, unshaven Eastern European women throwers, reminded me of the distorted half-animal creatures in *The Island of Dr. Moreau*. Johnson was on estragole, a fancy name for a veterinary product that adds muscle to animals before slaughter. H. G. Wells was on to body-shaping drugs nearly a hundred years before the Seoul Olympics; see his 1904 novel about giant human growth, *The Food of the Gods and How It Came to Earth*.

I made a small contribution to the way the historic 100 m was reported. Not being a sprinter, I did some reading and discovered that, contrary to appearances, all 100 m sprinters in fact slow down after about sixty-five or seventy meters. At the jam-packed media conference with Carl Lewis, I asked about that, and Lewis gave a thoughtful and informative answer. Next day, every journalist in Seoul had become an expert on the last thirty meters slow-down.

Well, the yellow-eyed villain didn't look as if he slowed down as he won that Olympic final in a world record, thrusting one huge, hubristic arm aloft, while the usually silken Lewis, who also broke the old record, gawked across at him in incomprehension. At the microphone, I had to find words of praise for something I deeply distrusted. I had to do the same twice that week for Florence Griffith Joyner's victories.

Three days later, one very early morning in the Olympic media village, the news exploded.

"Ben's busted!"

In an instant, thousands of journalists were shocked from hangover to feeding frenzy.

Heroes or villains? Nearly thirty years later, Johnson comes out as stubbornly naive rather than a calculating cheat. Lewis, clean under today's rules though benefiting from some leniency at the time, remains in every way a man of elusive, physical perfection and a psychological enigma. I knew that Linford Christie had tested positive for the stimulant pseudo-ephedrine because of the laps I was running with Mike Turner, who told me with conviction how Christie's positive test result was due to a ginseng medicine he had innocently taken for a cold. No doubt Mike's advocacy as British team manager helped secure the narrow vote (11–10) that let Christie keep his bronze (eventually silver) medal. Mike was a very old friend. I kept my doubts to myself.

For me, there's no question that, ultimately, the chief villain was Primo Nebiolo, the Mafia knockoff who ruled world track and field, sold the sport on world records, and concealed the drug-taking that policy demanded. When a proposal was put to the International Association of Athletics Federations (IAAF) by Great Britain and New Zealand to increase the penalty for doping from two years to four, Nebiolo and his medical chief Arne Ljungqvist blocked it. I told that story when reviewing Ljungqvist's book, self-vauntingly titled *Doping's Nemesis* (2011). A nemesis does not fight for lighter punishment. Nebiolo's legacy was the critically diseased condition of world track and field in the years after his death.

This view owes something to my own observation of Nebiolo's autocratic conduct, to private reports from members of the IAAF, and to the investigative books *Lords of the Rings* by Vyv Simson and Andrew Jennings (1992), and Jennings's sequel, *The New Lords of the Rings* (1996). "The world's sports leaders have misled us on dope testing," they conclude (Simson and Jennings 1992, 185).

I include the Johnson–Lewis 100 m in a book mainly about much longer races not because I think doping in track and field has itself made history. In the big picture, it's a minor symptom of a much greater malaise: society's increasing dependency on drugs for all kinds of purpose, including performance enhancement in sports. Track and running were not conspicuous leaders in doping, even among sports. Bodybuilding, weight lifting, swimming, football, baseball, and, among endurance sports, cycling, were probably well ahead of running in dependency.

What that Seoul Olympic race did change historically was the world's awareness. Instantly, the "Ben's busted" sensation locked in place a profound global skepticism. Nothing would ever be sacred again. That loss of trust was what I already implied with my *Chariots of Fire* reference as they took their marks. No revelation or disqualification since has shocked us so sensationally. The disillusionment was deepened when the Canadian government appointed the Ontario Appeal Court Chief Justice Charles Dubin to conduct an inquiry into the Johnson case. His independent report (1990) exposed for the first time the extent of the problem and the complicity of the IAAF, International Olympic Committee (IOC), and their supposed medical commissions.

Since Ben was busted, there is a shadow in our minds over most world-class performances in every sport. Lance Armstrong and the Bay Area Laboratory Co-Operative (BALCO) case for sure deepened this universal disbelief, but it began the day the Olympic sprint gold medalist was exposed as a cheat.

How deeply does that doubt go in the sport we call running, as opposed to track? Confirmed cases of doping were scattered two decades ago, though many top performances aroused suspicion. See my reservations about Russian women in the 2002 London Marathon (chapter 15). The earliest major revelation was when world cross-country champion (2000, 2001) Mohammed Mourhit, a Moroccan-born Belgian, was banned for the blood-boosting drug erythropoietin (EPO), which is routine breakfast food for most professional cyclists. The next big name to fall was the Moroccan Abderrahim Goumri, who among the running media was one of the best-liked elite marathoners of the 2005–11 era. Goumri seemed to specialize in nearly winning but finishing second (London 2007, New York City 2007 and 2008, Chicago 2009), yet remained good-humored about it. One of his lines was that he had promised to marry his fiancée when he finally won a major marathon, and he would giggle mischievously when someone asked how she felt about the latest second place.

I knew that Morocco was one of the places where doping was most prevalent, and I'd written incredulously about Asmae Leghzaoui's supposed world 10K record in New York, a year before she tested positive. I ironically urged my readers to eat fish, I remember, after she claimed that to be the secret of her success during our interview. One of Goumri's training partners was Rashid Ramzi, who won the 800 m and 1,500 m world championship golds with a meteoric improvement in 2005, representing Bahrain although he was born in Morocco and was still living there. Ramzi and Goumri shared the same agent, John Nubani. It was all highly suspicious, but it's naive to think a journalist with no proof and no scientific knowledge could stand up at a media conference and say, "I think you're a drugs cheat, you will now kindly confess." We waited till Ramzi was caught by an improved re-testing procedure six months after his Olympic 1,500 m victory in 2008, and then Goumri became one of the first athletes to be banned on the evidence of his long-term "biological passport." Goumri's story ended sadly when he was killed in a car wreck in Morocco in January 2013, at age thirty-six.

Another elite who was entrancing company at media interviews was Liliya Shobukhova, the Russian who was supposedly the second fastest woman marathoner of all time, winning Chicago three times (2009,

2010, and 2011) and London once (2010). She used to run her last three miles with such unnatural power that we always suspected EPO (that is a known effect). The biological passport eventually caught her, though she received a lighter ban for providing information about doping in Russia. A lot of money went back and forth during the investigation, but Shobukhova showed no inclination to repay her very considerable prize and sponsorship earnings (or stealings, more accurately). She used to tell us in media interviews that she aimed to build a hotel, and no doubt it is doing very nicely.

The money in running is biggest in the marathon, and there have been enough proven cases now to make us suspect that doping, especially EPO, is widespread, though probably not as endemic as it has been among cyclists. It's important to say that, so far, it's only at the prize-money professional level, not yet in the midpack people's sport. Other forms of cheating, especially course-cutting and identity swapping (to obtain a Boston Marathon qualifier, most often), are bigger problems.

Doping's impact on running at elite level is grave; being covert, it leaves so much in dark uncertainty. Without intimate access to corrupt managers, it's impossible to know the truth. Some training camps in Kenya are like fortresses, as I said in chapter 10. Few journalists have crossed the drawbridge. When I obtained a copy of Dr. Gabriele Rosa's (2014) book, *Correre la Vita*, I had it translated so that I could read what the manager and medical advisor of so many top Kenyan athletes, including several who have been banned, has to say about drugs. The answer is nothing. Apart from one reference to his disapproval of "blood doping" (re-injection of the athlete's own blood to boost red corpuscle count), the issue is never mentioned in 330 operatically eloquent pages. What can be said, and with passion, is that those of us who love and work for this sport do so with a profound and unhappy distrust.

There is a high personal cost when people who have risen by dedicated effort to achieve so much are then subjected to public shame. Notorious recent cases are the Kenyan training partners Rita Jeptoo and Jemima Sumgong. Jeptoo had won the Boston Marathon three times (2006, 2013, and 2014) and Chicago twice (2013 and 2014), making her one of the biggest dollar earners the sport has known. She was banned in 2016, with the announcement castigating her for "deceptive and obstructive conduct throughout the proceedings." Sumgong finished second at Boston in 2012 but was disqualified for prednisolone, then reinstated, finished second at New York in 2014, and reached the summit in 2016, winning the highly competitive and lucrative London Marathon in April and the Olympic gold medal in Rio in August. That was the first time I have ever watched the finish of an Olympic marathon in glum silence. In April 2017, to the surprise of no one within the sport, she tested positive for EPO and was banned.

The tragedy is that Sumgong was the first Kenyan woman to take the Olympic marathon gold medal, a historic achievement if it had been genuine. Jeptoo's four Boston and Chicago wins made in total one of the greatest victory sequences of all time. But now we can't write those things. We must work in a kind of black hole of history, a vortex where basic facts swirl endlessly about, change, and disappear, leaving us always scrambling to remember what results still stand, who's been banned for how long, and who was on what when. History crumbles in my fingers even as I write.

Did these athletes even know what was being given to them? We know that East German sportspeople in the 1960s–70s had no choice about being injected, and probably no knowledge of the implications. In the current economic structure of running, much responsibility surely lies with the managers, but none seem eager to accept it. (Refer to Wesley Korir's comments about modern slavery in chapter 10.)

Can we get nearer the truth? There's no funding. When David Walsh investigated cycling, he had the resources of the London *Sunday Times* behind him. You need money for travel and financial support when the legal cudgels come out. In 1997 (October 22), Phil Hersh of the *Chicago Tribune* questioned with his usual acerbic vigor the meteoric improvements by African runners, linking them to the Chinese. But even Hersh had to base his attack on the implication of more African runners now living "near the sports 'doctors' in Italy and Spain," and the statistical unlikelihood of the world 10,000 m record improving by twenty-five seconds in three years. Implication and unlikelihood are not evidence. The only real investigation has been by the German journalist Hajo Seppelt, who lived inside Kenya and posed as a running agent to get the story on drug enhancement. His charges were quickly denied, then fudged.

My unhappiness about having to cover this topic is apparent. When Ben Johnson triumphantly thrust his unnaturally bulging arm aloft in 1988, he left a dirty trail behind him, and we smell and taste its murk during every race we watch.

12

September 30, 1990, Berlin

Running through the Berlin Wall

I ran just one race in East Germany. Three days later, the country ceased to exist. The 1990 Berlin Marathon went for the first time through the recently breached Berlin Wall, under the arches of the Brandenburg Gate, and for five miles through the bleak streets of the East. It was the Marathon without the Wall, the Run Free Marathon, the Run in Unity ("Einheit" in German)—consciously historic, avowedly symbolic, openly emotional.

We started from the Charlottenburg Gate to the music of Beethoven and Schiller's "Ode to Joy": "Be united, ye millions." And the race enacted the music. The 26,000 competitors and million or so spectators made that marathon (to use a few phrases from Schiller's poem) the most joyful, inspiring, divinely sparkling, world uniting, magically binding of all the symbolic celebrations of the reunification of Germany.

Things have not been easy since then for Germany, though the reunited nation has conducted itself with greater integrity and generosity than most others of the current era. Running, too, has had problems, but it, too, has shown moral strength. History will look favorably on our contribution and our frequent link with larger history. The Berlin Marathon in 1990 was a key example.

Through the Brandenburg Gate

The runners in Berlin in September 1990 celebrated, I'm happy to say, in typical runner style: more vigorously and less reverently than any concert-hall audience listening to Beethoven's Ninth, more spontaneously and less

19. Berlin Marathon (1990) results book celebrates the Run in Unity. Courtesy of BMW Berlin Marathon/ Sport-Club Charlottenburg.

tidily than any military parade. As celebrants, runners are lively but disorganized, good at movement, and hopeless at ritual.

Approaching the Brandenburg Gate at two miles, shuffling in that exuberant crush of slow joggers between the trees of Tiergarten, I thought of the other celebratory parades that had passed along this broad avenue to the ceremonial arch. The victorious Prussians marched here in 1870; the united imperial German armies set out to world war here in 1914; the Wehrmacht's tanks and swastikas threatened the world from this wide, straight road in the 1930s, announcing their faith in making Germany great again, the state that would last a thousand years; and, in 1945, the Allied armies paraded here to symbolize that state's humiliation.

Army after army, along the avenue, through the Brandenburg Gate. War after war.

This time, instead of goose-stepping ranks and sinister trundling tanks, there came an untidy, cheerful, motley mob of undersized marathon runners, as sweaty, scruffy, and high spirited as runners always are. Instead of uniforms, we wore stripes or flowers, Union Jack shorts or silver-fern singlets, Soviet "CCCP" T-shirts or Stars and Stripes tights, club colors from all over Germany and the world, baseball caps and wooly hats, tattered sweaters or plastic garbage sacks to discard if the weather warmed up, or whatever idiosyncratic mix we felt like wearing that misty morning.

Instead of guns and fixed bayonets, we carried spare toilet paper, which doesn't rate high on the dangerous weapons list. Instead of military marches, we ran to Beethoven, rock, jazz, rollicking German folk tunes, or whatever the curbside bands and boom boxes played to stir us on.

And instead of saluting some medal-draped dictator as we passed under the Brandenburg arches, we clapped, cheered, raised our skinny arms in victory, hugged each other, paused to pat the stonework for luck, openly wept, took pictures, posed for pictures, exchanged cameras to take each other's pictures, ducked clumsily around to go through the Gate again, got in each other's way, got bumped and hugged and squeezed and smeared with other people's sweat, shook hands, joined hands, did miniature Mexican waves, linked arms, said "guten Tag" and "Vereinigung" to innumerable Swedes and Italians, and got kissed by some soggy-bearded foreigner. Finally, reluctantly, we were pressed forward in the shuffling jam of runners to move down the great avenue of Unter den Linden.

Nobody minded. Even when we had to walk or jog in place, jostled and squashed together, nobody grumbled or shoved. To save congestion at the gate, the organizers had appealed to the runners to go around it rather than through the arches. Nobody did. In this marathon, there were more important things to do than run a fast time.

For me, the important thing was to be there. I had an injury, had scarcely trained for four months, and knew that I couldn't race well over that distance and shouldn't even try. I went because it was going to be so much more than a race, and because of a kind of longing to clear the shadow of Berlin from my life. Running, so elementally simple, can often work like that.

The Sound of the Doodlebug

My earliest memories, from age three onward, on England's southeast coast and then in south London, are of Germans—of their bombs whistling down in the night, leaving heaps of rubble where childhood friends' houses had stood. One of my first words was "bombsite," meaning the ruin of a neighbor's home, the garden deep in weeds, with shattered remnants of walls to hide behind, a wonderful place for little boys. We played war in the overgrown debris, invading Berlin and Tokyo with toy pistols made of twigs. For some months, my family lived in Southend, on the Thames Estuary and directly under the flightpath of bombers in both directions between Germany and southern England.

The engines came every night. "Are they theirs or ours?" someone would ask as the family roused and stumbled for shelter. We were adept at telling the difference in engine sound, my parents used to say. I know for certain that the snarl of a petrol-driven propeller plane still hits some deep nerve and makes my stomach sink. The up-and-down hoot of a siren sets my flesh uncontrollably creeping. More than seventy years later, those sounds mean fear.

"The Germans" meant that remote pulsing of engines—"they're theirs!"—invisible yet destructive. Night after night, the growling throb drove us into the stuffy cupboard under the stairs or the wire mesh cage of the metal-topped indoor shelter that doubled as a dining table. We would scuttle downstairs in our night clothes, clutching a toy for comfort.

Later, when I was starting school (about 1944), the noise the Germans made changed. It became a single, rasping, pulsating, approaching drone: the doodlebug. The V-1 flying bomb was its official name, for *Vergeltung-swaffen* ("Vengeance Weapons"), justified as repayment for the bombing of Germany's cities. With a petrol engine, it was the flying bomb, the world's first long-range missile. The Londoners it aimed to kill renamed it, with their irrepressible wit and with belittling onomatopoeia, first as the buzz-bomb, then the doodlebug. Say "doodle-doodle-doodle" in the back of your throat, and that's how it sounded.

Once you heard it, you hoped for dear life that deadly droning, doodling sound would keep on going, and so pass you by. You listened, held your breath, and waited. If you were unlucky, the chuggling growl of the engine suddenly cut off. There came a terrible silence, then slowly the thin, rising whistle as the missile fell. Once I saw a woman blown down the steps of a railway bridge that I had just run across with my mother as the whining terror fell and exploded to earth nearby. I can still see her bleeding knees.

Strictly speaking, there was no German up there. These were pilotless missiles, "as impersonal as a plague . . . as though the city were infested with enormous, venomous insects," Evelyn Waugh wrote, in his war novel *Unconditional Surrender*. A child doesn't make those distinctions. "The Germans" were always in the sky above me. I was six when the war ended. I can't remember any time when "the Germans" were not part of my consciousness.

When I could first read the papers, the news was all about the Cold War and the 1948–49 Berlin airlift. When Chataway beat Kuts in 1954, I was fully conscious of the Cold War significance. I learned German as a teenager and began to visit Germany. I felt no hostility, though the memories stayed. Germany was an emerging country, and I liked the people. Still do. Once I nearly took a job there as a broadcaster in Bremen, still a bruised and damaged city from the bombing of its port. I ran among the wreckage after my interview. I took hiking holidays in central Germany, loving the forests and enjoying convivial evenings in little country pubs, drinking beer and schnapps. As English, we were always warmly welcomed. In my twenties, I was the only German-speaking member of an English club athletics team visiting the Sauerland, the rural area around the Möhne and the other reservoirs that the famous dam-busters had devastated by precision-bombing with bombs that bounced on the water. In 1965, we were taken up to view the impressively rebuilt dams as a tourist outing. I spent exhausting evenings in bars shuttling from table to table to interpret twenty different conversations.

"'Ere, what's he sayin', Rog?" The summons came again and again across the room. There were three main topics: track times (of course), goodwill between Germany and England, and resentment of the dividing line drawn across their country. Time after time, I listened to anxieties about relatives out of touch, alive or dead, in the East, about the repression by the occupying Soviet army, and about the threat to us all that was barely a hundred miles away. Germanic togetherness would rise among the pilsner glasses.

"Ve vill togezer march, Cherman und Britisch, zis enemy in the east to drive out," I remember one rosy-faced, vehement Sauerlander urging us all late one night, while I struggled to remember the German for "not tonight, thank you."

The Wall

The Berlin Wall was built in 1961. For thirty years it scarred every thought of Europe. I saw it in 1977. It was the worst affront to humanity I had ever seen. I was in Germany that time to run for New Zealand in the World Cross-Country Championships, and we spent a week near the quaint old town of Lübeck, in the cold northeast of the country only a few miles from the wall. One bitter March day, I did my training with some new German friends. One had been brought up in East Germany but a few years earlier had been lucky enough to be "sold" to relatives in the West. That was a common way of boosting the East German economy, my friends said.

We ran from Lübeck until our path was blocked by the wall. Runners never like to be blocked; a busy road is bad enough. Freedom of movement is what running is about. Often a wall is a challenge, and I've had many a mischievous romp on English country estates or exclusive golf courses. But this was no joke. The barricade of concrete, topped with vicious coils of barbed wire, extended endlessly, high as a house, across the landscape. Guns poked out from dark watchtowers, unseen dogs barked, and spotlights swept back and forth in the gloomy March afternoon light like hawks. There was an expanse of bare dirt on our side between the wall and the border itself. Imagine keeping a strip of land hundreds of miles long only for killing. The worst thing you could imagine doing in such a place was to run.

We turned and set out quietly to jog back toward Lübeck, uncomfortably aware of the guns pointing across the bare dirt at our backs. I thought of a photograph I saw once in a newspaper of a workman in overalls doing some small maintenance job on top of the wall, with an armed guard standing over him.

Laying Ghosts

All these old memories, from the sirens wailing through my three-year-old consciousness to the gun turrets marring an international friendship run in my late thirties, lurked in my imagination when the wall, to our astonishment, fell in late 1989. I don't want to over-dramatize or exaggerate. Mine were common enough memories for my generation, not especially tragic or traumatic. My wife, Kathrine Switzer, felt at least as strong a pull. She was born in Germany as the daughter of an officer of the American army of occupation after the war, had spoken German as a small child, and had destitute German house servants as her first friends. We found and renewed an affectionate friendship with the most important of them, Kathrine's much-loved nanny, who had lived in East Germany for fifty years, compulsorily out of contact with the Switzer family. Anni, Kathrine's "second mother," became important to us for ten years until her death at age ninety-two, and we're still close to her husband Heinz and their family. Among my unusual fields of expertise, from our visits I gained a detailed knowledge of the running trails around the modest Saxon town of Senftenberg. It's good running. The ugly scars of strip mining from the Communist era have been transformed into a recreational tourist landscape of scenic lakes and woodlands.

When Kathrine returned to Germany as an idealistic, sports-mad young journalist to cover the 1972 Olympics in Munich, she found herself writing instead about the defeat of idealism like hers by forces of hatred. Eleven Israeli athletes were taken hostage in the Games village and murdered by Palestinian terrorists, who took cruel advantage of Germany's well-intentioned laxness about security. That massacre was one of the blackest moments of intersection between sport and history. Those of us committed to sport felt as if our home had been invaded. We would feel the same at Boston in 2013.

So, both Kathrine and I had ghosts to lay in Germany, and we thought the Berlin Marathon could help lay them. But our interest was more than personal. We share the belief that sport has significance far beyond the back pages, a key and creative place in twentieth- and twenty-first-century history. When it was announced that the marathon would go this time through the Brandenburg Gate and into the East, it seemed to us likely to become one of our sport's most significant moments. We wanted to be part of it, as in running you can. It's the only major sport where participants often outnumber spectators.

Kathrine has been a friend of Horst Milde, the Berlin race director (his equally capable son Mark has since replaced him), since they collaborated in starting women's running in Germany. Horst invited us to the marathon and offered us accommodation in a top West Berlin hotel. That was another temptation—an alluring contrast to the student backpack-and-bratwurst style in which we had each separately first toured Germany. The announcement that reunification would follow only three days after the race clinched our decision to make the trip.

First Run: The Death Camp

We had three runs in Germany before the marathon. Each was unforgettable; like stopovers on a journey through time. We flew into Frankfurt armed with rail passes, hoping that a journey by train across the old border would let us witness in close-up the last days of the DDR (East Germany). We got more than we bargained for. Choosing Weimar for the first overnight because of its place in literary history, we discovered beneath all the peeling-paint dinginess a decoratively classical town that in ten years would be restored into one of the great cultural meccas of Europe. The Goethe and Schiller museums were already open, and the theater was advertising a play by Václav Havel, then an imprisoned dissident writer who, in a reversal as absurdly unlikely as one of his own plots, was about to become president of Czechoslovakia, and later the Czech Republic.

But Weimar's few hotels were already full, as the people gathered in iconic places for the *Vereinigung* (reunification). A kind proprietress at one hotel made a reservation for us by phone at an outlying place—not far away, she said. "Mit dem taxi, zehn kilometer [ten kilometers]." On a scrap of paper, she wrote "Hotel Am Ettersberg, Buchenwald."

We arrived at night. As the taxi drove there, climbing high through the black woods, we glimpsed the sign flash in the headlights. Then we realized why the name seemed familiar: Buchenwald.

The hotel, we could see the next morning, is in one of a row of functional accommodation blocks adjacent to a parade square. We dared not think what kind of parades had been held there. The hotel now serves pilgrims to the site of one of the most horrific of Nazi Germany's concentration camps.

We ran early the next day. We had a marathon to prepare for. A chill wind whipped across the top of Ettersberg, and we ran in full tracksuits. It was still September. Laboring a winter up there without proper food or clothing would be a death sentence. Marked walkways lead you around the site. We jogged somberly, stopping where the signs said the workshops and crematoria had stood; at the great holes in the earth that had each held 10,000 bodies; and at the quarry where thousands more, "the strongest and fittest," the sign said, had been forced to slave until they dropped. There is a terrace at the edge of the high escarpment of Ettersberg with monumental stones engraved with the names of the twenty or thirty nations whose people died here. It overlooks a view that would be picturesquely beautiful if the air had not been so dank with mist and sadness. The place was a concentration of horror.

We jogged on to look at the memorial tower at the highest point on the site and the statue showing radiant prisoners welcoming their Soviet army saviors in campy ardent-socialist-realist style; very impressive, provided you didn't know that Buchenwald was liberated by troops of the American Third Army, not Soviets. With a deepening cynicism, I read everywhere the signs that commemorated "the heroic anti-Fascists" who had died here. Among all the political lies, I found not a single hint anywhere that the reason they died here was because they were Jews. Compassion for Jews was never part of Communist Party doctrine. Nor was concern for truth.

Less surprisingly, there was also no reference to the fact that the occupying Soviet Union continued to use Buchenwald for five years after the war as an internment camp for dissident Germans, or alleged "anti-Stalinists." It had a reputation then, according to the taxi driver who drove us away later, for viciousness and massacre as terrible as the Nazis had inflicted. He may have been right. Some German friends later told us that in 1945, their survival depended on being taken prisoner by the Americans rather than the Soviets.

The whole place was an offense, a reminder of the worst that humans can be and had inflicted on each other in my own lifetime. But what offended me most was that such an appalling monument to inhumanity, a place where people would go to grieve for those who had innocently died, should be reconstructed as a vehicle for superficial political propaganda. Orwell's Ministry of Truth had been busy at Buchenwald.

On our morning run around the site, we felt incongruous, wearing the festive colors of modern sports clothes in that melancholy place, but it was very early and we meant no disrespect. Better a couple of sad joggers than a parade of yet more soldiers. I felt conscious, as I did at the wall in 1977, of my good fortune at having been free to run all my life. The people before us here had to march under guard to hew at the quarry. We could trot down on the springy autumn grass. The most basic of the many pleasures of running is that freedom to move over the surface of the earth.

In the taxi back to Weimar train station, we were held up for twenty minutes while a convoy of Russian tanks and tractor-trailers, hauling vast, long, cylindrical missiles, trundled ponderously out of a hidden site below Buchenwald, on to the road east and down the hill. A week ago, or perhaps only a few hours ago, these monstrous descendants of the doodlebug had been armed and aimed at London. Today they were leaving. We felt we were witnessing the moment of turning in a tide of history. Our taxi driver cursed them every inch of the way.

Second Run: The Divided City

The second prerace run was in Berlin, through the pleasant paths and woods of the Tiergarten and, magnetically, to the Brandenburg Gate. It was like a street fair there that day. Hawkers sold wurst, postcards, and fragments of the demolished Berlin Wall. The wall must have been as infinitely subdivisible for sale to tourists as Shakespeare's supposed mulberry tree. They also sold Russian army uniforms and paraphernalia. I was tempted to buy a greatcoat and uniform for my American brother-in-law, then a colonel in the Pentagon, to wear to work.

For all the noise and tourist kitsch, it was profoundly moving to jog through the Brandenburg Gate and simply step from one side to the other. We ran almost jubilantly along the 200-yd.-wide strip where the wall had stood. Kathrine warned me about unexploded mines or cartridges, but I ran there anyway. The Germans can be trusted to tidy up, and it seemed to matter. I wanted to be one of the first to run there. I went back to Kathrine full of a new idea: they should make the whole strip, indeed the whole east–west border, into a landscaped linear park for runners, walkers, and cyclists; a permanent, active commitment to the freedom of movement, stretching from one end to the other of the city or the nation.

And the Germans did it. Some years later, I did run a section of the Berliner Mauerweg (wall trail), which takes you on foot or bike around the old east–west border, 160 kilometers or 99 miles.

We were puzzled, as we ran back from the gate, by the long lines of buses parked the entire length of the avenue; there were hundreds of elderly motor coaches, all from Poland. They were marked Gdansk, Wroclaw, Szczecinek, Poznań, etc. Everywhere we went we saw Polish people shopping, standing in lines, scurrying from store to store, or staggering back to their buses loaded with washing detergent, tape recorders, beer, VCRs, tampons, cigarettes, toilet paper, electric shavers, and windbreakers. Discarded supermarket carts littered the pavements as the buses, sagging and overloaded, trundled slowly away eastward.

We pieced the story together. Until reunification, Poles could freely enter East Germany and now, with the wall gone, they had free access for the first time to West Berlin, city of affluence. They were shopping here in busloads. Perhaps they would resell the scarcer goods back home, or perhaps they were the appointees of their family or community. They had until Tuesday, after which the Poland/Germany border would close and visas be required. The Poles had their own urgent race to run, with just four shopping days left to the end of their brief Christmas.

Third Run: The Olympian Who Was Not Allowed to Run

The third of our historic prerace runs was another stop on the time machine, taking us farther back, to 1936 and the imposing neo-Roman Olympic Stadium, the Third Reich's hubris in monumental concrete. We ran there along with 10,000 visiting international athletes on the "World Breakfast Run" the morning before the marathon. It was a riot of fun: a cheering stream of people, more scampering than jogging, giggling and clowning like kids on their way through the streets, and then milling about in a frivolously un-Nazi manner around the stadium.

The 1936 Games at that stadium are known more vividly than any other early Olympics because Leni Riefenstahl's great film has left images in our minds almost as powerful as if we'd been there. Slipping away from the jolly crowd, we found the grand archway where the names of the gold medalists are carved. We were looking for some special names, which in different ways meant a lot personally. On reflection, they each also relate to the themes of this book.

I looked first for Jack (officially John) Lovelock, the light-stepping New Zealander whose world record 1,500 m victory came from his scrupulously scientific preparation, brought to perfection in a race he justly described as "an artistic creation." That race left him with an almost mythic place in New Zealand's shared imagination. I'd written about him as a cultural icon, a subject in fiction, drama, sculpture, and other arts, and I'd contributed to better understanding of his accidental early death in the New York subway in 1949. As I looked at his carved name there in Berlin, I thought not only of Lovelock's perfectly executed victory but his lesser known streak of impish mischief. The story goes that as New Zealand's flag bearer at the obtrusively militaristic parade of nations at the opening ceremony, he led his small team to make their formal eyes-right salute to honor a minor stadium worker with a broom and a Hitler-like moustache, instead of the Führer, whom the kiwis passed with eyes impassively straight ahead.

Next, I found the four engravings of the name of Jesse Owens. The great African-American sprinter has always been praised for the smooth beauty of his running, which strikes me as an almost patronizing way to define an athlete of such rare competitive intelligence and flawless craft. Under huge pressure from national expectation, crowd adulation, and Hitler's disapproval, Owens attained peak performance fourteen times in four very different events in changing and often difficult conditions (look at the cut-up cinders of his 100 m lane, or the rain for the 200 m final, or the pressure created by no jumps in the first two rounds of the long jump). Owens's running and jumping, and the openly demonstrated affection between him and his blond German rival Lutz Long, affirmed sport as a compelling positive, despite all Hitler's vainglorious racist propaganda.

The next name we sought was Kitei Son (Japan), whose marathon victory over Ernie Harper (Great Britain) makes such a memorable sequence of Riefenstahl's film. In fact, Kitei Son was Sohn Kee-Chung, a Korean who was compelled, along with bronze medalist Nan Shōryū (Nam Sung-yong), to represent the nation that occupied and ruled Korea at that time. Sohn Kee-Chung gained the ultimate recognition as a Korean when he ran into the stadium in Seoul in 1988 to light the Olympic flame. But he is engraved as Kitei Son in Berlin. He and Nam, like Rhadi ben Abdesse-lam (chapter 4), Mo Farah (chapter 10), Khalid Khannouchi (chapter 15), Meb Keflezighi (chapter 20), Ed Whitlock (chapter 21), and others, show that questions of individuality and nationality are more layered than it was permitted to believe in Germany in 1936.

The fourth name we wanted to see was not there, as we knew only too well. But we had a private mission of paying respect to its absence. We wanted to make a quiet tribute to a good New York friend whose name should have been inscribed as a gold medalist in the 4 x 100 m relay, Marty Glickman. In 1936, Marty was one of two Jewish athletes who were dropped from the USA's final relay selection by the team management in deference to the Nazi hosts' racial preferences. They had been brought to Berlin as part of the squad and had practiced for that role. Jesse Owens was the only USA team member to protest the decision, earning Marty's lifelong gratitude. More history. So soon after we saw Buchenwald, the story had even more meaning.

We jogged the back straight for Marty, the second leg that should have been his part of the relay. Marty had a distinguished career as a sports broadcaster, but he never forgave that injustice. He and Kathrine were both graduates of Syracuse University in upstate New York, and for a while he was something of a mentor to her in her television commentary work. Later, he and his wife Marge were good friends, whom we saw often in New York and who visited us in New Zealand. I told Marty's story in my columns. He later told it in his autobiography, *The Fastest Kid on the Block* (1999). The story became more widely known after it appeared in the Jesse Owens biopic *Race*. When Marty died in 2001, we felt glad to have paid our small, private tribute to him, there on the Berlin Olympic track, jogging the relay leg that he was not allowed to run.

The Marathon

No one was excluded from the Berlin Marathon the next day. It had many debts to pay. Visiting competitors had contributed to a fund to assist East German runners with travel and accommodation costs. We were all determined this should be the marathon with no wall. The results were appropriate. The women's winner was a young medical student, Uta Pippig, who in the first weeks of 1990 had simply stepped across where the wall had been to live and run in the West. The first man was an old friend from down under, a droll, cheeky Australian with a lopsided grin who calls himself "the boy from Ballarat," Steve Moneghetti. Earlier that year, Kathrine and I were the public-address announcers when Moneghetti ("Mona," as he was known) placed second in the 1990 Commonwealth Games marathon in Auckland. In Berlin, he strengthened his place in running history with the world's best time of the year, 2:08:16.

My own race, as I have hinted, was more of a sightseeing tour of Berlin's history and my own memories than a serious competition. While Mona and Gidemas Shahanga were doing their own Berlin airlift out front, back in the pack it was more like a carnival than a race. The moving crowd chattered and cheered, and under every road and rail bridge along the course they performed a kind of vocal Mexican wave, a jubilant shout that echoed back and forward along the long, moving mob.

The spectators were just as noisy. They waved and cheered, and we waved and cheered back. Two or three deep, they chanted, or beat bells or gongs, or clapped in unison. German spectators are highly rhythmic. There were no German flags. The chants were for running clubs, not for Deutschland.

Through the eastern sector, the crowds thinned and became quieter. The people looked watchful and withdrawn here, like dogs that have been much kicked and hesitate to romp. No wonder, when we looked at the Orwellian bleakness they had lived among for forty-five years. We reached Karl-Marx-Allee at four miles: block after oblong block of dull flats as far as you could see. Everything was angular, hard-edged, and soulless.

Covering many buildings and trying to conceal their drabness were giant inspirational murals, Soviet-realist-style pictures of workers working, students studying, housewives house-working, and everybody radiating communal good spirits and happy work. The images looked like mere mockeries against the barren reality of the homes. It was the marathoners who brought to that grim street the genuine communality of people sharing something they had chosen to do.

As we turned back across the Spree River toward the west, there were views of an older Berlin, a city of culture and learning and spirituality that had been shuttered. We passed baroque domes, gothic spires, the once-distinguished Humboldt University, and the elegant roofline of the Platz der Akademie, with its wondrous ensemble of *Schauspielhaus* (theater) and the French and German cathedrals. In there, the world has since discovered, is one of the most beautiful squares in Europe and a concert hall of exquisite shape, sound, and decor. We had heard a Mozart concert there the night before the race. That evening, we sat by chance with an elegant Englishman who told us he was a London private tailor, and that he regularly visited East Berlin to measure and fit expensive suits for senior Communist Party members. It is indeed a strange world.

The race moved on. Now we were running on Leipziger Strasse, almost back at the border, near Checkpoint Charlie. Looking up, I saw on the walls of an old library the pockmarks of bullet holes—scars on the face of history. Potsdamer Platz, where the wall stood over one of the most notorious killing-grounds, was still just a space, a wide vacuum of bare, sandy earth, winding away between the buildings into the distance. Even from the warmth of our mobile carnival it seemed creepy, a threatening place, a gap, disconcertingly empty in the middle of the great city. The youngsters who were gunned down there, and the dogs that howled and hunted them, and the guards who held the guns, and the searchlights that flickered in the dark, had not quite gone. The place teemed with sinister shadows. Even the runners went quiet for a few moments.

Then we were back among huge cheering crowds again as we re-entered the west, among the color and life and energy that were still missing in the east. We passed glittering shops and big, pretentious hotels, landscaped canals, archways of balloons, and choruses of cavorting children. A brass band oompah-pahed for us in the authentic lederhosen beat.

At eight miles, we were running through Kulturforum, a modern arts complex built (rather hastily, I thought) to replace the older galleries that for thirty years had been locked away behind the wall. Outside the National Gallery I read the signs for an exhibition called "Zwischen Romantik und Realismus" (Between Romanticism and Realism). It described my condition exactly. The first eight miles had been a ceremony of purification, inspiring and joyful, though perhaps idealistic. Runners are indeed great romantics. You must be a romantic to put up with running marathons. But "realismus" was making itself felt. You can't run, rejoice, and rubberneck all at the same time for an hour without starting to ache. There were eighteen realistic miles still to run. And my injured leg was twangling unromantically, too.

So, a bit before ten miles, where the course considerably passed close to our hotel, we two scarred veterans of many a completed marathon chose, for once, romance over realism, slipped through the cheering crowds, and sidled surreptitiously into the plush foyer of the Hotel Grand Esplanade. It's so plush that there was a television in the bathroom, and I watched the rest of the race through a consoling froth of bath bubbles and steamy coffee. If you're going to wimp out, do it in style.

If that dereliction makes this whole narrative a fraud, so be it. But I prefer to agree with what Steve Moneghetti said, echoing President Kennedy, at the awards ceremony (yes, I rose from the foam in time to be there): "I feel like a Berliner. I'll remember this win for the rest of my life. The race was inspiring, historic and very significant for the cause of freedom I represent."

Reunification

We all felt like Berliners, finishers and wimps alike. I felt, even in the bath, that I had accomplished my goal in coming to Germany. There was one highlight still ahead: the night of reunification itself. There was talk of demonstrations and violence, but all we saw were quietly happy Germans standing in the broad avenues near the gate with a slightly watchful and cautious air of fulfillment. The runners had been much more upbeat and demonstrative, but many of us were foreigners, and we had been through less pain than the Germans. Nor did we have their cause to feel nervous about what mass jubilation can lead to. The vast crowds waited patiently for midnight, cheered the moment of reunification, and oohed at the fireworks.

But the best and most significant part came two or three hours earlier. Driven by some undefined compulsion, we all, that whole huge agglomeration of people, crowded on both sides of the Brandenburg Gate, crept and shuffled slowly from both directions toward and through the arch, around the press of bodies under the stonework, and crept and shuffled slowly back again toward the relative space four or five hundred yards away. It had the inevitability of being a small twig in a very slow stream. We moved slowly, hardly perceptibly. But we moved. We passed from west to east, or from east to west, and back again. Under the gate, we were jammed close against the slow mass of people shuffling from the other side, squeezing by us under the arch with the same mute and almost instinctual purpose, without hostility or showing papers or being shot.

That strange, shuffling, slow mass movement was uncomfortable and probably dangerous, yet the night would not have been complete without doing it. The official symbols of reunification were the music and lights and speeches and fireworks, but the gathered people created our own. It was our slow, communal passing through the arch that truly symbolized the historic opening of the once fatal border. The runners did it first, and the shuffling crowds followed their footsteps. Movement has meaning.

In fifty years, Germany had inflicted on me image after image of destruction and restriction—the mesh metal shelter-cage in the family living room, the whine of falling bombs, the overgrown ruins of neighbors' houses, the wreckage of Bremen, the evil hooded figure on the balcony at the Munich Olympics, the murderous Wall of Lübeck, the death-pits of Buchenwald, my friend Marty's story of injustice. Now I had a new image: a gate that I had run through. The 1990 Berlin Marathon laid the German ghosts of my private memory. It also symbolized the public reunification of a great nation.

13

April 15, 1996, Boston

A New Way to Celebrate

I should never have done it. I was badly injured, with hardly any training for two months; it was utter folly. But the 100th Boston Athletic Association Marathon was the biggest celebration ever of the history of running. How could I not be part of it? Twelve years earlier, on my first visit to Boston, I'd broken the over-forty record with 2:20:15, mostly run into a horrible cold, wet headwind. So, although I'd run Boston only once, I felt I'd earned a place in the old race's hundred-year story.

Because so many runners wanted to take part, it somehow became more a community celebration than a sport. The 100th Boston Marathon in 1996 was a race with much grander significance, and every runner was intensely aware of that extra meaning.

"Hey, we're in history!" one jubilantly cried to the nervous crowd as we shuffled our way from the buses to the prestart village.

Runners are pragmatic people. Our minds are generally on curbs, corners, and drain covers, split times, water, blisters, and chafing. It doesn't occur to us when we pause for the national anthem before the start or gobble bananas at the finish that we're sharing in age-old rituals of ceremonial music and festive feasting. When we pass hundreds of zealous spectators chanting "Go, Scott! Go, Scott!" (the guy running next to me for ten miles had "Go, Scott" on his shirt), we don't reflect that we're refashioning an age-old custom of parades and processions. But it is so.

Every culture has its ways of celebrating health and heroism, communal purpose and individual accomplishment. The most universal elements in any human festivity are movement, music, feasting, and praise

The amazing thing is, it worked. It really worked. Sure, [...]ays[...] can point to a long line here or a timing error there, but that will all soon be forgotten. What will be remembered—for at least a century—is that the B.A.A.'s Guy Morse and the thousands who worked for him not only pulled off the 100th running of the Boston Marathon, but

Running's Greatest Day
THE 100TH RUNNING OF THE BOSTON MARATHON • APRIL 15, 1996

20. *Running Times* called the 100th Boston Marathon "running's greatest day."

for special individuals. You will find those elements in celebratory rituals in every culture in the world. The 100th Boston Marathon had them all.

It had other elements that go equally deep. The impulse to pay tribute to the land, and to your ancestors, is universal. Those tributes were fundamental in ancient Greek myth and ritual, and they're the basis of oral ceremony among Native American and other cultures, like the New Zealand Māori. If you speak on a Māori marae (meeting ground), the unfailing convention is to begin by acknowledging the ancestors and the land of your hosts.

To run the Boston Marathon is to enact in a modern way those age-old cultural rituals. By running an unchanged route over the same stretch of road, we pay tribute to "the land." By following a century's history of heroic achievement, we pay tribute to our "ancestors." The celebration of the 100th Boston, and the millions of words spoken and written about it, were special tributes to the old course and the meanings that generations of runners have given to it.

Don't think I was high on crowd support or an age-group personal record. On the contrary, I suffered more and performed worse than ever before in forty-five years of running. My throbbing knee was swollen like a watermelon for weeks afterward, and I never again want to hear the chant of "Go, 2-7-1-7, you can do it!" as long as I live. My race was a miserable, personal worst disaster.

Yet the 100th Boston Marathon was a day of wonder.

Friday Morning

I was in Boston only as a writer for *Running Times* and *New Zealand Runner*. My first stop was the elite athletes' press conference, held in the Fairmont Copley Plaza's Venetian Room, all glittering chandeliers and marble pillars. It certainly was not the setting I grew up with; as I wrote in chapter 8, I date back to the days when the changing rooms, the judges' stand, the spectator seating, and the awards podium were all the same single park bench. The golden glitz of the Venetian Room made me wonder if I was on the wrong planet. Emil Zátopek or Buddy Edelen would have been astonished. The prize money would have changed their lives. Even in 1965, Ron Clarke ran world records on a scruffy cinder circuit ringed by a rusty old chicken-wire fence and a dog track.

More than the furniture has changed. Where else could you witness people who are confined to wheelchairs being interviewed as sports stars? Not in any patronizing lump-in-the-throat way, but quite naturally, because they are supreme athletes. Our sport by its inclusiveness has changed many attitudes for the better.

Another changed attitude is in the way Western culture views black Africans. Read Nobel laureate Doris Lessing to understand how subconsciously deep the contempt used to go in colonial days. Here, in 1996, when the team of fifteen Kenyans stood up to take applause, the whole Venetian Room went still. A hundred hard-nosed journalists were, for a moment, silently rapt with admiration. However dramatic Monday's race might prove, it would be hard to surpass the pure theater of that moment. It proved the point in chapter 10 I make about running's leadership in this change.

Friday Afternoon

Kathrine and I drove out to Hopkinton to check the course. The start area was covered in snow, but I was looking for clues to its real character, something more structural than our era's surface clutter of cars and commercialism. It's hard now to find much that John J. McDermott might have noticed when he led the race in 1897. He would have seen some of those old elms, perhaps, and the Ashland graveyard, some of the scattered churches, a stone wall or two, and a few pillared verandas.

Looking beyond the stone walls, I began to discern patches of land where swampy pools still lingered. Where the landscape has been left unpolished, it is strewn with big, rugged, primeval, moss-covered rocks, evidences of a terrain that has lain there since before Pheidippides ran to Sparta.

And soon came the hills. Racing a marathon seems so much a thing of the immediate moment, three or four hours of urgency and effort, that it is well to be reminded of the earth's much longer timescale. Part of that scale is the hills. They are forever. They pre-date and will outlast every kind of road surface, every runner, and all our human fuss. They're the structure. I was glad of the chance to see their heave and surge for a few moments without the throbbing crowds and moving mass of runners who would soon cover them. (By the way, if you doubt that Boston's first ten miles are significantly downhill, try running the course in reverse.)

Friday Evening

There was a function at the "100 Years of Boston" Exhibition, high in the John Hancock Building. The mounted photographs were fascinating: everything from Tom Longboat to Moses Tanui. And, of course, of Jock Semple attacking Kathrine Switzer. I pretended to be grumpy about traveling 8,000 mi. to look at a glass case containing my wife's old sweatshirt.

Saturday Morning

More than forty past winners gathered at the Breakfast of Champions. The occasion vibrated with the sense that it was unrepeatable. Many of them, the great names of a global sport, scurried around from table to table, begging one another's autographs. Each seemed modestly to understand that he or she was only one piece in the greater jigsaw of history. They were there (almost all of them) to admire the others, and to celebrate the larger story.

During the formal proceedings, some of the older men were on the verge of tears. Their lives had perhaps been quite ordinary between that long-ago moment of victory and this present moment of its commemoration. That was certainly true of one I know well, Dave McKenzie of Greymouth, New Zealand, who in 1996 still lived in the same house and worked the same long hours as a newspaper printer that he did when, in 1967, he traveled overseas for the first time in his life and won the Boston Marathon in a course record.

As they filed into the gilded banquet room, it was almost as if my nomadic life paraded before my eyes. There was Ron Hill, who was my team captain when I ran for England; Allison Roe, who was with me on the New Zealand team eleven years later; Dave McKenzie, from my years on the South Island in my early thirties; Rob de Castella, whose first major track victory at age eighteen I announced when Australia sent a team to Queen Elizabeth 2 Stadium; Geoff Smith, who won Boston the year I set the masters record ten minutes behind him; Lorraine Moller, who I ran with in the 1970s and was maid of honor at our wedding in 1987; Amby Burfoot, who has sometimes been my American editor; Bill Rodgers, often a co-speaker in recent years; John J. Kelley, a fellow man of literature; and Toshihiko Seko, whom I'd met when I was guest speaker in Japan.

One thing was impressive. The champions, even the oldest, all seemed fit, dignified, and vigorously alert. Being a marathon champion does no harm to the character, it seems.

Saturday Afternoon

I began to feel restless and dissatisfied. I had been a runner too long to be content as only a scribe on the fringes of a race as momentous as this one. I began to argue with myself. How could I fully experience such an event, fully enough to write well about it? How could I truly understand it, if I only watched it on a television screen in the media center? Or standing at one spot along the course? I fretted and moped and dithered until I could have played Hamlet without make-up. So, I took my injured leg for a jog.

There must come a time in life, I told myself sternly as I ran by the calmly flowing Charles River, when the rashness of youth gives way to wisdom and self-knowledge. At fifty-six, I had surely reached that point.

Well, if so, I had gone right on by.

The history and hoopla and the sheer magic of the occasion were too much for my frail maturity. I went to the expo, gulped, and picked up my bib number. That decision would cost me a lot of pain and end my elite racing career for nearly twenty years. I have never regretted it.

Sunday

I had my best personal moment, one that made me feel I belonged. There was a brief ceremony to dedicate the new Boston Marathon Memorial, specially created for the centenary. It's in Copley Square, a few yards from the finish line; an elegant design set flat into the paving. Many people miss it, but it's well worth a visit for any runner. It shows a map and contour plan of the course, encircled by the names of all past winners—the land and the ancestors again.

There's a nice Tennyson quotation, from "Ulysses," where the poet imagines the aging hero calling his veteran sailors back for one last adventure:

Made weak by time and fate, but strong in will
To strive, to seek, to find, and not to yield.

The poem is a surprise, because it's not about the famous heroic years of Ulysses's youth, but a bunch of old guys bored with retirement, heeding the call to return to action, "to sail beyond the sunset." Appropriately, the names of past Boston champions etched into the memorial include the masters' winners. I found mine. I'm one of the ancestors now, with a small place in history, but on that cold Boston day back in 1984, I was out there, strong in will, striving and seeking, and so found a victory.

I'm proud my name is inscribed there. It's the only way I know to get my name on a monument without being dead.

Monday Morning

I wanted to be a face in the crowd, not a privileged, invited elite. I wanted to savor the full centennial experience, to see what it was like in the real people's race. I wanted to write about the real experience of being in the biggest field in the history of the marathon: 38,708 entries, 36,748 started. So, in the chill of the early morning, I lined up with the regular runners for the yellow school buses to Hopkinton. Arriving there, disgorged into a school parking lot, there was a colossal bottleneck around the corner of the school building, and it took an hour to squeeze through from the bus drop-off into the "Athletes' Village." The jam-packed runners were without exception patient, calm, and benign. The jubilant extrovert summed it up: "Hey, we're in history!"

The gods must have known it, too, for they smiled. We were wedged almost immobile in that bottleneck, and then were left wandering about without cover for hours. After the finish, the long, shuffling line to the gear buses was interminable. The day before the race, viciously cold rain had lashed Boston; the day after, it was torrential. In those conditions, 36,748 lightly dressed runners would have suffered helplessly. But race day was sunny and pleasant (until you were seriously tired). A different roll of the weather dice and there would have been deaths. I would probably have been one of them. Seriously.

The 100th Boston Marathon

At last the gun fired, and we were in history. When a million or so humans (counting runners, officials, volunteers, spectators, and media) strive strong in will to make an occasion positive and significant, they do it. Never had I seen good spirits on such a scale. There were people encouraging you ("Go, Scott!" "2-7-1-7, you can do it!" "Or-rye, Noo Zealan'!") almost every step of the way. From Wellesley onward, you ran through a ceaseless, crashing surf of sound.

I have called it a procession and a parade, and that works both ways. We paraded for the crowds: Go Scott, the Canadian flag-bearer, the ten-man caterpillar, the tiny microchip Japanese woman, the Viking, the flowing-hair blond from Texas, the body-painted Puerto Rican, Marty from Connecticut who graciously thanked every volunteer whenever he took water, and among them all, one in 36,748, me.

As we runners processed along, it seemed as if the roadside and its crowds were parading past us: people, banners, boom boxes, blossoms, church choirs, grandparents in deck chairs, beer parties, convenience stores, bluegrass music, children's palms outstretched for high fives, beribboned dogs, gas stations, hooting trains, Wellesley students ("At last! Some men around here!" their sign read), and long lines of proffered orange segments (hospitality, too, is basic to celebration). It all flickered by: a postmodern montage of discontinuous fragments, a mobile theatrical show, a new way to celebrate old traditions.

It was all a lot of fun, but something important was going on. Running has become a distinctive modern form of celebration. The big city marathon or road race is an unprecedented affirmation of communal values: the freedom to move, the right of assembly, the individual's right to health and happiness, complete inclusiveness without consideration of ethnicity, class, religion, or politics. It works so well as celebration because running is essentially movement, and movement is essential to good celebration. Dancers and processions, marchers and floats: there must be movement. That's why the British, in their clever, old-fashioned way, pop the king or queen into a coach with prancing horses and trundle them around the streets; that's why New York has ticker-tape parades, with festive movement along the streets and festivity showering down from above; that's why Christmas parades and homecoming parades and graduation parades and military parades are still so important, even in this age when community has become so diverse.

That's also one reason why running had become so important. I'd glimpsed it in Berlin in 1990, but here in Boston I understood it. With its mass numbers and city routes, running is a new way to celebrate.

On movement, let me pay tribute to the people who run marathons between three and four hours. In my sub-2:20 days I underestimated you.

You don't win many awards, but you are real runners, and tough. Cruising at a little under seven-minute miles, I was among thousands, all trained, fit, prepared, competitive, focused, resolute. When I folded, they poured past, and I realized how consistently fast you must run to go under four hours for a marathon.

My story is a small dot on the canvas of that historic race, best told briefly. But, having chosen to run, it's the only story I can tell. I slid along comfortably, 1:31 at halfway, running on memory, I suppose, hobbling just a little on my injured knee but not seriously conscious of it, enjoying the whole experience, happy at the pace, and unable to go slower. It was a historic event. How could I just jog it? At seventeen miles I felt smooth and strong, almost floating. The background training over so many years was paying off, making up for the lack of recent miles, so I thought. I began to plan a push, as in the old days.

"Get past Heartbreak," I told myself. "Then go for it."

But suddenly, at eighteen miles, I was walking. There was no warning, no crisis, no decision. It just happened. I stopped running. My race ended. The tank ran empty. It felt as if somewhere there in Newton, there is a dark, fetid hole, invisible to the eye, like some dire vortex of fantasy fiction. I fell straight into it. I was powerless, a tattered rag on two bent sticks. Two laborious miles later I was sitting on the curb behind the crowd with my shoes off, rubbing snow onto my aching knee. At seventeen miles I had been an elite athlete heading for an age-group place, confident and bouncy. At mile twenty-one I was a broken-down has-been on the slag heap of running history.

Dropping out was not an option, not this day. I had enough shreds of pride to know I needed to finish the 100th Boston. Slowly, I put my shoes back on, and very slowly I rejoined the moving throng.

The rest is the sketchy lingering of a bad dream. Jog to some landmark or sign. Reward myself with walking a while. A confusion of faces and voices alongside. A cascade of thousands racing past me. Faces peering from a clanking T-train car. The feeling of utter helplessness. The feeling of utter hopelessness. Only a kind of numb instinctual purpose to keep moving, like a wounded animal. Mile markers. Drain covers. Music. Crowds. "Go, 2-7-1-7!" "Oh, shuddup," I muttered. You get grumpy when you're really wearied. Our usual social inhibitors cut off. Somewhere I moved slowly past the resonant pulsing percussion of Japanese drummers. It seemed to take an hour for the throbba-thumpa-throbba-thrumpa beat to fade away behind me. It's a sound I shall associate for the rest of my days with despair and misery.

The last 385 yd. took me nearly two minutes. But I got there. No ecstasy, no victory, no name on the memorial, no "rejoice, we conquer!" Only the grim sense that a set task had been grimly completed, like digging a ditch. I crossed the line. Done.

Then I nearly did the dropping-dead bit from the Pheidippides story. It took an hour to shuffle slowly along Boylston Street to the end of the chutes and the gear bus at Boston Common. I was shivering uncontrollably, like after anesthetic, barely able to stay on my feet. If the day had been cold and wet, I would have been in real trouble. My admiration increased for the midpack runners who must tolerate these crowded delays. An hour later, Kathrine found me near-comatose in the hotel bath, the bathroom filled with steam.

Monday Evening, Reflections in the Bath

So, I was part of running's celebration of its own history. I hit the wall and finished in 3:44. It's not a heroic story, nor a dramatic one. Like many before me, I was not trained for the distance.

But more than that, it was just a plain old commonplace Boston Marathon. The course called the shots. The downhills tempted and deluded me, the uphills broke me, the last miles teased me with some easier bits, increased my suffering through the hard ones, and eventually permitted me to finish. The course was in charge. I was merely one of hundreds of thousands to have enacted its strenuous script.

Yet the day was a success. I did become part of history, a truly significant celebration in running's new way. Berlin in 1990 was significant, as I have described, but there the runners were part of the celebration of a historic event outside running. At Boston, we were it. Our sport was the history, we were the celebration. Together, those two marathons marked the beginning of an understanding of how significant running has become in the wider context of modern global society. That significance would make itself known, for worse as well as better, in the next two decades (see the following chapters).

Stride after stride, year after year, runner after runner, from the fifteen men who lined up at Metcalf's Mill in 1897 to the multinational millions who contributed in 1996 and since, our tribe of runners has been busy creating Boston's meanings.

14

September 11, 2001, New York

Affirming Our Freedoms

Part 1: Central Park

It was what Mark Twain once called "one of those rich and rare fall days . . . where it is heaven to be out of doors." In the golden afternoon light, looking north from our apartment, Central Park glowed deep green like a forest, under a sky of cloudless blue. A perfect day for running. But at our backs, we knew, from downtown, a gray-yellow smoke-cloud was slowly rising, drifting, and spreading. It marked the fallen towers. We also knew, only too well, why no planes flew across that lucid sky.

We heard the news first on radio, then watched on television as the twin towers fell, numbed with shock. Kathrine was getting ready to go to work as usual, until I protested. "You work in a fifty-story building. For all we know, they might be bombing every high building in New York," I said.

It takes a while to accept that the world you know has changed. Perhaps my wartime childhood has left me at some level always ready for the fall of the doodlebug. My concern about the younger generation in the modern world is that they have no concept that it can all end.

Our apartment looked over Central Park, but from the roof of our forty-four-floor apartment building, we could look south and see the rising cloud of smoke and dust. We soon retreated to the television. Kathrine's brother, retired from the US Army, still worked some days in the Pentagon. We needed news.

It was the appeal for blood donations that finally drew us outdoors. Finding the Amsterdam Avenue Red Cross Center overwhelmed, and our

21. "A slim monolith celebrating a civilization's sense of beauty and aspiration."
Egyptian obelisk, Central Park, New York, 2001. Photograph by Roger Robinson.

blood groups not required, we drifted back to the park. We walked and quietly talked, trying to sooth the insistent painful flicker of those terrible images.

Maybe we could even run. Central Park seemed the right place, since for New York runners (as we were then) the park was our magnetic center, our church, our garden, our earth. Call it habit, or reassurance, or even defiance. By running, we declined in that simple way to comply with the plot to disrupt our lives by force. The dogs were out, too, and children in the playgrounds, though even they seemed to play more quietly.

On such a day, you're not sure what is appropriate. There are no precedents. We ran in the spirit that a musician that afternoon might have opened the piano and begun to play. There are as many ways of running as there are of playing music, from jubilant to solemn. Just as music that day would be melancholy, we began our run in a mood of reflection or reverence, and for that reason soon went separate ways. This is the music of my run that day.

My first thoughts were of other occasions when I'd run in times of danger or crisis or grief: near London at the height of the Cuban Missile Crisis, on the day after the news of the Munich Olympics terrorist outrage in 1972, and under the grim shadow and menacing machine guns of the East–West German wall near Lübeck in 1977. Runners know how life can come from our simple rhythmic music of movement over the earth. And so I ran to my favorite corners of Central Park. Shakespeare's statue at the entrance to the mall reminded me of Henry V's "once more unto the breach" speech:

> In peace, there's nothing so becomes a man
> as modest stillness and humility;
> but when the blast of war blows in our ears,
> then imitate the action of the tiger;
> stiffen the sinews, summon up the blood . . .

There has been much argument about the connections between sport and war. I reflected on them under the trees along the East Drive. Obviously, many sports originated in military training, even in weaponry like archery or the javelin and discus. Pheidippides was an army messenger. Marathon was a battle. Much of the language of sport derives from warfare. Even in running, that least violent of sports, we speak of "tactics," "attack," "break," "surge," "fighting to the finish," "beating" and "killing" the opposition, "leaving them for dead," victory and defeat.

But that doesn't mean, I was thinking as I ran, that George Orwell was right when he irritably argued that sport is merely "mimic warfare." That misses the point. A sport like ours is an advance on war; it is a highly developed way of expressing human competitiveness, physical excellence, the need to confront a challenge, and the impulse to strive. It provides the adventurous combat that young men especially are programmed to seek. Sport is essentially cathartic; it channels the impulse to conflict, it allows life to be reaffirmed out of contest, and it has done so ever since ancient Greece.

That's why it seemed appropriate to run that day, to stiffen the sinews and reclaim life out of destruction. It seemed better to be running in grief than sitting in the apartment in shock.

Up on Greywacke Knoll, between the Great Lawn and the Metropolitan Museum of Art, I reached Cleopatra's Needle, the Egyptian obelisk. In the New York City Marathon, when you're struggling with the last big hill, and even most days in training, you run right underneath the obelisk without noticing it. Today it put things in proportion. It looks strong and placid. At 3,500 years old, the obelisk is the oldest work of human hands in Central Park. It rises (the guidebook says) sixty-nine feet from the hilltop, where it has stood since 1880. That's a mere sliver of time in a life span of 3,500 years. At ancient Heliopolis, after the Romans moved it down the Nile to Alexandria, it was one of a matching pair.

So, I thought, as I ran by it and headed toward the reservoir, that ancient civilization three millennia ago also celebrated its success, wealth, and sense of beauty and aspiration by building twin slim monoliths, tall oblongs at the water's edge that thrust symbolically from earth to sky. If the people who committed the attack saw our towers as emblematic only of excess and vanity, they were wrong.

Around the Bridle Path to the West Side, every patch of sand and grass, every root and rise and hollow, every tree and bench and squirrel and water fountain was just as usual. The only thing not as usual was the blissful weather and the people. There were very few, and those who were there walked or sat in quiet. When I ran out of the trees and around the Great Lawn, I saw again why. Into the clear blue of that rich and rare day, slowly taking shape as a cloud above the skyscrapers of midtown Manhattan, rose the gray smear of smoke. Two weeks later it hung there still.

Almost home, I was running on the sandy slope up to Tavern on the Green, a few yards from the finish line of the New York City Marathon, when I passed, on the grass, a golden retriever chasing a stick in his amiable goldie way. I envied his benign innocence. Going about his life so simply, he brought to mind one of the best of all war poems, Thomas Hardy's "In Time of 'The Breaking of Nations.'" He wrote it in 1915, amid an earlier slaughter. (Well, he began it in 1870, but these things take time.) Instead of describing battles and the fate of nations, the poem speaks simply about the scenes of ordinary life that continue even in times of war:

> Only a man harrowing clods
> in a slow silent walk
> with an old horse that stumbles and nods
> half asleep as they stalk.

The plowman, the seasons, work on the land, and, in the last lines, young lovers whispering together—these are eternal, the essence of life, the poem affirms:

> War's annals will cloud into night
> ere their story die.

"Only a dog chasing sticks," I thought. It would make a nice line, and a less painful image to carry home than those searing in my head as I began the run.

Columbus Circle was almost deserted. In my mind's eye I seemed to see the moving shadows of runners criss-crossing it, as they did every evening, heading for the park, happy to enjoy their share of the late sunshine of that rich and rare fall day. Many of them would never run again.

Part 2: Running in the Aftermath

September 12, 2001

The day after, I met my friends Greg and Jack as usual for our midday run, and as usual we jogged around the Central Park reservoir. But nothing was as usual. The park was just as it had been when we ran on Monday, two days ago: bright with late-summer foliage and flowers, the water of the reservoir shining. But looking across from the West Side to the south, you could see the awful smear of yellow-gray smoke drifting upward from Lower Manhattan.

Usually we three would talk about plays and books, but that day we were like everyone else in the world, compelled to share the sense of enormity. And there was the old human impulse to find ways to make such a vast tragedy personal, to find someone affected to identify with, to exchange anecdotes. Greg, Jack, and I were fortunate. We knew no one killed. But the stories of near-misses were beginning to come in. Victah Sailer, America's best running photographer, who at that time was also a New York firefighter, was heading home after night duty when the first plane struck, and he got back into Manhattan after the towers had fallen. Tracy Beverly, wife of my friend Jonathan Beverly, editor of *Running Times*, was on a subway train under the World Trade Center at the moment it was hit. My wife Kathrine's much-loved brother Warren was scheduled to be at a meeting in the Pentagon that Tuesday morning, but the meeting was canceled, so he turned the car around and drove to his regular workplace. Our lives might otherwise have been irrevocably changed.

Thousands of lives were changed, in great ways or small. America's government responded in ways that shaped the world. Jack's work as a Broadway stage manager was threatened by the closure of all New York theaters. Kathrine had to cancel the major Avon women's race scheduled to be run in three days' time. I had already emailed Jonathan Beverly to suggest that we should delay the feature we were writing together for *Running Times* about the reception of foreign-born American runners, a controversial subject that was best left a while (see chapter 10).

And so, we three old friends talked, like everyone else in New York, exchanging stories, trying to make some sense of it, seeking to ease the horror. Where were you, what did you see, how did you react, who shared it, how has it affected your routine?

After the run, I sat down and wrote the narrative of my 9/11 run in Central Park that was the longer origin of the first part of this chapter. The running magazines received hundreds of submissions that week from readers who had the same impulse to express how running helped them understand or cope with the significance of that terrible day. Bookstores reported a spike in sales of poetry. My account, a stream of consciousness cadenced in the dying fall of sorrowful music, was chosen for publication by *Running Times.*

September 13

The wind changed. In Central Park, three miles from Ground Zero, for the first time you smelled acrid smoke as you ran.

September 15

Allan Steinfeld of New York Road Runners and Mayor Rudy Giuliani issued an announcement that the marathon would not be canceled. It had been a difficult judgment call in such an anxious context, and behind the scenes there was a lot of argument. Allan reported later that the deciding factor in the debate was the symbolic value of the marathon going ahead. Despite the risks, despite the costs, this most irrepressible of cities must not be seen to be cowed.

It is pertinent to the subject of this book that the marathon was seen as the iconic symbol of the city's spirit. It was an important expression of the people in a time of crisis.

The same decision was made in Philadelphia for the Distance Classic (half-marathon), which now proudly promotes itself as "the first sporting event held in the northeast following the 9/11 terrorist attacks." Then came the Marine Corps Marathon in Washington, DC. The logistics of implementing that marathon were mind-blowing. Race director Rick Nealis has reported on how many agencies he had to placate, bring onside, and work with. His race came a week before the New York City Marathon, and the event is conceived as an annual people's festival that gives a human face to the US military. The decision to hold it in the aftermath of the fatal attack on the Pentagon created a hugely emotional statement of affirmation. That Marine Corps Marathon was one of the most significantly historic of all running events.

But I was in New York, and this is an eyewitness book. I can write only of how that traumatized city ran through the aftermath.

September 16–30

Counselors say that at times of trauma, running can give you empowerment, making you feel less vulnerable, more in control of your own actions. For me, it's the old rhythmic movement, the contact with the earth (and trees, grass, birds, dogs, and squirrels), that keep the bruises from sinking too deep; and the conversation of my friends.

But my three-block jog to reach Central Park every day was like running a gauntlet of grief. Every pole, every sign, and every bin on Broadway, and many walls and windows, carried fluttering, frantic, homemade computer-printed posters with pictures and details of someone "missing." "Last seen Floor 98, WTC . . ." How could they cope with the thought of what their loved one went through on that floor? How could the rest of us cope with the thought of what the survivors were going through, with no information, no certainty, no closure? Putting up those posters at least gave them some sense of taking action, until the time came when they knew they had to stop hoping.

On the way to the park each day, I ran past the Fifty-Eighth Street Firehouse, two blocks from our apartment. Six men of Engine 23 died when the towers fell. The sidewalk was soon covered with mounting heaps of flowers and candles and photos. "When we ran out, you ran in," said one grateful inscription. Every day there were more flowers, more grateful messages. They covered the sidewalk, spilling out onto the street. The traffic patiently drove around. For David, a friend from New Zealand who visited on his way home from Europe, the Fifty-Eighth Street Firehouse remained years later the most indelible memory, and we exchanged notes about it on September 11 every year.

October 10

The marathon adopted the slogan "United We Run." We put a sticker on our apartment door. It reminded us of Berlin's "Run Free" and "Marathon of Unity" in 1990. It seemed to affirm not only the resilience of America (and for me, all Western culture, which I am proud of) but the value of running as an image of peaceful unity to set against divisive violence. I'm proud of that, too.

You could also buy a defiant version of the American flag with the words, "These colors don't run." I didn't share the Bush White House's "bring 'em on" bellicosity that was becoming America's official response, because I believed justice should come from a coordinated international police action, not arbitrary military invasions. But I much admired the American nation's deeper resolve, and noted with approval when it was expressed in metaphors drawn from running rather than shoot-'em-down cowboy movies.

October 15

Mayor Giuliani was urging New Yorkers to support Broadway theater. We chose the Rocky Horror Show. It opened with a sudden unannounced bang-crash of music. In the audience, we all jumped out of our skins like frightened kids. It made you realize what a nervous knife-edge of fear and suppressed horror we were living on during those weeks.

October 27

It became permissible to go downtown. Previously the limit had been Union Square, which had turned into a candlelit shrine. We decided to walk/jog down to see Ground Zero late one night, when work on the site was over for the day. It was probably not a good idea. The air down there was still thick with smoky dust, like a drifting, pungent, yellow-brown mountain mist that made everything shady and half-visible under the lights. It was hard to form a coherent impression. It was all a dismal confusion of scraps, litter, rubble, grimy vehicles, broken buildings, oil drums, and rusty metal reinforcing rods lying about, with everything covered thick in dust, dust, dust.

For me, the lasting image was of half-wrecked buildings, ripped open and their insides exposed, like bodies with the entrails falling out. As a small child, I was surrounded by half-shattered buildings exactly like that in wartime England, and had hoped never to see them again.

"This is where I came in," I muttered. (We used to say that at the cinema in the days when you showed up in the middle of a movie.) We'd planned to support local business by finding a meal in the area, but couldn't bear to stay in that gloomy acrid brown haze. For a while we took refuge in a bookstore, but every shelf was thick with ash.

October 29

The runners began to arrive for the marathon. At a press conference, a Russian, Lyudmila Petrova, asked for a minute's silence for the victims of September 11. A South African, Elana Meyer, said, "Initially I was really scared about coming here, but the way the people of New York stood up and stayed united gave me the courage to come." Kenyans, Ethiopians, Italians, and Romanians all said, "If we don't run, the terrorists will win." Every runner, not only these elites, felt they could contribute something by running. I had felt the same on September 11 itself. Perhaps it's the elemental nature of running that makes it capable of being a statement, an affirmation. You wouldn't, I think, feel that playing tennis or golf symbolically defied the terrorists, but I only know that's how we all felt about running.

November 1

Race promoters from Milan, always good friends of the New York Road Runners, put together an evening of song by famous Italian stars, "Rinascere Insieme, Let's Run Together," a gesture of support for New York. The audience was all runners, most of them Italian, and they affirmed that they were indeed "together," waving their marathon race packets to supplement their applause.

November 2

Kathrine and I were dinner guests at New York Athletic Club. The club had lost twenty-one members on 9/11, a devastating number for one organization. Always it's the personal story that goes deepest, and one we heard that night was of a young NYAC member who had been convinced at age twenty-nine that this was the happiest year of his life. He had a great new job, got engaged in August to a woman he madly loved, and was accepted in the lottery to run the marathon. The perfect triple, he called it, laughing with delight. On September 11, a rich and rare fall day, he woke at 6 a.m., ran six miles, kissed his fiancée goodbye, and went to work at his new job, which was on one of the upper floors of the World Trade Center. He never came home. Multiply that story by three thousand.

November 4

I had another memorable moment as a marathon spectator, but it was darker than my glimpse of Abebe Bikila in Rome in 1960, and more anxious than when I watched Buddy Edelen in his white T-shirt break the world record at Chiswick in 1963. This time I was on Fourth Avenue, Brooklyn, waiting anxiously to see if the 2001 New York City Marathon would reach the three-mile point in safety.

At whatever risk, overcoming shock, grief, fear, anger, and despair, 30,000 people ran in an incredible human flood across the vast Verrazano-Narrows Bridge in that New York City Marathon eight weeks after 9/11. Special ceremonies marked the start. Many runners carried or wore an American flag, or their own national flag; many others ran with a victim's name or picture on their shirt. The traditional blue line marking the route was red, white, and blue for parts of the course. As they crossed the bridge, every runner looked across to their left, to the gap in the waterfront skyline where the slim twin towers should stand.

We all feel an impulse to give personal meaning to a large-scale tragedy. People all over the world had phoned or emailed us after September 11, wanting some personal reassurance in the face of an event that seemed so apocalyptic. On race day, my own anxieties of the last two months distilled into worry about Kathrine.

She left early, as she did each year, to join the television crew, with her commentator's headset and microphone, riding in a motorcycle sidecar alongside the top women. For my job as a print journalist, I was on the course, following the race by subway. (This was before I began doing online reports from the media center.)

Not until they reached Brooklyn would I know that the race, 30,000-plus runners, and my wife, were safe. In an open sidecar, she was utterly vulnerable. Real personal anxiety emerged, from wherever I'd suppressed it, for the first time since September 11. I knew from Allan Steinfeld about the precautions, the guards, the police divers under the bridge, and the observers from the air, but those were anxious days. At last, the runners came flickering up Fourth Avenue toward me, with the usual entourage of cops and vans and cameras, all intact, and the leaders flitted past, unbelievably fast as they always are. There was a glimpse of Kathrine's unmistakable hair flying from under the helmet and headphones, some runners I recognized, the accustomed broadening of the stream behind the elites, the stream turning into a river, then a flood, then a surging ocean, filling the entire road, spilling over the curb, the same old eager mass field bobbling along, all familiar, my world, known, alive, safe, in motion. It is, I thought, as the relief flowed, only another race.

Yet it was more. Undeterred by horror and grief, that 2001 running of the New York City Marathon symbolized, more than any other single event, the resolute continuing life of New York, of America, and of Western global culture after the attacks. Thirty thousand men and women is a lot, plus the largest spectator crowd in the race's history, and all who supported and reported them. It's no exaggeration to say that they affirmed with some courage that we value the freedoms and opportunities our society provides, including the freedom for men and women to run freely together.

America and the West have behaved badly in many ways, but our libraries, galleries, theaters, parks, hospitals, bridges, and towers, our peaceful crowds, the equality we give to women, our (mostly) welcoming acceptance of foreigners, our religious tolerance, our systems of governance, our schools and universities, our sports, and all running events, with their utterly nonjudgmental inclusiveness, testify to values that any society should be proud of. Thirty thousand runners embodied them, their faces jubilant as they crossed the finish line.

Watching that mass affirmation convinced me more than ever that modern running has meanings beyond sport, and that it is too important to close down. It has become a potent mix of shared spiritual experience, an expression of communal consciousness, a form of group therapy, and a symbol of city and national spirit. Those may sound pretentious, but tell me which one didn't apply at the 2001 New York City Marathon.

15

April 14, 2002, London

The Best of Times, the Worst of Times

> You can be one of the greatest, if God gives you the strength. But
> you cannot be the only one. Paul Tergat and Haile Gebrselassie
> inspired me when I was washing dishes. To beat them today, that
> does not make me alone the greatest.
> —Khalid Khannouchi

The new world record breaker was paying a modest tribute to the heroes
he had beaten. He was also offering a critique of our culture's simplistic
greed for celebrity and one-and-only heroism. The stony-hearted British
press room burst into applause.

I'll follow Khannouchi's advice. It's hard to avoid hyperbole any year
writing about the London Marathon, so for the 2002 race I'll say only that
it was one of the greatest of all time, and treated us to many of the best
times ever run. Fourteen years later, when I was reporting again from the
2016 London race, it was 2002 that was cited as the paragon of intense
competition that produced a world record. Its impact on the statistics by
which we chart our sport are still felt: a new men's world record, the second fastest ever male and female, the best women's-only performance, the
fastest debut times for both men and women, four national men's records
(USA, Kenya, Ethiopia, and Italy), and two national women's records
(Great Britain and Russia).

The impact of the actual races may last even longer, for their intensity,
passion, and suspense were the stuff of legends. Asked if she would be
watching a video of her run, Paula Radcliffe said, "I doubt it. I have it in
my mind." It is in the minds of all who witnessed it.

22. Paula Radcliffe triumphs in London: "They should name a pub after her."
2002. Mark Shearman–Athletics Images.

It remains there with such clarity because of race director Dave Bedford's innovative arrangement (later adopted by other major marathons) of starting the elite women's field forty-five minutes ahead of the men. Only thirty years earlier, women sat down on the start line in New York to demand equality and the right to start at the same time as the men. Now marathon running has become so huge, and women such a crucial part of it, that the need is for separation again. The elites need to race on their own terms, not paced and protected by attentive or attention-seeking men. The crowds and the media need to be able to watch them uncluttered. The best in their field need the risk and responsibility of being alone.

So, Paula Radcliffe was unimpeded, and so was our view, when after nine cautious miles her patience ran out, she lifted those bony knees, and she pranced away from Derartu Tulu and Susan Chepkemei. Alone she did it.

Alone, she took the awesome responsibility of that move, with the watching world clucking. Alone, she ran for seventeen miles, with the thought, as she later confessed (with her typical directness), "You'd better not blow this, or you'll be the idiot who didn't respect the marathon." Racing is about judgment, decision, responsibility, risk, and sometimes loneliness. Surely women's running has earned the right to those? No woman could better embody those qualities than Radcliffe.

Racing marathons is also about balancing passion with caution. After passing halfway eighty-three seconds ahead in 1:11:04, Radcliffe smelled home like a spirited thoroughbred. She surged from a 5:25 mile canter to two galloping 5:06 miles. But wisdom prevailed.

"When I saw 5:06 I thought, whoops, better slow it down," she said. The wondrous 2:18:56 outcome confirmed her judgment. Nevertheless, Catherine Ndereba must have wondered what would have happened if Radcliffe had known earlier than the last half-mile how close she was going to the Kenyan's 2:18:47 world best.

A year later, on this same London course, with help this time from male pacers, Radcliffe fulfilled the supreme potential she showed in 2002. Driving as only she could through all barriers of pain and doubt, she obliterated the world record with 2:15:25. That stands, fifteen years later, as one of the superlative performances in running history. It set a high new standard for women's capability in the precise measure of endurance that the marathon provides. I wasn't there that time, or 2003 would be the race described here. But the London Marathon has been creative in so many ways, and Paula's contribution as a leading performer and spokeswoman has extended over so many years, that 2002 can be taken as representative of the ways they have made history.

Founded in 1981, the London Marathon led the running boom by making charities central to its mission from the outset, by committing itself to improve recreational spaces in the London area, and, when the numbers grew, by insisting that the elites, the competitive national runners, and the fun-seeking shufflers all have an equal place in this inclusive sport. It created its own kind of party by encouraging charity runners to wear fancy dress, so the spectator crowds are entertained by a procession of chickens, caterpillars, Shakespeare look-alikes, and even a deep-sea diver (whose wife, the tabloids gleefully reported, misbehaved while he was away taking eight days to clump around the marathon course).

There is always humor in London. One year, I jogged from point to point on the course and wrote my coverage by quoting the Londoners I overheard. The sponsor's name on the bibs was Flora margarine.

"Blimey," said a spectator, "there's a lot of girls called Flora in this race."

"Look, Livvy, look, it's Paula! It's Paula!"

"Oh, mum, I dint fink it was Bambi."

Paula was a celebrity on a scale I'd never seen before in this sport, not even Grete Waitz in New York. In 2002, in the last ten miles, we were gripped with suspense as she ran into undiscovered country, although in retrospect, her break and her dominant win seem as inevitable as Benoit's in 1984. Radcliffe's risk-taking attitude and the way she sometimes got herself into trouble always made me think of the old silent movie series, "The Perils of Pauline." Millions watched her sob when injury put her out of the 2004 Olympic marathon, and millions more watched her suffer diarrhea during the 2005 London Marathon. Winning is not easy, not always pretty. Radcliffe has proved in public what I said in chapter 9, that with the responsibility of racing comes risk, and that running's women have redefined being feminine.

But this time, our intrepid heroine was never in danger of dropping off the cliff. Quite the reverse. Defending champion Derartu Tulu looked sluggish all the way, slid down to ninth, and was reported to have a hip problem. Susan Chepkemei was caught by Japan's Reiko Tosa with two Russians in tow, and she promptly threw up on the carpet outside the Tower of London. Women have earned the right to do that, too.

Behind Radcliffe, two Russians, Sveltana Zakharova (2:22:31) and Lyudmila Petrova (2:22:33), came back with uncanny revivals in the last miles, and they finished with two- and three-minute personal improvements. The conditions were perfect for fast running. Or the revelations of 2016 about the prevalence of doping among Russian athletes may suggest other interpretations.

The best way I can describe the weather conditions is to say that there weren't any. No heat, no cold, no humidity, no wind, just 48°F/9°C of English mildness. Nothing to deter the men's race from being worthy of the field assembled, which is saying a lot. From the first mile in 4:47 and ten kilometers in 29:37, they ran on the very cusp of world record speed.

Even more surprising was that at 62:47 for halfway, there were still twelve there, several setting major personal bests at that point.

There should have been bodies hitting walls all over Wapping and the Isle of Dogs. But none yet faltered, and several tried their hand in front. Abdelkader El Mouaziz threw in one of his sudden pushes at eighteen miles, just like the one that won the race the previous year. But it's hard to make a break at a relentless 4:43–4:48 pace. As they headed back from the docks to the city, there were still six in it: Haile Gebrselassie edging in front, Khalid Khannouchi, Paul Tergat, El Mouaziz, Stefano Baldini (an Italian who would become the 2004 Olympic champion), and the astonishing Ian Syster, who went on to threaten the South African record held by his coach, Gert Thys.

And then, there were only the big three: Gebrselassie, Tergat, and Khannouchi. From that moment on, the twenty-mile mark on April 14, 2002, those three would monopolize the world marathon record for the next decade. Khannouchi already held it, as a Moroccan, and broke it again that day in London, now an American citizen. Tergat claimed it in 2003. Gebrselassie took over in 2007 and put it under 2:04 in 2008. We can see that threesome moment now as a historic one. At the time, all we knew was that three of the greatest runners the world has ever seen were skimming with that sublime fluidity of great marathoners along the Thames Embankment. Utterly unlike in origin, physique, running action, and personality, they demonstrated that we need better definitions than merely "African."

Later, at the press conference, I asked what each had been thinking at twenty-four miles, when no one in the world knew how it would end. Their answers were revealing.

Khannouchi: "You know you are in pain, but I was thinking, I can go those two miles. And I felt I betrayed a lot of people by dropping out of the world championship last year. Everything then was dark for me. Now I wanted to give the United States something better than a medal."

Tergat: "I was thinking, these are people with a lot of experience. I was thinking, something is going to happen. And it did."

Gebrselassie: "I was thinking, to win would be wonderful. I was thinking about being in front. But I could not."

And that is exactly how it looked. Gebrselassie the demigod suddenly got that puzzled frown and stiffened stride we mortal runners know so well. He drifted. Tergat, with his perpetual nemesis beaten at last and the world for the taking, could not make the decision to take it. He waited. It was Khannouchi, a man in search of identity and acceptance, who was willing to seize control and pay any price in effort and pain to keep it. He prevailed. Three times in the last mile he looked anxiously behind, fueled by fear, seemingly more conscious of the potential of Tergat's sprint than Tergat himself. Khannouchi earned his new US passport with a new world record: four seconds under his own 1999 Chicago mark. It was a gift he could offer to his new country, as the only American to hold it since Buddy Edelen thirty-nine years earlier. Winning, as he modestly said, "does not make me alone the greatest." But when you want to gain acceptance in America, it sure helps.

As for Paula, as everyone calls her, she is the ultimate English heroine: the ordinary girl-next-door yet capable of the extraordinary; extremely intelligent, with a first-class degree in languages and so confident that I've seen her conduct a media conference in alternating French, German, and English; always astute and scientifically informed when you ask about her training and racing; openly tearful when she is unlucky or fallible, yet more often radiantly triumphant; charismatically vibrant when that intelligent enthusiasm shines forth; and talented, yet her biggest talent is a huge capacity for sheer hard work. She loves the intense effort that training and racing demand; the harder it is, the better. She is a direct descendant of that uncompromising world of almost wholly male English running of the 1960s that I described in chapter 5. In wartime, she would have been a leader, innovator, and distinguished medal winner. Now that she has run her last elite race, the best thing the Brits could do would be what they have done for other female icons, like Britannia, Queen Victoria, and Nell Gwyn—name a pub after her. No more fitting tribute than a pint at The Paula Radcliffe somewhere between Tower Bridge and The Mall.

Looking back, the years 1999 to 2002 were difficult times for Kathrine and me. We both had high-level and significant jobs, 8,000 miles apart (I was now academic pro-vice-chancellor, shaping strategy and programs). It was a time of overcoming challenges and laying down contributions, but also of family illnesses and deaths. Kathrine's parents died in 1999 and 2001. She was very close to them. Being in New York on September 11, 2001, was another painful time.

Early in 2002, my much-loved mother and my sister-in-law died, and my father was declining fast. He was a complex and often difficult man who had overcome the disadvantages of impoverished origins and the accidental loss of one arm as a teenager. For his family, he was sometimes inspiring, sometimes angry and malevolent, and, at ninety-four, he was short of friends to support him. My main reason for being in England was to help with his care and give my beleaguered brother Allan some relief.

The 2002 London Marathon was run under a different shadow, the death of Queen Elizabeth the Queen Mother. Five days before the marathon, her funeral had processed along the same route as the marathon's last half-mile, from Parliament Square to Buckingham Palace. For those like me, old enough to remember the 1940s, it stirred memories of fire, darkness, and danger, and the city's resilient wartime spirit that she and George VI helped to sustain.

After the postrace press conference, I drove south along the route of the old London to Brighton Road Relay, and I turned off along Surrey lanes like those where I had run as a teenager, to the nursing home where my father was sinking. Like the Queen Mother, who died at 101, he was a long-lived survivor from those war years, and like her, his time had come.

It wasn't an easy switch, to change moods from the marathon's celebratory color and movement, from the buzzing energy of the race and the media conference, from a morning spent as witness to dramatic accomplishments on a world stage, to this fading, late afternoon scene of still, silent, small-scale decay.

"You should talk to him," said the matron. "Even though they seem asleep, often they can still understand you."

I sat by the bed as his breathing faded and the morphine pump clicked, and I told him about Paula's victory, how the British crowds loved it, and how the course goes through parts of London that he saw devastated in 1939–45.

"It was wonderful," I said, "to see 33,000 runners and a million spectators out in those same streets, all safe and happy. Runners came from all over, including Germany and Japan. Children were running about, instead of spending days cramped in the shelter like we did. A race like that changes the world. It was what your generation fought for. And when things started up again, it was volunteer sports officials like you who laid the foundations, revived the world at its best, and made great events like the London Marathon possible."

I don't know if he heard me.

16

February 26, 2011, and February 3, 2012, Wellington and Christchurch, New Zealand

Running Lifts a Fallen City

Part 1. A City Falls: February 2011

After moving to Wellington, I always enjoyed returning to Christchurch for university work, to race, or to do another stint of announcing at Queen Elizabeth 2 Stadium. In February 2011, I was due to announce at the third annual International Track Meet (ITM). A group of young Christchurch enthusiasts, including the adult sons of some old running friends and rivals, created this innovative meet. They were following in the enterprising footsteps of the team that put on the Christchurch Commonwealth Games almost forty years before.

The 2011 edition of the ITM looked good. Nick Willis was bringing in a group of near world-class middle-distance friends from America and the United Kingdom, coach Nic Bideau had committed strong runners from Melbourne, Valerie Adams was ready to give the meet the imprimatur of her Olympic gold medal quality in the shot put, and there was an almost-secure arrangement with Alberto Salazar for Galen Rupp to attempt the US 10,000 m record, with a Kenyan pacemaker. Heady stuff.

On top of all that, there was to be a unique extra for the fans. For the first time ever, an Olympic medal was going to be awarded in New Zealand. Nick Willis would receive his silver medal for the 2008 Olympic 1,500 m in Beijing, following his promotion from third place after the disqualification of the original winner for illicit drug use. World record breaker and Olympic gold medalist John Walker (now imposingly "Sir John") was due to make the presentation, while I would do the fruity voice.

I even had the prospect of some good-humored personal color. My main training partner in my Christchurch years had been Brian Taylor, a lovable enthusiast with a gift for leadership. "Brian always had the Pied Piper instinct," his mother once told me. With Brian's inspirational skills and my ideas, between us we'd brought the University of Canterbury club up from mediocrity in the late 1960s to be one of the best teams in New Zealand by 1974. We remained close friends, though an odd couple as personalities. Brian had a kind of pugnacious charisma, was deeply loyal, and was passionately opinionated. His idea of bliss was to drink beers and talk late into the night, increasingly loudly, with a bunch of his running mates. He used to remind me of a friendly old dog, happiest amid a gang of dogs, all grinning with their tongues out, tails wagging, bumping into things, barking, and getting into the edge of mischief.

Brian was now a very good coach, a potent motivator, and a vehement Lydiard disciple. When we talked by phone on the Monday of that week, he was warming himself up for the coaching seminar due to be held in Christchurch the day before the track meet, bracing to argue for Lydiard's ideas with Salazar and Willis's University of Michigan coach Ron Warhurst. That pair of feisty Americans struck me as unlikely to roll over and surrender. It was going to be an entertaining and potentially historic few days in a city I always enjoyed revisiting.

Then came Tuesday, February 22, 2011.

A bit before one o'clock, I was on my way to watch Willis and friends run a session of repeats at Newtown Park, the Wellington track. At 12:51 p.m., Christchurch was hit by a force 6.3 earthquake. That's not huge, but it was shallow and located exactly under the city. It struck suddenly up through the surface of the earth, and punched up into the central business district like a demonic fist.

I heard the first news as I arrived at the track. It took weeks for the full, terrible facts to emerge. Hit by that giant uppercut, buildings rose and fell back down. Some collapsed into rubble, including the nine-floor concrete Canterbury TV (CTV) building where Brian Taylor was head of an international school. Brian was killed instantly, with many overseas students, including some who had arrived in Christchurch from Japan only that morning. Conscientious as always, Brian had left a downtown lunch meeting to be ready to welcome the new arrivals, and at 12:51 p.m. he had just reached the building. He was probably in the basement parking lot. His gold neck chain was the only identification ever found. Nine floors of concrete in free fall were beyond even Brian's robust runner's resilience.

He was one of 185 people killed in the city, 115 of them in the CTV building. It simply compacted in a way that has since raised questions about its engineering design. One woman who worked on the top floor "rode it down to the ground" as it compacted, and walked out unhurt at street level. No other building collapsed so badly, but there were grave injuries all over the city. Eight people died and many were hurt when falling masonry crushed a city bus.

Although I'm writing here mainly about the impact on Christchurch, the wider loss was dire. Because of the deaths among Brian's students, many Asian families lost their only child. It's hard to imagine how it must have been to get the news that their loved son or daughter, perhaps leaving home for the first time, had been killed barely an hour after arriving in the country. That international tragedy became evident to me when I attended the memorial service on the third anniversary, before the 2014 track meet. More than twenty languages were spoken.

Instead of a highlight for track and field in New Zealand, we were left in February 2011 with a national tragedy. Like the rest of New Zealand (and a few weeks later, even more horrifically, like Japan) we had to find ways to carry on. We needed to figure how to fulfill our sport's function of affirming physical human life at its best, without demeaning those who had died or distracting the survivors and rescue workers.

In Wellington, still unaware of the scale of the disaster, not knowing yet that the track where Filbert Bayi ran his world record was wrecked, not knowing yet that my oldest Kiwi running friend was dead, we discussed the first news from Christchurch. Nick Willis immediately said, "We could put on some races here and raise money for Christchurch." I reminded him of the Olympic medal ceremony, and we agreed that would be an additional draw for spectators, if the Olympic Association agreed.

They did, as did the Red Cross, making the event a major fundraiser for the earthquake relief effort. Wellington's track officials (those indispensable and often-overlooked volunteers) put in a huge amount of work to put the meet together and prepare the facility. On Saturday, February 26, 2011, four days after the quake, I walked to the microphone inside the track at Newtown Park, Wellington, to address 6,000 silent spectators.

It had already been one of the most fraught and complex weeks of my life. Hour by hour, we absorbed the news from Christchurch, and we waited for information about Brian. He was one of hundreds missing. It all took me back to New York in 2001. Then something else happened. Two days after the quake, on Thursday, February 24, a book launch was scheduled at Victoria University of Wellington. I was led to believe it was for a new book by my colleague and friend David Norton. In fact, in secret, it was the launch of a Festschrift for me. The academic convention of the Festschrift, or celebratory writings, is that a new book is presented to a distinguished scholar, usually on his or her retirement. The convention is to assemble a collection of essays by colleagues and former students. To honor my unusual range of activity, *Running Writing Robinson* (Carnegie et al. 2011) reached further to cover my diverse interests as a writer, with contributions from the worlds of literary scholarship, creative writing, and running writing, including some by internationally known names.

The pending publication had been kept secret from me, planned as a flattering surprise, but with all the anxiety about Christchurch and Brian, I was in fact told a few hours beforehand. There had been a lot of discussion about canceling, but they went ahead because so much was in place and so many people had already traveled to Wellington. Someone had even been delegated to meet Brian off his scheduled flight.

I'm telling this personal story because it typifies the way a national tragedy affects many people who are not directly afflicted. People must have been getting married that week, or celebrating in other ways. At the book launch, it was hard for all of us to steer through our confused emotions. Gratitude merged with sadness, every laugh was on the edge of tears, every friend I greeted somehow included the friend I would never greet again. Kathrine paid a short, warm tribute to Brian, and Tim Chamberlain, publisher, editor, and another old friend, was a generous main speaker who perceptively commented that the week must be reminding me of my early childhood in London during World War II.

In a strange way, that night of conflicting emotions prepared me for the bigger public event two days later. I knew as I walked to the microphone on the infield at Newtown Park Stadium that it was going to be a momentous occasion for everyone there, probably one they will remember for the rest of their lives, as I will. It felt lonely standing there on the grass, looking up at six thousand people who wanted me to articulate their sense of significant emotion and help them come to terms with one of the greatest disasters ever to affect them.

I began: "In a week that has inflicted one of the worst tragedies in New Zealand's history, welcome, to an event that is one of the most positive in New Zealand's history—positive especially for New Zealand athletics, and the New Zealand Olympic movement. The tragedy in Christchurch, among many terrible losses, caused the cancellation of the planned International Track Meet. The track races and field events would have been in progress at Queen Elizabeth 2 Stadium at this very moment. The ceremony we're about to witness tonight is one way for Wellington and its athletics community to pay our respects to Christchurch and its athletics community, which we know has lost at least one senior and much-loved member."

After the presentation of the Olympic silver medal to Nick Willis, I asked for a minute's silence in honor of the people of Christchurch.

That occasion distilled the way our sport can contribute positively to a community, which is one of the subjects of this book. That night we managed together to express feelings that had seemed to lie too deep for words. The collective emotions—patriotic jubilation during the medal presentation, respectful grief during the silence, and exuberant fan fervor during the races that followed—had a rare intensity.

The climax was a memorable 1 mi. It was a perfect race to commentate on over the public address: fast, tactical, close, and exciting, with several of the leading runners needing to be identified and their credentials briefly established. Alan Webb (at that time America's best miler) did much of the pacemaking, and Lee Emmanuel from Great Britain was challenging for the lead when he fell with two hundred meters to go. The whole ground cried "ooooh!" in sympathy. The crowd of 6,000 moved out of the stand to cluster around the very edge of the track, just as we had done for Ron Clarke in London in 1965, but closer. Willis finally surged just clear of two young Americans. It was Willis 3:58.4, Will Leer 3:58.8, and Brendon Bethke 4:00.00. Sub-four still had magic, almost sixty years (at that time) after Bannister.

The crowd cheered all the way, and long after. They cheered Willis every time he waved to them, they cheered Emmanuel as he walked disconsolate across the track, they cheered Webb because he was a great athlete who this night had done the work to help his friends, and they cheered Leer because they loved his big mustache and ebullient spirit (and the women thought he was cool).

As in London for Zátopek in 1948, Chataway in 1954, and Clarke in 1965; as in Rome for Halberg and Bikila in 1960; and as in Christchurch for Tayler and Bayi in 1974, the crowd was part of the experience and helped to make the history. Being a sports spectator is not a passive experience. Some waited in line for an hour for Willis's autograph. All went home happy, or at least with feelings that combined acceptance of loss with affirmation of life—exactly why the ancient Greeks held track meets at funerals.

Part 2. A City Revives: February 2012

The shot rose, curved down, and plunked into the grass. A BIG one. Silence. All eyes were on the official holding the two flags, one red, one white. A long pause. Then he raised the white flag, and 3,000 people around him burst into a triumphant cheer, filling the arena with acclaim, as if Nick Willis had just won the Olympic gold medal.

"In a lifetime in track and field," I said over the public address, as the crowd chortled, "I have never heard an official get a cheer like that."

In simple terms, it meant that his first four shot put attempts got the red flag for a foot fault, but this time young Jacko Gill had hit one right. Many of the 3,000 spectators were sitting in attentive circles, right there on the grass around the shot area, to watch up close as Gill and the towering, genial women's multiple world and Olympic champion Valerie Adams were competing.

In less simple terms, the ebullient cheers for Gill (and the judge) meant that the people of Christchurch had come out of their damaged homes to enjoy a track meet. A year after the earthquake that destroyed much of their city and left structural fractures in thousands of houses, they stepped carefully over the cracked concrete and heaped liquefaction, they shook off the endemic anxiety and depression that became known as "earthquake brain," and they came out to watch some sport. They clapped in unison for Gill and Adams, they cheered wildly for Nick Willis and Will Leer, the American friend who beat him, they whooped for the school relays. They even cheered the officials.

It was testimony to the resilient spirit of that poor, battered city that the 2012 International Track Meet was being held at all. The earthquake totally wrecked the grandstand and other buildings at Queen Elizabeth 2 Stadium, left the world record track there looking like a recently ploughed field, and damaged or destroyed every building in the inner city, including many of historic value. In the subsequent fifty-one weeks, there had been more than 10,000 measurable aftershocks. That's more than one every hour, twenty-four hours a day, nonstop for almost a year. Many were the force of quite major quakes: the earth "with ceaseless turmoil seething." No wonder the people were ready to relax for a couple of hours.

It was emotionally draining even to return. For six mostly good years from 1968 to 1974, I lived and worked there, running happily with Brian Taylor or other friends along Christchurch's tidy, grass-verged streets and around its tastefully landscaped Hagley Park. Now I found wrecked buildings, sealed-off bridges, shops and cafés working out of shipping containers, roads scattered with rubble, historic old churches and modern multistory hotels being demolished by a swinging ball and a great grabbing claw of a crane, and fetid, gray, dried liquefaction lying everywhere. Everywhere.

A fine powder in the air from all the demolitions made your eyes itch all day. The mellow old university buildings on the town site where I used to lecture on Shakespeare, Hardy, and Jane Austen looked shell-shocked, with fallen fragments laid out like an archaeological dig. We parked for the track meet on the bare empty site where the Victorian architectural gem of the old girls' high school used to stand. The city's people looked watchful and wounded, like animals that have been mistreated. They reminded me of Londoners in 1945 or East Berliners in 1990.

"We just want to get on with life," runner Matt Smith told me. Under orders to carry key documents and his laptop whenever he leaves the office, Matt could no longer train by running to and from work.

They had been starved of top-level sport. Rugby, cricket, tennis, horse racing, track and field—all the city's famous sports facilities were wrecked. "Munted" is the word Christchurch adopted for wrecked, destroyed, unusable, damaged perhaps beyond repair. "Munted" saved them from using a different word. It's typical that people of English stock respond to disaster and danger by inventing a comic new word that helps them joke about it. In London in 1944 it was "doodlebug." In Christchurch in 2011 it was "munted."

Queen Elizabeth 2 Stadium, venue of the athletics and swimming at the triumphant 1974 Commonwealth Games, was munted. Legendary Lancaster Park where the All Blacks played in front of 60,000 ardent rugby fans, and Peter Snell broke the world records for 800 m and 880 yd. on grass in 1962, was munted. Gyms and squash courts all over the city were munted. The house where I lived for five years from 1970 to 1974, my base when I ran out to meet Brian Taylor for training, my destination when I was driving wearily back from the last day of being stadium announcer at the Commonwealth Games in 1974, and the home from which my two sons each set out at age five for their first day of school, was munted. When I walked by in 2017, looking for the tree from which the cats used to leap onto the roof and claim access through their private upstairs window, I saw that even the cats' tree was gone, as well as the house, replaced by a wasteland of scruffy weeds and scattered debris.

Yet only one year after the quake, Paul Coughlan, Craig Mottley, and Leyton Tremain, creators of the ITM, resolved, in spite of everything, to give the munted city the opportunity to watch quality track and field again, and to stage it at all risk in central Christchurch. Defy the daily quakes, they said, refusing to join the retreat to better facilities in safer cities. They found an atmospheric tree-lined grass cricket field where they could squeeze in a three-hundred-some meter lap, in the old English-style grounds of Christ's College, with pointy neo-Gothic buildings that could serve as the set for Harry Potter's Hogwarts.

Only a half mile from the cordoned-off, safety hazard Central Business District, it was a courageous decision, but an inspiring one for a city starved of positive experiences. It was like the decision to hold the austerity Olympics in 1948 within blitzed London, not in some unharmed provincial cathedral town.

The grass was mown to croquet-lawn perfection. The track was expertly surveyed. Once Adams and Gill confirmed they would compete, glossy new concrete shot and discus circles were laid, precisely to international specification. The announcer (me) was installed overlooking the track from the window of a third-floor classroom with Japanese phrases chalked all over the blackboard. A nearby classroom block was a taped-off semi-ruin. Results came up to me as they did at Rugby Park back in 1973, by a bulldog clip on a long cord dangling out of the window. You can't get more retro than that. This was not a high-tech twenty-first-century stadium. But it had spirit.

There was an extra dimension. February 3 was chosen because it was the fiftieth anniversary of Peter Snell's world records for 800 m and 880 yd. (1:44.3/1:45.1), on grass, at Lancaster Park. Snell sent a video message from Dallas, and several great names of running history were there in person: England's Bruce Tulloh, whose impudent challenge startled Snell into his record-breaking last lap at Whanganui in 1962; Dave McKenzie, Boston Marathon winner in 1967; Barry Magee, Olympic marathon bronze medalist at Rome in 1960 (who found racing in the dark so strange); Mike Ryan, Olympic marathon bronze in 1968; Dick Tayler, national hero on the opening day of the 1974 Commonwealth Games; and Valerie Sloper Young, who so nearly won an Olympic shot put medal in the same hour as Snell and Halberg at Rome in 1960, and did win medals at many Commonwealth Games. Their presence enhanced the sense that this was a day of history and of rebirth.

For the first time in many a decade, I saw crowds lined up for a track meet an hour before the gates opened. They stood on the sidewalk of Rolleston Avenue, outside the walls of Christ's College, alongside a grass

23. International runners on high school grass commemorate a coach and help a city revive: the Brian Taylor Memorial Race, Christchurch International Track Meet, 2012. Courtesy of Margo Flanagan.

verge that had once been impeccably clipped and green, but now was smeared with gray-brown heaps of liquefaction. They were determined to see some good track and field. They got it.

One of the races, the international women's 3,000 m, was in memory of Brian Taylor. The whole meet was in honor of the people of Christchurch who died, were injured, or survived to contribute to the recovery. By using running to affirm life and find closure after death, and by making a race into a historic statement that the community was ready to move on, we were following a very ancient tradition. It goes back to the ancient Mycenaean Greeks, who held games as funeral rites of commemoration. Literature's first narratives of competitive running, in Homer's *Iliad* and *Odyssey*, are accounts of funeral games. Competitive running, jumping, and throwing expressed grief and affirmed ongoing life in the same way that music and poetry do at our funerals. The tradition has become strong again in the last hundred-plus years. San Francisco's Bay to Breakers (1912) originated as a morale booster after that city's disastrous 1906 quake. The Comrade's Marathon in South Africa and the Peace Marathon in Košice, Slovakia, were both created to help remember the dead and restore life after World War I. There were many commemorative events after World War II, from the London·Olympics to local ones like the Wellington to Masterton Relay in New Zealand, in which club teams raced for the "Air Force Trophy," engraved with the names of the region's runners who gave their lives. The Marine Corps and New York City Marathons in 2001, and Boston in 2014, were hugely affirmative memorial events (see chapters 14 and 20). New races are created that add to the tradition, like the Oklahoma City Memorial Marathon in remembrance of those who were killed and maimed in the 1995 bombing, or the Flanders Fields Marathon for Peace in Ypres, Belgium, which honors those who died in that quagmire of horror in 1914–18 and who lie in the vast cemeteries that the course passes.

But sport is never solemn for long. One local runner, Jim Macdonald, who ran in the 880 yd. on February 3, 1962, remembered fifty years later how he hoped to run a good time behind the pace of Snell and the two guest Americans, Jim Dupree and John Bork, so he gave his wife his stopwatch to time his finish, since only the first three would be officially recorded. Snell was magnificent, breaking the world 880 yd. record by 1.7 seconds. Running well, though near the back, Macdonald reckoned he had run a personal best, possibly even a breakthrough sub-1:50. He was eager for news when he saw his wife rushing over to him holding up the watch.

"Look, Jim!" she cried, excitedly showing him where she had stopped the time. "Snell ran 1:44!"

17

August 17, 2012, Mohonk Preserve, New Paltz, New York

Running for the Earth

In the original story of Pheidippides, there's nothing about him dropping dead. The messenger runs 150 mi./240 km from Athens to Sparta to ask for help against the invading Persians. The big moment in the story—the only reason Herodotos included it in his history—comes during the run back, when the running messenger meets Pan, the pipe-playing, half-goat nature god. Pan gives him another message: to tell the city people of Greece that they have been negligent in their worship of him, god of nature.

Was it the hallucination of an exhausted messenger after three days' running? Or a cunning invention by the Athenian generals to boost their soldiers' morale before the battle? Some accounts have Pan whirling invisible about the battlefield, causing "Panic" among the invaders.

You don't have to believe in goat-footed gods for the story to have meaning relevant to our own age and the situation of our planet. Pan's message means that we need more contact between wild nature and human civilization. He was 2,500 years before E. O. Wilson in the hypothesis of biophilia, the idea that our evolutionary history has left us with a profound affinity with living things and an innate need for the close presence of nature. He was reminding humans that this contact also means we have responsibilities to the natural environment (to "worship nature").

I like that interpretation. I especially like the fact that it was a runner who carried that world-saving message. To the best of my ability, I've always tried to follow Pan's wish.

24. Running for the rhinos: runners lead in environmental and wildlife conservation at the Safaricom Marathon, Lewa Wildlife Preserve, Kenya. Courtesy of Tusk Trust/Safaricom Marathon, Lewa Wildlife Conservancy.

Running for My Local Environment

That's why I'm here, racing along a smooth trail cut into a tree-covered hillside on the Shawangunk Ridge, with glimpses through the dense leaves across forty miles of green New York State to the Catskill Mountains. That's why each year I race this Bridge 2 Bridge Run (5 mi.) in the Mohonk Preserve, near my American home in New Paltz, New York. It's one of three races a year that raise funds for the Mohonk Preserve, whose mission is custodianship of 8,000 acres of the Shawangunk Ridge, ninety miles north of New York City, a spectacular, unspoiled landscape that the Nature Conservancy designated "one of the earth's last great places."

The ridge is a long, 200-ft.-high hog's back of rock and forest that stands between the wide, tamed spaces of the Hudson Valley and the wild, heaving mountains of the Catskills. It's a place of high, bare cliffs and deep, tree-filled gullies, glacial lakes and waterfalls, rocky creeks and tall oaks, sparkling white spring laurel and polychrome fall foliage, concealed caves, vast vistas, towering falcons, resident bears, deer, coyotes, porcupine, turtles, toads, barred owls, silver foxes, snakes large and small, and gorgeous little orange salamanders after rain. Running there, I've met all these things of nature. It's a place that often gives you the sense that it has scarcely changed since the dinosaurs.

Yet for running it's comfortable, safe, and accessible. Late nineteenth-century enterprise tucked a rambling castle-like resort called Mohonk House just below the ridge and laid a network of trails through the forest, all on easy gradients and wide enough for horse-drawn carriages to trot guests along on scenic tours. It was an idealistic concept designed to preserve the land unspoiled yet give city-weary New Yorkers access to it after a journey by rail or river. Most of that land with its trails is now managed by the Mohonk Preserve Trust. It connects with Minnewaska State Park Preserve, providing in total more than sixty miles of well-maintained trails, without encountering a highway or an inch of concrete.

Enter runners. It's idyllic to run through such beautiful natural surroundings on a surface that's predictable and soothing (even for my two old legs). This place is the running equivalent of swimming in a South Pacific blue lagoon.

The races are designed to spread the word and to welcome and educate runners in what the preserve can offer them. Areas like this need friends. A proposal to develop part of the ridge a few years ago was narrowly headed off, in large part thanks to runner activists who opposed it.

Running has always had strong links with the earth and conservation. The connection goes back to my opening story of Pheidippides and the god of nature. Kenny Moore once described the 1970s running movement in America as "Thoreauvian." In England, hare and hounds cross-country started long before Thoreau. Running messengers in every culture bonded with the terrain they had to cross in such a personal way. I explore this connection fully in *Running in Literature* (2003), showing how the bond appears in literature from Pheidippides and the Old Testament's "man of Benjamin" through the running footmen of the 1700s and James Fenimore Cooper's Native American messengers, to Rudyard Kipling's poem "The Overland Mail," with its description of the running mailman's encounters with the environment of India:

Is the torrent in spate? He must ford it or swim.
Has the rain wrecked the road? He must climb by the cliff.
Does the tempest cry halt? What are tempests to him?

There's another tempest, with runners again moving in close contact with nature, in the poem that is often regarded as the best written about running, Charles Hamilton Sorley's "The Song of the Ungirt Runners." It has unforgettable images of running, the elements, and escape from authority, which I established in *Running in Literature* derived from Sorley's time coaching the men under his command for a cross-country championship during training for the front in World War I:

The rain is on our lips,
We do not run for prize.
But the storm the water whips
And the wave howls to the skies.
The winds arise and strike it
And scatter it like sand,
And we run because we like it
Through the broad bright land.

That's why I'm a runner, not a gym rat. Building my pecs or strengthening my core is only about me, but when I run I'm taking part in the world, interacting with the earth and the weather, fulfilling my nature, running because I like it. Once, as guest speaker for the Japan Marathon Society, I even composed a haiku in honor of my hosts:

Runners' feet feel earth
passing, as potter's fingers
touch rotating clay.

Most runners enthuse about the contact their running gives them with the elements and the broad, bright land. Trail running, mountain running, parkruns, mud runs, and other all-terrain variants are the most booming part of the still-developing running boom. Moving through natural terrain, participants are tapping into an age-old connection: the match between the structural rhythms of landscape and life forms (such as trees) and the neural and cardiorespiratory rhythms of the human body in motion, a connection explored by seminal twentieth-century writers on landscape like Richard Neutra (1954, 182, 361): "We have a consistent preference for rhythm [in nature], possibly reflecting rhythmic processes within our body."

When you run somewhere often, it becomes part of your being. When travel allows, I'm drawn back to such places, as more sane and normal people might revisit the scenes of past loves. I'm impelled to run once more on Wimbledon Common or the steep, sandy, heather-covered hills of Frensham, the autumn stubble fields around Cambridge, the green landscapes of Hagley Park in Christchurch, or Central Park in New York, and when I can still get to the skyline track high above Wellington, my runs up there are as they have always been, like being a bird. If I ever move away, no doubt I'll come back to run the tree-shadowed carriage trails of Mohonk. Through those runs I reconnect with my past and (as E. M. Forster put it) receive some help from the earth, which we all need.

"To run so many miles in any place is to learn the land so thoroughly that you make it part of your blood," I once wrote, after staying with Rod Sutherland, a friend who was a livestock quarantine officer on Matiu/ Somes Island in Wellington Harbour, and who trained there for a 2:21 marathon at age forty by running 100 mi. (160 km) a week around a sheep-track circuit slightly less than 1 mi. (1,502 m) around. Rod used to knock on the house window with one lap to go to ask his wife Ruth to run the bath ("Round the Island," *New Zealand Runner,* September 1990).

The runner's interaction with the real terrain is all the more special, I would add in 2017, because so much of the human race seems to prefer to experience the natural world only at a virtual remove, through a camera lens, or with their own face foregrounded in the inevitable, obsessive selfie. Runners do it for real. Their eagerness to experience nature directly, and to encounter its challenges, make runners a sympathetic target market for a conservation fundraiser, as the Mohonk Preserve's board has recognized.

"The best way to get runners, hikers, and walkers to support our mission of protecting this unique land is to introduce them to the area through their primary interest. Our three races a year give participants a physical and emotional connection to the land that we hope will lead some to become ongoing supporters. We offer all runners a special preserve membership. Top priority is to put on a really well-run race. The running events are among our best fundraisers, even though we restrict entries to minimize impact on the land," said Norman Goluskin, vice president of the Mohonk Preserve, a world-class over-seventy runner, and my frequent training partner.

The running events have lured many New York city-dwellers upstate to experience the leafy trails, the views of the Catskill Mountains, and the unpolluted air. Have they changed the world? They help stop that treasured part of the world from changing, which is equally good.

The Greenline Half-Marathon is another fundraiser and consciousness-raiser for Shelby Farms Park, a 4,500 acre nonprofit nature haven in Memphis. It's run mostly on rail trail between the park and the city, and the race also proudly describes itself as the "first sustainable sports event in Tennessee." More than that, this twenty-first-century park ambitiously advertises its mission as "to define and shape a great city." Why not? That's what Central Park did for New York 160 years ago, and Hagley Park in Christchurch, New Zealand (I've run thousands of miles in both those parks and love every inch of them), and many other nineteenth-century cities nationwide and worldwide still benefit from the same foresight. The human craving for exercise or recreation (in the literal sense of creating yourself anew) in natural surroundings has brought incalculable benefits in conservation.

But the car-crazed twentieth century, obsessed with its sprawltopias of highways and malls, forgot about parks, to its shame and our profound loss. People wanting exercise and some greenery are lucky if they get a reclaimed railroad, and runners have always been prominent in saving and using those. Twenty years ago, I wrote in *Running Times* how runners in the 1960s invented the concept landscapers now promote as the "linear park." I don't want to make excessive claims, and I'm not intimate with the modern history of landscape, but back in the 1960s–70s, runners (including me) were the first humans I ever saw using the bumpy, disused rail line north of Cambridge, the fetid, rat-owned Grand Union Canal towpath in

Birmingham, United Kingdom, the River Parks trails in Tulsa, Oklahoma, the banks of the River Torrens in Adelaide, South Australia, and the narrow, runner-beaten foot track around Hagley Park. We romped over the open common lands of England, reaffirming in our own way the public ownership of Wimbledon Common, Ripley Common, Frensham Common, or Midsummer Common, to name only some where I have logged many personal miles. Runners were the first to make use of Desierto de los Leones, a forested ridge outside Mexico City that in the 1990s became one of the most famous training locations in the world.

"When I first came, there was nobody here," recalled world record breaker Arturo Barrios, when Mike Sandrock (1992) visited and wrote about the hundreds of runners working out there. A sign at the entrance reads: "If you run in the forest, plant a tree," and even the later running hordes leave the forest spotless, Sandrock reported.

The world's most famous running recreational trail was definitely the idea of a runner. Inspired by European cross-country, Steve Prefontaine suggested to officials in Eugene, Oregon, and at the University of Oregon, that a running trail be built through Eugene's Alton Baker Park in Lane County. After his death in an auto wreck in 1975, the trail proved the most apposite possible memorial, and hundreds run Pre's Trail in his memory (as I have done) every day.

In the 1950s–70s, when runners were still an eccentric but enterprising minority, we ran on forest fire breaks, old field tracks, around cemeteries, along beaches (I claim an unofficial record for a session of interval 400 m on Castaway Island, Fiji, because no one else would be crazy enough to do it), by rails and rivers, and of course around golf courses (I have been shouted at on some of the world's most exclusive). Long before linear parks were fashionable, "groomed," and passable to bikes and strollers, we ran on any uninterrupted linear route of dirt footing and no traffic. I argued in *Running Times* that all golf courses should by law have to retain a perimeter trail for walkers and runners to repay society for occupying so much land, and I hold by that contention. Now landscape conservationists tell us that linear parks have added value.

"Twenty-six years ago, when we initiated the concept of a river trail with the local Rotary Club, if I had talked about developing an ecological corridor their eyes would have become glazed. But talk about a track to walk and run on, and their eyes lit up. Later would come suggestions of putting in some planting. So, we could also create an ecological corridor. Running and other forms of recreation have been the catalyst for ecological improvements. Now we call it a 'linear park,' as it gets more visitors than any of our regional parks," said Ross Jackson, a landscape architect in New Zealand and former elite runner, in 2017.

There's a longer history behind this theme. The oldest recreational spaces were simply open land in its natural state, used for walking, riding, or hunting. Then the nobility enclosed their hunting grounds, previously called "chases," and invented the concept of the "park," from the now obsolete word "parrock," meaning to shut off or confine within limits. Recreation spaces became places of ownership, enclosure, and security, the extreme version of which was the garden maze or labyrinth, associated in myth with virginity. In some Scandinavian myths, the young men hold orienteering foot races to be first to reach the female prize at the heart of the maze (Fenton 1993). The parks of royalty and the aristocracy, like St James's Park in London (enclosed as a deer park by Henry VIII in 1531) or the Tuileries Garden in Paris, passed into public use. As urbanization increased, new midcity parks were created: first, Joseph Paxton's Birkenhead Park, near Liverpool, England; and, most notably, Frederick Law Olmsted's parks in North America. Runners have been using Olmsted's Central Park at least since the visiting English star Alf Shrubb eluded a mounted policeman who took exception to him training there in 1907. Shrubb used his cross-country multiterrain and gate-vaulting skills to outrun the horse. I once wrote an article pretending to be out for a run with Olmsted and his partner Calvert Vaux, who guided me around Central Park and my other favorite landscape among their work, Mont Royal (Royal Mountain), in Montreal.

So, runners have led, or were among the leaders, in a move to reverse the enclosure of recreational space, to claim the freedom to go as far as the river or forest goes, and not to be confined in the walled garden, the park, or the labyrinth. At the least, by pioneering all those areas and routes, including those that became linear parks, and thus ecological corridors, running has begun to make a different kind of history and to change the world environmentally. It's only a beginning to the huge task we all face of saving the earth and making it better, but I think Pan would be pleased.

Edible T-Shirts

One of my missions as a writer has been to advocate for running to use its economic and political power as leverage (that trendy word) for the environment. That way it could reclaim its historical position, as in old cross-country, as an embodiment of the bond between humanity and the land.

One obvious way is to become a role model in sustainability and recycling. Running grew so fast, and issues of hygiene for so many participants took such necessary priority, that big races for a decade or so threw out mountains of plastic or waxed paper cups, sponges, and other waste. The first beginnings of a change in thinking and behavior that I know of came in about 1996, in Kansas City, where Bob Mann, a runner, race organizer, and lawyer, joined a nonprofit group called Bridge the Gap (BTG), whose mission was to help businesses and other organizations think and act environmentally. Through Mann, BTG quickly forged a historic "green" alliance with the Kansas City Marathon.

"BTG could supply hundreds of volunteers while also educating a group of people already inclined to 'think green'—namely, runners," wrote Mike Lundgren (1999, 41). BTG added its members to race committees, guided purchases like T-shirts, race numbers, and paper, eliminated plastic race packet bags, and established the guiding principle of "waste minimization."

"Tile, terra cotta, even the city's own street bricks were used as race awards. Recycled radiators were turned into beautiful picture frames for award winners" (Lundgren 1999, 41). By the third year of BTG involvement, despite rapidly rising entries, the marathon reduced its landfill garbage from two full truckloads to six bags. In *Marathon & Beyond*, Lundgren set out ten points as "green advice" for race directors.

Considering the disparate, noncentralized nature of the sport of running, this kind of environmental thinking gained widespread priority remarkably quickly. Lundgren described how runners were eager to comply with new requirements, like where to deposit yogurt cups, even in a snowstorm the first year. I've carried a water cup myself more than a mile to find a collection sack to drop it in, and I see many runners do the same. In 2003, Frankie Ruiz of PR Racing and the Miami Tropical Marathon wrote an email to the editor of *Running Times* requesting data "to support the assumption that runners are more environmentally sensitive and socially responsible than the average person." The data were provided six years later.

"My research shows that 68.3% of the race directors polled have had a positive change of attitude about green initiatives in the past 18 months," Keith Peters of Eco-Logistics, and author of the *Road Race Management Guide to Greener Running Events*, told me in July 2009, and the situation has continued to improve. Many races now advertise their eco-friendly or "green" policies along with their "fast" or "scenic" courses. (I did an informal survey of race flyers and websites in 2015 and those were the most frequent buzz words.) Another industry leader was the San Francisco Marathon, which committed to extensive sustainability changes, including compostable drinking cups and goody bags, electronic instead of paper finishers' certificates, and bicycles in place of race vehicles. Most big races now follow these practices and have added more.

No one has yet taken seriously my suggestion that race T-shirts should be edible, but the joke makes a real point. It was almost overtaken by reality when Peters told *Mother Jones Magazine* in 2011, "some races are looking for organic or sustainable fiber T-shirts." The Kansas City Marathon had already rejected the cheaper, bleached T-shirts. "Environmental leadership" includes recycling your garbage, but entails much more. Our thriving sport, with its record of creativity, must seek creative ways to repay the debt to the earth we run.

Visionary Venues

One way to repay that debt is to contribute areas of landscape that enhance the earth, as some other sports have done. Some golf courses are works of art; some horse race courses enhance the environment, provide priceless open space amid urban sprawl, and are available for multiple use; cricket greens and baseball diamonds add charm and green space to the English village and the American suburb.

Running is unusual in that we borrow our venues rather than build them. We don't need a diamond or gridiron, courts or goalposts, bunkers and greens. We simply find a stretch of road, or the streets of a city, or someone else's park or farm, and one day a year we make them our own. On race day, we surge along like a huge mass carnival. We leave not a trace behind. Our typical building material is balloons. One day, there is a technicolor finish photo-op archway. Next day, pop! Gone.

For a *Running Times* feature called "Visionary Venues," I visited several specially created cross-country courses. Rim Rock Farm at Lawrence, Kansas, is the home venue of Kansas University (KU) and combines idyllic landscaping and tough hill running with works of art: giant silhouette sculptures of great KU runners like Billy Mills and Jim Ryun, as well as one of Coach Bob Timmons, who bequeathed the land.

The idea spread. Billy Lamb, a graduate assistant for Timmons in the 1960s, later designed the Choctaw Trails course for Mississippi College in Clinton, Missouri, which is used for high school and college cross-country up to championship level and is praised for its European flavor and spectator-friendly access. In Canberra, Australia, Rob de Castella designed a new cross-country facility for racing and training on land restored after devastating forest fires. It has quickly become a vital resource, green and challenging. Other running venues that enhance the land include Winter Hill Farm in Henniker, New Hampshire, and Camp Olympic Park, near Emmaus, Pennsylvania, where Budd Coates of *Runner's World* (an elite marathoner of the 1980s) established a cross-country course around a cornfield. Camp Olympic Park now hosts a mix of farming and recreation that Coates calls "agri-cross." Several courses were established in New England by John Morton, a ski Olympian and coach, who created a new profession as designer of sports trails in natural terrain.

Some famous visionary courses have been built on the pioneering footsteps of runners. It was runners who used the dirty, rutted, rat-infested reservoir path in Central Park, New York (I write from personal experience, including the rats), as a training circuit. Joe Kleinerman, one of the founders of New York Road Runners, recalled near the end of his life that "in 1927, I started running around the reservoir. The park was filled with runners, mainly from the many schools in Manhattan." Numbers of adult runners rose in the 1940s and 1950s, and Kleinerman organized group runs on the park's bridle paths in the mid-1960s.

"Even Jackie Kennedy showed up. It was remarkable," he said (cited in Sherman 2003). A fervent lobbying campaign by runners and cyclists led to Mayor John Lindsay closing the park to weekend traffic in 1968, a historic victory. It was doubly historic because it enabled the New York City Marathon to be created in 1970, using the now traffic-free East and West Drives to circle the park, a venue the race used until the equally historic move into the streets in 1976. Eventually, under the new Central Park Conservancy (founded 1980), the bridle paths and reservoir path were cleaned up and became fit for presidents to run there, as Bill Clinton did. In 1994, the reservoir path was declared the Jacqueline Kennedy Onassis Reservoir Jogging Trail, and it became a tourist attraction and a visionary venue.

Runners ran through untrodden sand dunes and forests on routes that have become iconic recreation trails, from Balmoral in Scotland to the spectacular Motu Trails in New Zealand's Bay of Plenty; runners defended beloved training areas like Hagley Park in Christchurch or linear parks like the River Parks in Tulsa, Oklahoma, from ever-avaricious roads and highways. Germany and other European countries have always had their hiking routes, but elsewhere today's global choice of recreation trails owes a lot to the pragmatic pioneering of runners and their more recent allies, the mountain bikers.

Futuristic novels and movies dream of high-tech cities soaring to the skies, with superlative high-speed public transport. My vision is of cities interfused with natural places and interlaced with networks of green trails that enable runners, walkers, and cyclists to traverse the urban area in contact with the earth and without hearing an engine or setting foot on concrete. Olmsted had it figured out. Look at all the different routes in Central Park, with carriages, people on horseback, and walkers all separated, often crossing but never encountering each other.

Track and field has been building venues since ancient Greece. They get worse and worse. Our age has created nothing to rival Delphi's spiritual mountainside juxtaposition of temple, athletic track, and theater. The problem is the modern sport's obsession with records, and therefore conformity, which denies any connection with nature and any sense of local character. The typical high school track, with all those crisscrossing lines and standardized equipment, looks more like a research laboratory than a place for play. Even the old rural steeplechase, the race that began as a spontaneous choose-your-own route romp across hedges and streams, has been cropped and tidied and made to conform. All so we can obsess about records.

Modern tracks seem unnatural and anonymous. Any track could be any other track. "The replacement of geography by geometry," John Bale (1994) calls it in *Landscapes of Modern Sport*. The latest low point was the dead-flat, weather-free marathon on an impeccably smooth car-racing circuit that in May 2017 was used in pursuit of the totally artificial target of running 26.219 mi./42.198 km in 119.9 minutes.

That may be part of the reason most runners have no interest in track and prefer road racing, where each course has some distinct character. I'm sentimental enough to want athletics tracks to fit into and enhance their natural settings. I know three that do. The Lake Tahoe venue for the high-altitude 1968 US Olympic Trials kept its character as a glade in natural mountainside forest. The 400 m all-weather training track on the Nike campus at Beaverton, Oregon, cuts through a woodland grove, so that the athletes disappear into trees halfway round the lap and re-emerge coming off the bend. And in my New Zealand home town of Wellington, the Newtown Park track sits beneath a steep wind-breaking hillside, in part covered with evergreen trees, and the rest the grassy lower slopes of the Wellington Zoo. The starter must pause during the clamor of the chimpanzees' afternoon mealtime (always reminding me of the university staff club). A few years ago, Newtown Park was the world's only running stadium with its own elephant. Elderly and placid, Kamala browsed the grassy hillside above the 200 m start. For many years as stadium announcer, I tried to save her nerves by opening each new track season with an official warning: "Kamala the elephant, please do not be alarmed, as the starter is about to fire his gun for the first race."

Environmental Initiatives

I also look for races that have environmental initiatives and those that exist primarily to benefit the earth. It's an inspiring thought. Right now, trees are growing where none grew, water flows clean, parks help cities breathe, and scores of young rhinos are blinking their way to their own place on the earth because of running and runners. That's what I mean by creative environmental leadership. Here is a selection.

The Bank of America Chicago Marathon is a major sponsor of Gateway Green, a project for establishing trees in that concrete city. Volunteers have planted as many as one hundred trees at a time, reaching the initial target of 15,000 by 2015. The marathon focuses on plantings alongside sections of its course, which is no easy task when you realize that every sapling requires a hole to be broken through the sidewalk, with enough earth, water, and sunlight available for the tree to survive long term in a climate of severe extremes.

"We aim to do about a half-mile per year," said race director Carey Pinkowski, who also reminded me that the marathon contributes to improving the running trails through Lincoln Park and to other park and youth sport projects.

I checked out several marathon course plantings. One alleviates the squalor beneath the Dan Ryan Expressway. Some are in neighborhoods way outside the usual tourist comfort zone. But we run their streets. We should leave some improvement behind us. Don't look yet for an overarching canopy or grand avenue. The newcomers are stringy little saplings that you hardly notice as you fight for a parking space. Yet already, I thought, they modify an ambience otherwise dictated by the Honky Tonk Barbecue or the Hyundai and Pontiac dealerships, bringing a hint of repose to clattering streets. In time, they will improve the oxygen and lower the summer temperature. They will be trees in the city, a gift from the marathon to the streets it borrows.

New York Road Runners (NYRR) in 2016 announced a partnership with the Trust for Public Land to fund a visionary transformation of New York City's decrepit public-school playgrounds into "state-of-the-art, green, community playgrounds." That ties in with NYRR's highly successful youth running programs. All life forms are to some degree shaped by their environment, especially in early life. If money from running can help New York City kids to be shaped by clean, green nature rather than dirty, cracked concrete, it will be a good step toward changing the world.

Martin's Park is a Boston project that by 2018 will have created a thirteen-million-dollar park in the Seafront District, next to the Boston Children's Museum, in memory of Martin Richard, who died at age eight in the 2013 Boston Marathon bombing. The Boston Marathon's major sponsor, John Hancock, is among the supporters.

Trees were the seed of the Eye-Q Two Cities Marathon in California's Fresno and Clovis communities. The race is an alliance with the Tree Fresno Trust, and every runner is a donor. The course is mostly off-road, yet on wide asphalt surfaces, and it explores the area's network of parkland recreation trails alongside and sometimes below the car-dominated streets. Some of the trails were once railroads, affirming the alliance between running and the Rails-for-Trails Conservancy, the nonprofit organization dedicated to transforming America's disused railroads into recreational linear parks.

We completed a tree-themed Fresno weekend by driving to the nearby Sequoia National Park and paying respects to one towering sequoia that has been quietly growing there for 2,500 years. "This was a sapling," I said, "when Pheidippides met Pan on the way back from Sparta."

Two other tree events, an ocean apart, are the London Tree-Athlon, a 5K in London's Battersea Park where every runner contributes to Britain's Trees for Cities charity and receives a sapling in the race goody bag; and the Oak Tree Half-Marathon in Geneseo, New York, which supports the Genesee Valley Conservancy and awards winners a wreath and an oak sapling grown from a local acorn.

Tradition as well as trendiness underlies this connection between running and trees. Winners at the ancient Greek games received not gold medals but crowns of wreathed leaves—olive at Olympia, laurel at Delphi, pine at Isthmia—symbolizing the games' celebration of the sacredness of nature. The 1936 Olympic Games in Berlin revived the tradition, presenting each winner with an oak sapling. At least two flourish today as mature trees, one planted by Jesse Owens at Rhodes High School, Cleveland, Ohio, the other by Jack Lovelock (1,500 m winner) at Timaru Boys High School in New Zealand. Many believe that an oak at Ohio State University is another of the four won and was planted by Owens.

The Virgin Money London Marathon is guardian and benefactor of London's sports fields. It adopted them as part of its original charitable mission in 1981, and it donates millions of pounds per year to improve sports spaces or protect them from housing development. The sports grounds of Birkbeck College in West London were neglected and vandalized until the marathon saved them in 1986, at a cost of 850,000 pounds. Now renamed the London Marathon Playing Fields, they teem daily with sports action.

"Recreational space is a vital part of every community," said former race director Dave Bedford, whose own world record–breaking running career was founded on the grassy hills of Hampstead Heath, north of the city.

The Run for Central Park four-miler is a fundraising partnership between New York Road Runners and the Central Park Conservancy, the body that restored the decrepit old park of the 1970s into the environmental masterwork it was in the 1860s. In my years as a Manhattan runner, Central Park was my track, my gym, my social center, my sculpture collection, and, as I wrote in chapter 14, my church, my garden, my earth. This race is an opportunity to repay a big debt. From 2009, the conservancy made the event even greener by giving only earth-friendly awards and planting flowers in honor of each winner.

Trail running, a rapidly expanding offshoot of the later running boom, often accepts responsibility for the trails it uses. "The Tarawera Ultra, one of the world's biggest long trail races, arranges for volunteers to put in over 500 hours of work on the tracks, benefiting all users year-round," said New Zealand multisport journalist James Boorsinn. The highly international race is also making it a condition of entry that all runners show evidence that they have logged some volunteer hours on trails near their homes.

The parkrun movement has rapidly become a huge global player in using and promoting parks. Started in the United Kingdom by Paul Sinton-Hewitt, "parkruns" are, yes, runs in parks: 5K, every week, totally free, totally open, operating through modern technology. You simply print your own barcode, show up any Saturday at any parkrun in the world, and check results online. That's it. With a few on-the-spot volunteers, it almost runs itself. From one event with thirteen runners in 2004, there are now hundreds every week. The movement has been slowest to take off in the United States, mainly because of insurance issues. It's booming everywhere else. Problems may arise from the scale of this success, especially because of the heavy use of venues funded by others, but that would be easily solved.

Heavy-Hitting Conservation

Now some real heavy hitters enter the story: rhinos and elephants. Nearly twenty years ago, Ian Craig, a runner who founded the Lewa Wildlife Conservancy on family land in Kenya, had the idea of a fundraising race to let runners experience that iconic high plains terrain. He partnered with Tusk Trust, a conservation charity, and Kenyan telecommunications giant Safaricom. Bruce Tulloh was identified as the ideal race director. Former European 5,000 m champion, scientist, and writer Tulloh lived for a while in Kenya, coaching runners like Olympic medalist Mike Boit, and so he brought in support from the Kenyan elite running community.

The Safaricom Marathon/Half-Marathon annually features Olympic medalists, as well as attracting local runners, Kenyan and overseas corporate teams, the British and Kenyan armies, and travel groups from all over the world. Catherine Ndereba, Paul Tergat, and the late Sammy Wanjiru have all starred. It is little exaggeration to say that millions raised from runners have saved the white rhino and Grévy's zebra from extinction. In the first ten years of the race, numbers of these animals have more than doubled. While we were there in 2008, the white rhino population rose by one more happy little armor-plated bundle to 112. That's progress. Lewa holds more than fifteen percent of Kenya's white rhino population (*Safaricom Marathon, Tenth Anniversary*, program book, 2009). Elephants, lions, and giraffes also thrive there. On race day, the animals are shooed off the course by a buzzing helicopter, so there is no likelihood of a runner becoming lunch, though no one seemed quite relaxed about being last.

Lewa and Tusk Trust are important as innovators in African conservation because they insist that their work lies not only with animals but with local tribes. One beneficiary of the marathon is the Northern Rangelands Trust, which supports community conservancies across two million acres of tribal lands, nurturing "the re-establishment of the wildlife landscape." The people living near the conservancy are made beneficiaries, given employment and schools, and shown that their best economic prospect lies in preserving the wildlife, not poaching it. Women are especially targeted for economic empowerment. Local people jammed the postrace awards in the thousands, including Masai in full beaded glory. There was an exuberant children's race, and participation in the main races by local business teams gave me one more unique experience in my lifetime in running—for the first time, I saw slow, tired Kenyans.

A different kind of conservation motivates the popular Pasig River Marathon in the Philippine capital, Manila. The race is dedicated to cleaning up the fetid Pasig River, one of the world's most polluted waterways. "The government and private sector have joined hands in moving to eliminate the 'toilet bowl' reputation of the river," wrote the *Manila Bulletin* in February 2009. The marathon is a crucial catalyst, with 9,000 runners bringing publicity for the environmental mission. Like the Athens and Boston Marathons, it also celebrates a historic journey for freedom; the race follows the route taken by patriot Rajah Sulayman during the Spanish invasion in 1571.

The Kepler Challenge Mountain Run in New Zealand's Fiordland National Park is another race that helps endangered species. In 2006, it set up "Operation Birdsong" for native birdlife, especially the kiwi, threatened by imported stoats and rats. Race proceeds have bought and maintained traps every two hundred meters around the 38 mi./61 km of the course. Sixty sharp-fanged bird-murderers were trapped each month in the first year, declining encouragingly by more than half in recent counts. Kiwi numbers are harder to measure, but their cry has been heard, and hikers and runners report increased evidence of their twiggy footprints. The kiwi is a nocturnal, shy, flightless, and therefore vulnerable bird, so it is not a photo op to amaze your Facebook friends.

Improving the environment is not about human instant gratification. That shy little brown earthbound bird matters, too. What better use could there be for running's wealth and power? There is still much to be done and much waste to eliminate, but I like to think the nature god Pan did well when he chose a runner to carry his message back to Athens.

18

November 4, 2012, New York City

Season of Storm and Stress

When Superstorm Sandy hit the US Eastern Seaboard six days before the 2012 New York City Marathon, I was 8,000 miles away, coping with a smaller tragedy. I'd made a fast, unplanned trip back from the Hudson Valley to Wellington, New Zealand, to attend and conduct the funeral of a friend, David Carson-Parker. David was not a runner, but he was an important friend, the one who was staying with us in New York right after 9/11 and was so moved by the tragic toll on the nearby firehouse. Despite the distance and the narrow window before I had to work as a journalist at the marathon, I made the decision to go back to participate in an important rite for a community I belong to.

The big public funeral was done, and the small private farewell. As the early flight to Sydney lifted off from Wellington, it veered round Mount Victoria and gave me an exquisite view in the dawn light of David and Jeremy's house, perched on the steep hillside, that elegant art-crammed home where they had hosted so many memorable dinner parties. Now Jeremy was alone. While the storm was battering the New Jersey seaboard and New York City, I was on the return journey, kicking around Sydney Airport for ten hours with a burning sore throat from the virus I'd picked up. I simply couldn't talk, even when I met Kurt Fearnley, a contender for the wheelchair race in New York and someone else whose long journey might prove unnecessary.

I got as far as Los Angeles, but there were no onward flights to the East Coast. I was stuck in a motel near the Los Angeles Airport during the fraught days that followed. My news from New York and its marathon

25. The New York City Marathon passes people's streets, stores, and homes, 2012. Courtesy of Les Potapczyk.

came from television and online sources, including the *Runner's World/ Running Times* website that I was supposed to be writing for. On the Monday of marathon week, Mayor Michael Bloomberg announced that the race would go on. I finally made it to New York and the race media center in Central Park, ill and exhausted, on the Friday afternoon. Ten minutes later came the counter-announcement that the race was canceled.

There was a lot of controversy about the lateness of that decision. I felt it was not irresponsible, from the evidence I had been able to access in Los Angeles. The media stories and images that I saw covered only Lower Manhattan and coastal New Jersey, where Governor Chris Christie schmoozed with President Obama among the wreckage of Seaside Park. I looked that up and found it's on a precariously exposed spit, forty miles from the marathon course. There was nothing on television to suggest the city itself had been so ravaged, no coverage from Staten Island, nothing from Brooklyn, and apart from a fire in Queens, nothing from anywhere on or near the marathon course.

So, unless you were on the spot, and outside Manhattan, the scale of the disaster within the other city boroughs was not apparent until late in the week. A friend who comes from Staten Island and has brothers there could not contact them, and even he was not aware for five days how severe their problems were. It would have been less troublesome and less expensive for everyone (including Kurt Fearnley and me) if the race had been canceled earlier, and it was an error of judgment, or timing, to think the race could benefit the city in the way the 2001 marathon did. That came eight weeks after the 9/11 attacks and could therefore be a triumph of healing. Six days is very different, with flood water still in many basements.

But the eruption of resentful criticism toward the race and the earlier decision to proceed took everyone by surprise. It's natural for humans at times of distress to look instinctively for someone to blame, but that time it was suddenly running that was castigated on social media and subjected to indignation in the tabloids. The *New York Post* made heartrending front-page images out of the generators that the New York City Marathon had hired for the race's medical headquarters, slanting the story to make it look as if the marathon had somehow appropriated the generators and was selfishly depriving the suffering people of Staten Island and Queens of vital resources. More seriously, race volunteers were reporting that they had been opposed by residents along the course when they began to set up equipment.

Such hostility was unprecedented. Running is rightly proud of its popularity and public esteem. We are inclusive and welcoming, we stretch every race to bursting point to let in more people, and we love to see the restaurant signs that say, "runners welcome" and the ecumenical church services for runners worshipping in T-shirts and tracksuits. We exuberantly relish the vast crowds that cheer us along their streets. We congratulate ourselves on taking over whole cities on race day, convinced that our appropriation is benign. All that is true, and has been documented in this book, but now we had to do some soul-searching to understand that it was not the whole truth.

The New York City Marathon in 2012 (a race that didn't happen) made history because of its importance to the understanding of the relationship between running and its host communities, and I would say to running's understanding of itself, its mission, and its reputation. There was no coherent debate, and no agreed consensus, since running has no structure or process for that, but there was heated discussion in every club room, running store, and media center, and on every long Sunday group run, probably all around the world. What follows is my personal response, and I was admittedly sick and jet-lagged. But change did subsequently happen, especially in New York, so I don't believe I'm alone in this interpretation.

As a historian, I tried to think of precedents. There had been large-scale last-minute cancellations before: the 1995 Osaka Women's Marathon was canceled after an earthquake, the 2011 Nagoya Women's Marathon after the March tsunami, the International Track Meet in Christchurch, New Zealand, after the February 2011 earthquake (chapter 16), and many races around America, including the Avon Women's US Championship, the weekend after the 9/11 terrorist attacks. All those cancellations affected invited elite athletes, sponsors, media, charities, and city authorities, as well as causing major local inconvenience and economic loss. Yet none provoked the kind of resentment that surfaced in New York in 2012.

New York City didn't come to a stop that week. Other ongoing events and activities could have been subjected to anger and acrimony. Running alone was targeted, presumably because nothing else has the scale and public visibility of the marathon, and nothing else takes over the streets. Throughout this book, I have recorded the growth of running as it became a new form of celebration, an expression of communal catharsis, or an incarnation of unity and hope. Now other implications seemed to have emerged.

One realization is that being big and important is two-edged. It creates responsibilities. The initial decision to proceed with the marathon seems to have been largely Mayor Bloomberg's, and made for economic reasons.

"We have to have an economy. There are an awful lot of small businesses that depend on these people [the runners]. . . . For those who were lost, you've got to believe they would want us to have an economy, and have a city go on for those they have left behind," Bloomberg said.

Running knows it makes a positive economic contribution, which races use as leverage in securing community support. The New York City Marathon, in fact, was the first to research and quantify it, and to use it in negotiation with authorities. Now Bloomberg was adding an element of obligation, a dependence on running, and therefore a commitment to sustain that contribution even in (to put it mildly) difficult circumstances.

As criticism grew, the race appealed to its charity résumé, including the huge contribution made by what was then the Run for Kids program, and quickly rebranded the 2012 marathon as a fundraiser, offering a million-dollar donation to superstorm relief and volunteer resources and equipment for relief work. It was sincerely meant but it didn't help. The sport of running still came out looking self-absorbed and obtuse. Its top executives reeled. People who have devoted their careers to creating and putting out good news about running were perplexed and ravaged now by two weeks of dispute and negativity.

The story of modern running has been so positive that in recent years its community support has been taken for granted. The problems on the ground in 2012 were not in Manhattan, but Staten Island, Brooklyn, Queens, and the Bronx, making evident a disparity between the festive mass of affluent and international runners and the local, workaday streets, small stores, and modest apartments that courses like New York's pass through. The demographics suggest that few runners live in such locations. Entrants in big city marathons like New York are in general from a highly educated, affluent, and almost entirely white upper-middle-class segment of society. Entering a big race is expensive and brings other expenses with it.

I may be sensitive to this because I began running by going outside my team at a private high school to run in club "harriers," a sport that in the context of class-conscious mid-twentieth-century England was remarkably inclusive, and comfortably so. When I ran for England in 1966, the team was like a socioeconomic microcosm. One member came from land-owning wealth, another was a housepainter who because of childhood illness had received only three years of education. He ran best on the day. Our hierarchy of respect depended entirely on your finishing place. One of the great bonuses of my life as a runner has been that it enabled me to mix on easy terms with a much more varied range of people than in my other life as an academic; as I once wrote, "making friends from the entire cross-section of society, right down the social scale to lawyers and politicians."

In America, too, there has been a huge change from the early and middle twentieth century, when marathoners were the dedicated, hard-scrabble, blue-collar manual workers described by Pamela Cooper (1999) in *The American Marathon*.

So, it has long troubled me that modern running, for all its proud inclusiveness, does not, in fact, recruit from the whole of society. In 2012, trying to understand the hostility, I began to think there may be a touch of arrogance about our demand that other people's streets be closed for us, their traffic stopped, and their businesses shut for the day. Can we, I wondered, continue to expect poor people to come out on their streets to cheer for rich people?

That may put it oversimply, but others formed similar conclusions. Since 2012, New York Road Runners have made a committed effort to reach out to communities outside Manhattan, creating new events in areas of the city that had been neglected, or in 2012 alienated. One key slogan for the marathon is now "Run New York. Five Boroughs. One City." They are putting major resources into expanding their successful kids program, rebranded in late 2017 as Rising New York Road Runners. Another positive development is the flourishing Black Girls RUN! organization, founded in 2009. I don't yet see any overall effort to change the sport's demographic profile, but wider social and political forces may be at work.

"I have taken too little care of this," says King Lear about the disparity between kingly pomp and the raggedness of the poor, while he is contending with a similar dreadful storm. Sandy reminded me, and I hope others, that we should take more care about the omissions, disparities, and perhaps complacency within our sport. It also confirmed, as I wrote in the previous chapter, that running's economic success carries the responsibility to use it well. And it showed everyone that running has now attained a scale and importance that inevitably will bring scrutiny, criticism, and perhaps unwanted attention or exploitation.

Six months after Sandy, that unwanted attention happened. At the next major American marathon, in Boston on April 15, 2013, the sport of running paid an even heavier price for its combination of prominence and vulnerability.

Footnote, 2017: Another test of running's active role in modern history came five days before the 2017 New York City Marathon, when a lone terrorist murdered eight people and injured eleven by a truck attack on the West Side bike path. The next day's marathon-related public events were all canceled as a sign of respect, and every subsequent event, including the race itself, opened scrupulously with an expression of sympathy. The program went ahead, sometimes mutedly, without public or media criticism. The 2017 New York City Marathon became again what it had been in 2001, and what Boston was in 2014: a public affirmation of resilience, freedom, civic spirit, and continuing life. The sport's cathartic value was reaffirmed over and over, at the highest level.

"This day is incredibly important for this city and this country," is how Mayor Bill de Blasio greeted 50,000 runners at the start-line on Staten Island.

The mayor also emphasized the race's inclusiveness: "Live and let live, everyone together, it doesn't matter what background." As a sport, we have not yet perfectly implemented that ideal, but since 2012 we have moved a lot closer, perhaps most especially in New York.

19

April 15, 2013, Boston; April 21, 2013, London

The Boston Marathon Bombings

As the winners cross the line at a major marathon, journalists like me in the media center are already writing our first short-version race report for almost immediate website posting. Then comes a high-pressure period of about two hours when you compile a more in-depth report, attend the medal-winners' media conferences, ask questions, and insert new information and salient quotes into your story. All that in a crowded, excited, and noisy media room with continuing finish-line action and press conference discussion on giant screens. It requires an ability to detach and focus, especially if, like me, your role is to provide a report that offers more considered and articulate interpretations of the whole race than is available to the television viewer or most immediate coverage. It's the kind of thing that used to appear in a print magazine two months later. With only minutes to work in, I'm trying to craft eloquent, expert insights in the middle of bedlam.

I sent that kind of coverage of the 2013 Boston Marathon men's race to the editor for immediate posting about two hours after the winner crossed the line on Boylston Street. In a result with few well-known names, I decided to give emphasis to the strange pacing and the complexities of the "teams race" rivalry between Ethiopia and Kenya that wouldn't be apparent to the casual television viewer, but which I'd picked up as a strong subcurrent in the days before the race.

I was just approaching my last paragraph, summarizing the emergence of a new Ethiopian cohort led by winner Lelisa Desisa, when the media director of the Boston Athletic Association suddenly called for

26. Finish-area volunteer Les Potapczyk captured this image of the first bomb exploding at the 2013 Boston Marathon. Courtesy of Les Potapczyk.

silence from the side doorway of the main press room where we were working, in normal life the gilt Venetian Room of the Copley Plaza Hotel, two hundred yards from the finish line. The buzz of many conversations faded, and those of us in the process of writing reluctantly looked up from our laptops, sentences half-formed in our heads.

"There has been a serious incident at the finish line, and this hotel is in police lockdown until further notice. No questions can be taken at this time," he said. (I'm working from memory, and at the time barely half my mind was on his announcement).

Quickly, people were on their cell phones. There had been an explosion, probably a bomb. I had no immediate personal anxiety. Kathrine had come by after finishing her television duties at the finish line to give me a quick pat on the shoulder as I worked. I knew she was safe in our room two floors up in the Copley.

My report was due. I kept writing.

I pressed "send" on my coverage and went straight to our room. I still knew almost nothing. Kathrine had heard the boom of the two explosions and then the sirens from the street below the hotel. She was absorbed in the television, worried about Lisa Hughes, her WBZ-TV colleague who had stayed on at the booth to continue covering the people's field after Kathrine and Toni Reavis left. Lisa was still on air, sounding distressed but still wholly professional. She was safe. That was about the only thing we knew.

You start thinking of friends and colleagues who might have been hurt: Rhonda, whose predicted finish was about the time the bombs went off, her husband Rich who might have been in the crowd, Les and Bob and Jimmy who were volunteers in the finish area. That's when the horror of it bites.

We also knew that as soon as the news broke worldwide, people would worry about us. We fired off a reassuring email to family and close friends saying we were safe. My sons commented later that they seem to get these messages from me fairly often.

Before we had time to worry much more, or begin to grieve, the phone rang. The media frenzy had started. At first, we responded, feeling some responsibility to provide information and a degree of interpretation from within the sport. I felt a special commitment to New Zealand, and did several interviews. But each one we satisfied only multiplied the demands. It was like lopping off the Hydra's heads. We learned that night that there are thousands upon thousands of media outlets, and in a crisis like that, every footling breakfast show of them wants to show its audience that they have their very own eyewitness on the spot.

We were scarcely valid for that. When the bombs went off, Kathrine was in a hotel room and I had my nose in my laptop. Now, in police lockdown, we knew only what we were seeing on television. We were desperately weary, after two very short nights and several hours of intense work, and emotional about what had happened, and I knew I had to start again at 5 a.m. to try to reach Logan Airport and fly to London for the next marathon assignment.

However, we tried to staunch the flood. The requests for interviews became demands from all over the world, even at 3 a.m. from people who knew we were trying to grab some desperate sleep. We both work for media and believe in good journalism. But that afternoon and night we felt exploited.

When my own online editor Scott Douglas emailed to ask if I could provide a reflective piece on what the attack meant for the sport of running, and for the running community, that was a different matter. I was in Boston as a team member, and my role as a writer is to reflect on significance, context, and depth, not merely report. I agreed to try.

Here is what I wrote between phone calls. Because it gives a sense of immediacy, the actual scene, the story still developing, and my thoughts and emotions in process, I quote it intact. Though intended only for *Runner's World Newswire*, it was picked up by other outlets, like the *Guardian* in the United Kingdom. Subsequently, it has been widely cited, and in one instance (in Tulsa, Oklahoma) the paragraph about running as a source of goodwill inspired a new race, dedicated to international peace.

Boston Bombings: A Loss of Innocence
What will happen to big-city
marathons' openness?

Boston MONDAY, APRIL 15, 2013, 5pm.

Three hours ago bombs killed and injured people at the finish line of the Boston Marathon. I feel as if my own family has been violated. Worse even than that, after a lifetime of writing about how running is one of the most positive forces in the modern world.

I've been in Boston five days. I've been at media conferences, parties, meals with fellow writers and a running travel group, and I've had crowded hours at the expo. I ran among lots of runners alongside the Charles River, I stood and cheered on the sidelines of the 5K and street mile, and today I reported the race from the media center, surrounded by journalists from around the world. There has been not one moment in all five days that has been anything but warm, friendly, supportive, generous, benevolent in the fullest sense. Until now.

I'm not just being warm and fuzzy. Marathon running has a long tradition of celebrating, commemorating, and affirming life. The original Olympic marathon in 1896 was to commemorate the man who carried the news of a victory for freedom. The first Boston Marathon a year later followed that idea by honoring the ride of Paul Revere, not on his actual route, but always on his day, Patriots' Day in the State of Massachusetts (that's why it's on Monday). The London Marathon, to be run next Sunday, was created with charities as part of its original mission. This very Boston Marathon mourned and honored the school-kids who were gunned down a few months ago in Newtown, CT, not far from here. Out of respect for them, this year's race was started for the first time in 117 years not with a gun but with an airhorn.

Even without that special purpose, marathon running is a sport of goodwill. It's a sport where if a competitor falls, the others around will pick him or her up. It's a sport where no one ever boos anybody. It's a sport open to absolutely everyone, regardless of gender, age, ethnicity or any other division you can think of. It's a rare occasion when tens of thousands of people assemble, often in a major city like New York, Boston or London, for a reason that is totally peaceful, healthy, non-political, and well-meaning.

If you're losing your faith in human nature, look at marathon crowds, standing for hours with no seating, no cover, no bathrooms, to cheer thousands of strangers. Or look at our sport's volunteers, on whose shoulders the whole sport rests. I spent time on Saturday with friends from Buffalo and Niagara Falls, race directors and volunteers who travel the East Coast giving their skills and labor to other races. Bob Kaminsky, Jimmy Moran, Jimmy Cummings, and Les Potapczyk told me they would be "working security at the finish line." Right by where the first bomb went off. I've been frantic with worry. I heard only minutes ago that they are safe.

Our problem is that this marathon world of goodwill and prelapsarian innocence has made us so vulnerable. Ever since the New York Marathon went ahead eight weeks after the horror of 9/11, my wife Kathrine Switzer and I have feared exactly what happened today.

We often discussed it, but almost superstitiously never shared our worry with others. Our sport, we know too well, is such a great photo-op, and global media coverage is guaranteed. Modern murderers like those things.

I'm spending today explaining to media from England to New Zealand that it's impossible to make a marathon course totally secure. The police sniffer dogs were out at 8am this morning checking the finish area, so the bombs were presumably planted later, by someone who wandered in behind the crowd. How could you stop it?

It's too soon to say where we go from here. Our sport is still in shock. The first response is pity for the victims; and then defiance. We believe our sport's innocence has value. We will go on running marathons. If you're trying to break our society's spirit, it's a mistake to start with runners. But we may have to accept constraints. The World Cross-Country Championships were much diluted by the demands of modern security, meaning they always have to be held on closed circuits instead of genuinely across farmland or open country as they should be. Could we run marathons on safe closed circuits that can be readily policed? That would a loss. How can you reconcile that with the essential notion that the marathon is a journey, and a celebration of the community or the environment it passes through?

I just received a press release from the London Marathon, where I'm due to travel tomorrow morning, to say they are "reviewing security arrangements with the Metropolitan Police." How do you reconcile that need and that language with the essential innocence of the marathon?

At this moment we're still in "lock-down" in the Copley Plaza hotel, the race and media headquarters. I don't know when I can get out or whether I can fly to London tomorrow. Our hotel window looks down on Dartmouth Street. Every other year at this time, five hours after the winners finished, that scene has been jammed with happy and tired runners, making their creaky way to the Family Reunion area just around the corner. Every other year, we have looked down on a scene of mass but quiet jubilation and unity.

Today there's nothing moving out there. The street is lined with back-up ambulances, fire-trucks and police vehicles, including a massive black thing out of Mad Max called "Massachusetts Police Incident

Command." I'm grateful they are there today. But it's a sight I never wanted to see at a marathon.

Then I flew to London. The moment I emerged from the hotel to hunt a taxi at 4:45 a.m., I had to elude a dozen prowling camera crews, all sleep deprived and frantic to fulfill orders to get "on-the-spot comment," preferably from someone who would burst into tears. It was like dodging through a wolf pack.

London, of course, was full of concern for Boston, which I described in one prerace article. I went to the media conferences, wrote previews, and on race day reported the men's and women's elite races. I wrote with special enthusiasm about the victory of Tsegaye Kebede, one of my favorites, a good-humored man who is intrigued by his own rise from extreme poverty. Totally engrossed as the race approached, I was one of the few people who did not follow the breaking news drama from Boston of the hunt for the Tsarnaev brothers.

I did take an evening off and got lucky with a last-minute ticket for the National Theatre's excellent *Othello*, set in a modern military camp. This book isn't confessional, but since I'm near the end, I might risk revealing that I may be a compulsive truant. When I was a high-powered professor of literature, I used to sneak away from academic conferences to go for a run; now that running is my business, my idea of an illicit night off is to sneak away to a Shakespeare play. I really don't know which is Dr. Jekyll and which is Mr. Hyde.

When the 2013 London Marathon was all over, and I'd done my job, all reports sent, and I was beginning to nod on the long-distance bus journey from London to Ross-on-Wye in Herefordshire, to visit my niece and family, an email arrived from *Runner's World*. They urgently wanted a final summary of how the London Marathon responded to the Boston bombings.

So as the 6 p.m. National Express snarled its way through Swindon, Cirencester, and Cheltenham, moving randomly in and out of Wi-Fi connection, I returned in thought to the images and conversations of the six days since I staggered off the flight from Boston. True to the eyewitness mission of this book, I leave the article intact for its authenticity as immediate evidence of this latest encounter of running with history.

'Run4Boston' Is the London Marathon Message
Sunday's marathon showed the global unity
of the running community.

Monday April 22, 2013, 8.15pm

"Run4Boston" was the theme of Sunday's London Marathon. That caption was on hundreds of rapidly printed T-shirts worn by runners and spectators, and on homemade banners flourished by the crowds. From Prince Harry handing out the awards and Tsegaye Kebede dedicating his victory, through to the last finisher and the smallest spectator, the race turned into a gigantic affirmation of support for the runners and spectators of Boston.

The biggest message came from the sheer numbers on London's streets. When Edna Kiplagat, second in the women's race, said, "I had no fear," she spoke for 39,000 runners and an estimated three-quarters of a million equally defiant spectators. Not one, it's almost certain, was deterred by what happened in Boston.

"I come to show we still run, we are not afraid, they do not win," said Karl, a Swede among a group of runners I talked to at the East Croydon train station before the race.

"We owe it to the poor bastards that got killed and maimed. I'm running for them," said Frank, a Londoner on the same train.

"It was bad to do that. My mum says running is good so she's still going to run today. I think she'll be alright," said nine-year-old Olivia anxiously.

"The marathon raises millions for charities, like the one my husband runs for. We're not going to let them stop that," said Connie.

The mood was upbeat as well as respectful. The thirty-second silence before the start was scrupulously observed by the huge assembly of runners, but immediately followed by an exuberant outburst of applause and cheering. The solemn silence was for Boston. The happy cheers were for the undeterred, undiminished, positive resolve of the sport of running.

Men's champion Tsegaye Kebede, who comes from poverty in
Ethiopia and has seen plenty of suffering at home, summed it up,
when he said his win was "for my family, the runners of Boston."

Every runner I saw wore a black ribbon, distributed at registration.
Many had black armbands. Some spectators wore yellow and blue, and
Boston Marathon jackets and Red Sox hoodies were everywhere.

"Many of the marshals and volunteers wore black ribbons, as well,"
said Lisa Jackson, a race volunteer on the course, and best-selling running author. "Many runners wore Boston T-shirts that were sold at the
race expo, to raise money for the Boston victims fund. Also I spotted
several runners who, instead of their own names on their shirts, had
the word 'Boston,' encouraging spectators to cheer for that name."

All the top finishers at their media conferences struggled with limited English to express their sympathy. Every speaker, every celebrity
interviewed, every official race announcement, and every newspaper
editorial over London Marathon weekend insisted that this marathon
and every marathon and road race must go ahead.

Security was thorough but I saw nothing extreme, little more than
at any large-scale marathon that closes parts of a city. My briefcase was
never checked on my walk to the media center, though my usual narrow walkways on the perimeter of the Tower of London were blocked
off. Marathon CEO Nick Bitel implied on Wednesday that most of the
extra provisions would be unseen, and I suspect there was CCTV coverage of the sidewalks along the entire course. But CCTV is standard
almost everywhere in London, as many signs advise you. The "7/7"
subway and bus bombings (July 7, 2005) taught Londoners to find a
means of non-intrusive security.

There were plenty of cops, but no guns, of course, and no military that I saw. We were steered around on wide walkways or roads
that were no doubt under observation, but it was all good-humored.
No cops are more jocund than London cops when they're on crowd
control and double pay.

Access to the media center was controlled by a security man who
looked like a stand-in for James Bond's old mate Oddjob, but such
guards are standard issue these days. The finish area was restricted
entirely to people with accreditation, and it was not possible to get
behind the crowds and the bleachers as the bombers did at Boston. We

can't control the entire course of any marathon, but the photogenic start and finish areas of our big marathons need to be taken off the "soft target" list.

The London mood was lightened, I think, by the successful end of the Boston manhunt before marathon day. Earlier in the week, every British runner I talked to had inventive proposals for what should be done to the anatomy of the bombers when caught. After Saturday, resentment was put behind them and the whole emphasis was on getting on with running. And getting on with cheering for runners, as this marathon is an annual folk festival of costumes, charities, and celebration.

This is not just a British story. At the Hamburg Marathon in Germany, also held on Sunday morning, runners wore "Run for Boston" wristbands and observed a pre-start silence. I heard from friends in Vancouver that many of the 48,000 people in the Vancouver Sun Run wore Boston blue and yellow, and made donations to the Boston fund. The race director of the Melbourne Marathon in Australia emailed to thank me for my week's writing about Boston, and to say "at our race later this year we plan to show our support for Boston and keep promoting the positive aspect that running brings to so many people in all walks of life." No doubt many more races will show the global nature of the support.

Nothing can alleviate the tragedy or justify the evil that was done. But it has had the unexpected consequence of making running more aware than ever before of its own extraordinary resilience, and the strength and loyalty of its international community.

I pressed "send." I slept the few remaining miles to Ross-on-Wye.

20

April 21, 2014, Boston

Running Makes History: The Race of Redemption

> And this time next year, on the third Monday in April, the world will
> return to this great American city to run harder than ever, and to cheer
> even louder, for the 118th Boston Marathon. (Applause.) Bet on it.
> —President Barack Obama, Interfaith Memorial
> Service, April 18, 2013

The year after the bombings, everyone wanted to return to Boston to run,
to cheer, or in some way be part of that year's marathon. It was going to be
redemption, affirmation, catharsis, closure, healing, defiance—a race more
laden with meanings than any race in history, a race historic before it even
happened.

If you're skeptical about the theme of this book, the potential intersection of running with history, you must have been some place other than
Boston on April 21, 2014. As Boston Athletic Association President Joann
Flamineo said, "There are moments when this race gets elevated beyond
sport."

For the *Runner's World* website coverage, I was allocated the men's race.
The plum assignment from the American viewpoint looked to be the
women's race, with Shalane Flanagan a strong candidate for the outright
win, one that would have made her an instant legend. It turned out otherwise, something no one predicted.

Sometimes being a writer is a privilege. Sometimes for a writer, just as for
a runner, there is a special challenge to rise to. I opened with this paragraph:

27. Meb Keflezighi makes history with the perfect race of redemption, Boston Marathon, 2014. Fay Foto. Courtesy of Boston Athletic Association.

Meb Keflezighi gave Boston and America the victory the whole country longed for, but scarcely dreamed hope for, in the most emotional and significant of all 118 Boston Marathons. He did it with a courage and determination that the nation can be proud of. If Boston and America were to find healing from last year's horrific finish-line attack, there could be no better resolution than by an American winning this Boston Marathon (in 2:08:37). Boston today was a field of dreams.

I then chose to do what I was pretty sure no other writer would: write about the tactics, the technique, the drama, and what was happening inside the minds of the contestants. Symbolic victories in sport don't happen because the rest of us are craving a symbol. They come because someone has done the work and delivers at top level. And this time, to be frank, it happened because other elite runners failed to produce their best on the day. I pulled no punches about how feebly the star-studded field performed when they let Keflezighi get away.

What was happening? Very little, it emerged. This pack of five sub-2:05 men, seven sub-2:06s, this phalanx of highly-paid professionals with 14 major marathon victories among them, couldn't find one with the initiative or the racing instinct to start the chase. I suppose they figured a guy who came into the race ranked 16th on fastest times, and who won his Olympic silver medal when most of them were in high school (2004) wasn't to be taken seriously.

The break stretched at thirty kilometers to 1:20, and still the chase didn't begin. Of five highly touted Ethiopians, only one finished. That mass failure, whatever its cause, was puzzling, but doesn't detract from the deep resolve and impeccable judgment of Keflezighi's performance. That's where I wanted to put the emphasis of my report.

I kept on timing the gap to Chebet. It was a silent drama: 17 seconds, 14 seconds, 12 seconds, 9 seconds, 8 seconds, 7 seconds, 6.8 seconds, 8 seconds, 8 seconds, 8 seconds. . . . He was holding! Chebet was suffering. Starting the real pursuit so late, and alone, he chased so hard that he ran the 23rd mile in 4:31, we learned later. That's brilliant running, but it cost him. At 25 miles, you could see him struggling on a small uphill. Chepkwony was making little impact. Keflezighi was going to do it!—if he could hang on.

Around the final corner into Boylston Street, he crossed himself, and committed to the last minutes of unrelenting effort. Whatever we say about the dream script, and however we feel about the emotion of this most timely American victory, this was above all a runner show-ing how a runner can get the best from himself. To put it simply, on a course where the first half is notoriously faster than the second, he ran a six-second negative split, impeccable pace-judgment. He used every downhill, he cut every tangent. However many strides this marathon took him, Meb never put a foot wrong.

So running reclaimed its own most historic marathon. It wasn't done by hype or flags or swelling movie music, but by good, hard, skillful running. The bombing had rebranded our iconic marathon as a disaster location, a pretext for exploitation, and a setting for violence-complicit Hollywood feature movies or shallow emotive books. Meb's 2014 victory brought such perfect resolution because it helped us reclaim it as a footrace. From my own inbox over those days I can affirm that the level of interest among the global running community was unprecedented. All were ecstatic about Meb, whom I called "the ultimate runner's runner."

The resolution on the grander scale was also positive. The sport of running, so vastly transformed from how it was at London in 1948 or Ber-lin in 1990 or even Boston in 1996, had to take stock and reflect on its new identity. The Boston bombing, even more violently than Superstorm Sandy six months before, showed the responsibility and risk that go with our sport's size, social importance, and media visibility. Again, we had to grow up a little, accept that our zest and beneficence may sometimes provoke hostility, that our prominence may get exploited, and that we will need measures to protect ourselves. Again, we had to absorb the new real-ity that our importance brings responsibility to use it well.

But the bombings did not traumatize, terrorize, or diminish running. Quite the reverse. There's a streak of defiance in every runner, and at

Boston in 2014 it came to the surface. The attack only made runners feel more stubborn than ever about continuing with our strange preoccupation. We feel more closely bonded with each other, and more valued by society. And we know that our sport's survival has a larger significance.

"We have not let evil overcome goodness" is how Boston's usually pragmatic race director Dave McGillivray expressed it. From Obama's eloquence to countless sermons, blogs, and editorials, marathon running became the metaphor du jour for affirming our society's resilience, its adherence to principles of freedom and community, and the generosity and courage that unite us at times of difficulty.

Perhaps the selfie-obsessed "me, me, me" of today's society reverted to something more like "the concept of sacrifice for a larger idea than one's own self-improvement," as Tom Derderian wrote in *New England Runner* (May/June 2014).

Keflezighi at the time had no doubt of the symbolic significance of the 2014 Boston Marathon, nor the special meanings that an American victory would carry. He later revealed that he had sent a prerace text message to the other top American, Ryan Hall, wishing him well, and urging that one or other of them should win, "for USA." He ran with the names of the victims of the 2013 bombings written on his bib. And throughout the race, he revealed, he was chanting inwardly, "Boston strong, USA strong, Meb strong."

Keflezighi's win was the perfect image in another historically important way, which I didn't have space for in the immediate postrace report. I have touched on it in chapter 10. As I finish this book, immigration has become a major issue worldwide, with millions desperately seeking opportunity or safety, received often with fear and subjected to fomented hatred. Keflezighi's historic win reads as a defiant riposte. A refugee, he is a member of a large immigrant family that has already achieved at high level in education and the professions, making huge contributions to American society. He sometimes jokes that because of his running, he is the only sibling out of ten without a higher degree. That personal narrative makes him one of millions in history who arrived with nothing and went on to live their lives as a positive, creative response to the country that accepted them. Nothing could be a better counterbalance to the negative, destructive response from those less typical immigrants, the Tsarnaev brothers. In that, too, Meb's win was the perfect ending.

Meb can also represent the many people from every kind of modest background (Zátopek, Bikila, Edelen, Clayton, Khannouchi, Tulu, Loroupe, Kebede) whose lives find opportunity, significance, and community through running, not least the thousands of women in many countries who have been brought from the domestic fringes into an admired role in this remarkable sport.

Again, a little perspective. Two thousand five hundred years ago, the Greek poet Pindar celebrated a long-distance running champion who had been forced by civil war to leave his native island of Crete. Pindar's poem might have been addressed to many of the runners today who live and race in America or elsewhere because of strife in their countries of origin, usually Africa. It could be a poem of tribute for Meb Keflezighi.

> Great runner, four times victor at the Games,
> but for a war you would have known no fame.
> Though exiled from the bubbling springs of home,
> your swift pace made a new land's fields your own.
>
> —Pindar, Odes, Olympian XII, 470 BC,
> translated by author

21

July 27, 29, 1989, Eugene, Oregon; October 2, 2016, Syracuse, New York

The Fire of Youth under the Creases of Age

As always, I started cautiously and began to work through the pack as we approached the one-mile marker. Bobbing ahead I could see twenty or thirty big number 40s and 45s, the age-group indicator we all wore high on the back of our shirts. All good. It was 50 I was anxiously looking for. At World Masters Championships, especially your first year in the age group, you never know who will come out of the woodwork. In training in Northern Virginia that hot, humid summer, I conjured up a fictitious Japanese runner whom I named Toshi. Toshi had just turned fifty and was a fast, fanatical trainer who used to move alongside and challenge me (all in imagination) in the last mile of every session, to make sure I dug deep.

No Toshi. No Steve James, whose only too real name I had seen on the start list with a jolt of fear, because he had been the Oxford superstar in my first university year when I couldn't even make the Cambridge B team. Amid the bouncing, crowded pack ahead, I saw no 50s, though I couldn't yet be sure. Maybe I'd be able to save something for the track 10,000 m.

Then a glimpse! On a slight up slope at about the mile, there, close to the front: 50. Did I? Yes, there it is again, in the thick of the front pack of 40s and 45s. A green singlet; 50, for sure this time. Oh damn. I've got a real race. But for a world title, it should be.

I tracked him, hoping he'd gone out too fast, waiting for him to slow, not wanting him to know I was there. As I worked past more 40s and 45s, I saw him clearly. I saw nothing else. Don't ask me to describe the Eugene

28. Roger Robinson leads Jim McNamara early in the 10,000 m, World Masters Championships, 1989.

scenery. Only two things filled my consciousness: that green singlet and the course, every tweak and turn and rise and fall of the road, to ensure I made the best use of every foot of the 10K we were racing over.

On the third mile, I edged carefully closer. Irish, surely, with that green singlet over such pale skin. Lean, light haired, angular, a little taller than me, slightly stooped, with the flowing, springy stride of a runner who knows what he's about. Running strong. I was ten yards back and I hoped invisible, but in line we worked through all but the best 40s. A lot was going to depend on that first mile, which he'd run ten seconds faster than I did. Would that be his fatal error?

At three miles, I found myself closing. Was he slowing? We passed five kilometers, but I missed the time, focused so intently on my pace and position, and his. I came alongside, paused, then let him see the 50 on my back, a nasty surprise, a worm to eat into the core of his confidence. Then I waited for the moment.

"How do you decide the moment to make the break?" people used to ask me, because I always had to be a tactical racer, having no finishing sprint. "I smell it," I would say. Boxers and fencers watch each other's eyes, wolves look for the limp that identifies the likeliest victim, but runners race side by side, and you must go by some sense of your opponent's weakness at the very edge of your peripheral vision. It comes from instinct, or experience.

It was a bit before four miles that I caught a whiff of doubt. On a longish uphill, he slipped back, only a few inches, but enough. You always know. I held that tiny lead for a long minute. Racing, I have often said, requires ice-cold judgment combined with blazing hot passion. When you wait like that, there's a buildup of potential energy. You're near full stretch but the battery is recharging. At every stride, the mind is assessing how you feel and how he looks. Then you sense (or smell) the moment. Now, get the gap, build it, build it, hold your pace at crest, never toppling over into oxygen debt, screw your courage to the sticking place and keep it there through the last mile to the finish (32:13, an over-fifty world championship record).

We spoke only briefly after the race. There were other races to come. He was Jim McNamara. We had raced before, though neither of us knew it, when he placed forty-ninth for Ireland and I was sixty-seventh for England in the 1966 International Cross-Country Championship in Rabat, Morocco. A nice thought that all the big guns from 1966—El Ghazi, Michel Jazy and Tracy Smith, Ron Hill and Roy Fowler—were retired or no longer able to compete, not at top age-group level, and it was McNamara and Robinson from obscurely back in the Rabat field who this time had just gone head to head for a world title. The tortoise and the hare fable has always been a favorite.

Three days later at those World Masters Championships in Eugene, we raced again. It was the track 10,000 m, and we set a full stand at Hayward Field screaming with a duel people still talk about. That time the race was for fifty-plus age-group runners only, so we were out front, clear of the field after four laps. Jim read it right. He sat on me. I'd met my match in cunning as well as speed. I pressed and surged, kept the rhythm high, did all I knew to draw his sting, but he held on. A long attack on (I think) the fourth mile didn't work. One last feint and surge nearly dropped him on lap 23, but this time he wasn't going to be broken. It was simple, like Chataway sticking to Kuts. He picked his spot and sprinted away. I was born with no fast-twitch fibers. He killed me. He ran 32:13, exactly the time I'd run on the road.

So, honors were shared and we were both happy that way. It's strange how you bond after two races like that: strangers pushing each other to the very edge of the will, learning each other's innermost character. I soon realized that Jim was a warm, sincere, and modest man. Quietly, we shared the life stories of persistent grafters, modestly talented but never outstanding ("I was almost good," I told Jonathan Beverly for his book about lifetime competitors, *Run Strong, Stay Hungry* [2017]), yet who both loved running and racing too much ever to feel it was time to stop. There in Eugene, age fifty, each with a gold and a silver medal, we quietly shared the feeling that our long, patient years of work were rewarded. We didn't talk together about our plans for the rest of the week, but it emerged that somehow, we had each concluded that those two races were enough. When he won the track 5,000 m I sat with the Irish team and cheered for Jim loudest of them all. He became an honorary Kiwi the day I won the cross-country.

We never met again. We exchanged a few letters (he didn't ever get into email) and when he died in 2016, I felt I'd lost a dear friend, however briefly we'd known each other. He had kept racing well, setting many Irish age-group records, and even racing for Ireland in a masters international cross-country after he knew he had cancer. He was a much-loved coach with his lifelong club, Donore Harriers. His death left many Irish runners "heartbroken," one emailed to me.

"I saw an article you wrote about running competitively in your 70s. Jim was the same. He was still competitive and wanted to get a few more Irish records," wrote Florence Curley of Donore Harriers. "Gentleman Jim" they called him, a man of special quality and gentleness, and I would endorse that except for one ungentle moment when he slammed past me on the last lap of the 10,000 m in Eugene in 1989.

Jim McNamara and I didn't exactly make history, but there are reasons for lingering over those races. Running is extraordinary in the way it gives solitary pleasure ("a lonely impulse of delight," to choose an Irish poet in Jim's honor) yet also forges some of the closest and most respectful friendships you will ever know. That's relevant to the upsurge in running among older people over the last four decades. We value solitude. We value friendship.

Historically, our two races in Eugene in 1989 were a key part of a World Masters Championship track meet that was a key part of the burgeoning masters movement that has, beyond question, changed history in its effect on medical and social attitudes to the capabilities of older people. (For the main progression of masters running, see appendix C.) To put the transformation perhaps oversimply, I think that Eugene was the first masters sports event where there was not a single moment of ageist condescension. The competitors, the spectators, the officials, the announcers, and the media treated every race in every age group as a top-level international sporting competition, period. Women and para-athletes have gone through the same process of earning respect unqualified by the "oh, wow, that's incredible at that age" (or "for a woman") mindset that dominated public perception of masters events in the 1970s. Coverage in those early days always focused on the tumbles over hurdles, the pathetic pole vault failures, the six-inch long jumps, the back of the pack shufflers, the competitors carried off on stretchers, and anything that confirmed the deeply engrained human view that old people venturing into extreme physical effort are only embarrassing. One of the earliest articles to refute that and treat aging positively was my "Running through the Mid-Life Crisis" in *Heroes and Sparrows* (1986), though previously in the *New Zealand Runner* (1984) and later reprinted in *Runner's World.*

"The pleasures and rewards of running are immeasurably greater for me at 46 than they were at 16 or 26. . . . We are looking at a social movement whose contribution to community health, improved lifestyle, and changing values will be one of the crucial cultural developments of the late 20th century" (Robinson 2011, 204, 208). I got that right.

I knew perceptions were changing the year I was running top fifty at age fifty at the New York City Marathon, and I heard a guy in the crowd in Central Park call out in astonished approval, "Hey! There goes an *old* guy!"

I enthused about Eugene 1989 in an article titled "How the Olympics Ought to Be" in *New Zealand Runner.* Hal Higdon wrote an equally positive piece for *Runner's World.* "Catch them at a distance, watch the legs without looking at the ageing face, and you could believe every time that these were champions in their prime," I wrote (Robinson 1989, 36). That made Eugene an early marker in a transformational process that led, among much else, to representations like the 2017 BBC documentary "The Pacemakers," which takes a group of over-ninety 100 m runners as they prepare and compete for their world age-group title and treats their striving to win as seriously as if they were the contenders for the Olympic gold medal. That's a big change in social attitudes, and running led it.

That's why I started this chapter with my races against Jim McNamara. At fifty, we were running the 10K about two minutes slower than we did in our prime, but it didn't feel any slower, nor was the race any less intense. The physical and psychological commitment were total. In 2015–17, one of my main topics as writer and speaker became the right (you must use that word) of older people to push themselves hard physically. Race after race, people would show concern that I ran so hard—kindly intended concern, but nevertheless revealing a deep prejudice. Moderation, caution, they urged. Just have fun. That's ageism, and it's rampant.

"If anyone tut-tuts that a man of my age should not risk such intensity of physical effort, well, prove it. Why not?" I wrote in *Running Times*.

The prevailing belief has always been that older people who push themselves physically risk their health and look unseemly. Guillaume Depping's (1871) *Wonders of Bodily Strength and Skill* complains that it is "embarrassing" to see frail, elderly men even try to run, especially in front of spectators. There's a painful scene in Fanny Burney's novel *Evelina* (1778) where some arrogant gambling gents set up a race between two old women, "more than eighty years of age," who "hobble, stumble, and fall." The change from that to Libby James (see the end of this chapter) is the one I'm celebrating. No longer is the senile and ranting King Lear the image of old age. These days he'd be up on the heath because he's training for the London Marathon.

There are still prejudices to overcome. You risk your health, and it looks unseemly, we older runners are still told, even by implication. Well, that's exactly what society told women sixty years ago. Personally, running hard to the edge of distress is what I've done since I was thirteen, and I like it, or the way it earns the satisfaction of knowing I extended my body to its best possible performance. I believe that far from placing myself in danger of heart attack, I'm in fact giving myself the best possible protection against it. I can't prove that, and may be wrong, but neither is there any proof of how, exactly, older people who run hard are supposed to be damaging themselves.

The scientific research into exercise in later life points compellingly in the opposite direction, not only in longevity and life quality in general but in the reduction of joint disability and the effects of chronic conditions. It's running hard that best arrests the decline in muscle mass and strength (Wroblewski et al. 2011). The sports medicine profession has swung entirely behind the mantra "exercise is medicine."

For an eyewitness race showing historic change by older runners, my obvious choice in celebrity terms would have been one of the several occasions I raced or watched or was co-speaker with the legendary Ed Whitlock, the extraordinary Canadian who ran a 2:54:49 marathon at age seventy-three and a 3:15:54 marathon at age eighty, and thus redefined what is possible at top level at that age. But by being so extraordinary, so legendary, so inexplicably different, and by breaking records by an hour, Ed somehow confirmed the sense that there are norms, and that he was abnormal. I confess that I once subscribed to that by publishing my theory that Ed's mother had been abducted nine months before his birth by emaciated-looking beings with white hair in a flying saucer from a planet where there is no aging.

Whitlock was one of the most remarkable legends of the entire history of running, and of the human race. However genetically extraordinary he was, his performances were the most prominent in a process that has transformed notions of what is possible physically in the years after seventy. They received wide publicity, partly because they were so far off the charts, partly from astute promotion by Alan Brookes of the Scotiabank Toronto Waterfront Marathon, who also made a global figure of the reputedly one-hundred-year-old Fauja Singh. This was the first time such old runners had been publicized as promotional celebrities, not as stars of the past, but as current elite competitors.

The first famously "fast old man" was probably the English/South African/Rhodesian breaker of ultra-run records in the 1920s and 1930s, Arthur Newton. English-born New Zealander Jack Foster ran at Olympic and world championship level into his forties in the 1970s, and he was succeeded in the public imagination by an older New Zealander, sheep farmer Derek Turnbull, who smashed all the over-sixty and over-seventy records. Joyce Smith and Priscilla Welch, both British, matched Foster in competing at top level into their forties. Welch defiantly won the New York City Marathon at age forty-two in 1987 when Fred Lebow declined on grounds of age to give her an elite invitation. Carlos Lopes won the Olympic marathon at thirty-seven. A dour Dutchman and major figure in Europe, Piet van Alphen, was the first to transform over-fifty standards, followed by two clerical Americans, Norm Green and Marion Irvine, who had the added appeal that Green was a Baptist minister and Irvine a Dominican nun and school principal (the first nun to appear in national magazines in singlet and shorts). Ted Corbitt, who in 1952 was the first African-American to represent the United States in the Olympic marathon, kept adding to his already legendary status as "the father of American long-distance running" by his 200-mile training weeks and high placings in ultra-distance races through his sixties and seventies, with his last race being a twenty-four-hour event in 2003 in which he totaled sixty-eight miles at age eighty-four.

All these achieved media and public reputations beyond running, and, partly by their sheer human variety, inspired many older people to try a sport once thought the preserve of the young. All lived up to my favorite description of older runners, from nearly two hundred years ago: "How good it is to see runners who look like a beautiful day in winter . . . who have kept the fire of youth under the creases of age" (translated from *Les Modes et les Costumes Provençales*, anonymous, c. 1850).

Millions of older runners want to run only for health and pleasure, but I hold to the belief that competition has its place for those who choose it, at whatever age. The ancient Greeks believed that through competition, humans can aspire most closely to the gods. Their word for competition was "agon," from which we take "agony," our word for extreme pain and for participation, as "protagonists." In that view of life, it's not just being there that matters, but contesting, striving to achieve your best possible.

If you prefer a Christian text, John Milton famously affirmed that the only way to attain the immortal garland of virtue is to line up in the race, face the competition, and commit to the very limit with whatever effort it takes. "I cannot praise a fugitive and cloistered virtue, unexercised and unbreathed, that never sallies out and sees her adversary, but slinks out of the race, where that immortal garland is to be run for not without dust and heat" (John Milton, *Areopagitica*, 1644; see Robinson 2003, 74–75).

In the early chapters of this book, I've described how the world was during my childhood and youth: one urgently in need of improvement, one that demanded and rewarded a rigorous commitment. That's probably why I still get my greatest fun from what I have called the "arduous joy" of competition; and through that I also find the deepest friendships with those I compete against. As an old runner, I want races that still feel like racing did when I was in my twenties, that make the same demands on preparation, judgment, and execution. I don't want my running to be a variant on line dancing.

I once heard the leading authority on the theory of leisure, John R. Kelly, explain that the most important thing in activities for the old is to avoid "violation of the continuity of the self." As we move up in years, Kelly said, we never identify as "old person," whatever younger people may think they see, but as the same person we have always been, grown somewhat older. Therefore, the best activities we can choose are those that respect that continuity. This whole book is in one way my tribute to the insight I gained that day from Kelly, its narratives showing that the seventy-eight-year-old author of this chapter is the same narrator and the same thinker as the nine-year-old who watched Emil Zátopek in 1948.

I have some nine-year-old weaknesses, too. I'm doomed to be remembered in our sound-bite culture for what has become my best-known line, which even made *Readers' Digest* as well as numerous books of running quotes. I was being skeptical about the "listen to your body" mantra.

"If I listened to my body, I'd live off toffee-pops and vintage port" (*New Zealand Runner*, October 1987, 16).

There's not much literature yet on older runners, apart from some helpful how-to articles. There's a market for those. I once helped my friends Bruce and Sue Tulloh (2001) sell their *Running Over Forty* book at the London Marathon expo, and Bruce had to keep scrambling up on the desk with a felt pen to write in "and over fifty," "and over sixty," etc., on the poster to lure the many interested buyers of those ages. Whitlock sadly wrote no book. For three fascinating and different old runner stories, try Vince Boyle's (2006) life of Derek Turnbull, *The Fastest Old Man in the World*, Betty Jean McHugh and Bob Nixon's (2011) *My Road to Rome*, and *Expressions of Aging* by the fascinating actor-runner John Keston and Richard A. Lovett (2011).

Lacking books, here's a personal story. In my later years, I've conducted an interesting experiment on myself and some contemporary friends who asked me to advise them, John Barrington in New Zealand and Norman Goluskin and Dennis Moore in New Paltz, New York. We all had competitive aspirations, despite being seventy or thereabouts. I put us all on variants of my well-tried structure of a slow buildup followed by a progressive mix of long runs and long and short intervals (repeats), designed to achieve my "quantity of quality" goal (if you'll be racing for forty minutes, you need to have totaled forty minutes' quality in training).

The concession I made for us being old was to require more recovery: two or three light days between hard sessions, and longer jog time between the repeats. I wrote about Norman, "he could do a 25-year-old's training because he got a 70-year-old's recovery." The file where I kept my notes on his progress was titled "Norman Conquest."

In each case, it worked. John placed third over-seventy at the New York City Marathon, Dennis progressed in three years from a sixty-seven-year-old beginner who had only jogged one mile with Radar the dog to a Boston qualifier and over-seventy winner at the Goodlife Fitness Toronto Marathon, and Norman reached what he described as "the best shape for a race of my whole life," even though ill-timed Lyme disease deprived him of the World Masters Championship medals he should have won. And I proved that it is possible to start running again at seventy-five after five years off, with one partial knee replacement, and in three years win US age-group championship races at 5K and 10K and attain PKRPRs (that's post-knee replacement personal records) of 22:16 5K, 47:38 10K, and 1:46:57 half-marathon. Next challenge: another comeback, this time with a total replacement on the other knee.

I'm aware that we all owe much of this to modern medical science and surgeons' skill, which eliminate things that in the past would have finished us off, or made us doddery. In an earlier generation, I would have spent my seventies in a wheelchair, not racing on the roads. Was it hard to come back? My weeks began to total more than eight hours of running and included intense intervals or repeats. Dennis and Norman accuse me of carrying a whip. But did we "have fun"? Few things in life have been so enjoyable, or so rewarding. The one absolute guarantee of feeling positive about your own aging is to be improving at something. It's even better when shared with friends. Those three years were an unexpected but profoundly enriching late-life bonus.

"It's not often in this life you can enjoy the dawn at twilight," I wrote.

My other great stroke of good fortune as a runner was that I turned forty in 1979, the very moment masters running developed. A set of new opportunities gave me once again a close-up view on history as it happened. Races like Hospital Hill Run in 1980 (chapter 8) began to give awards (not yet money) to over-forty masters. I went to the United Kingdom to win my first British masters title (5,000 m track) and the World Masters Championship, 10K road, in Scotland, only the fourth time it had been contested. I returned to America to run the Virginia Ten Miler, one of the first big road races to define itself as a lot of races within one race. They put a guy on a bike with a flag alongside the leading master, as well as the first woman. Then I won two races in Hal Higdon's Brooks Masters series, another innovation and the first time a sponsor had seen the potential in masters running. I wrapped up my year of masters marvels with my debut marathon, 2:22:15 at New York City, winning the new masters division and a lovely silver bowl engraved to my perpetual delight: "New York City Marathon, 1980—1st." Sorry, Alberto.

Runner's World selected me as number one for that season, the first time they had assessed rankings for masters. All these opportunities were new. So was the hugely successful World Masters Track and Field Championships in Christchurch, New Zealand, in January 1981, only the fourth for that rapidly expanding event, yet suddenly the biggest adult track meet in history at that date. I won a gold and a bronze, and I was outsprinted in a close and tactical 5,000 m by three runners who embody the international reach of masters championships in that early era: Michael Connolly of

Ireland, Trevor Vincent of Australia, and Renato Da Palmas of Italy, with South Americans and Japanese also in the field.

Thanks to the development of masters, I became a frontline participant in the running boom. At thirty-four, I'd semi-gracefully morphed into an official, as older runners traditionally had always done; stadium announcer, in my case. At forty, with defiant delight, I was morphing back again, back to being an athlete, more competitive than ever, and with greater incentives: world-level competition, travel, even some financial support. With those incentives, many others kept on racing. That generation of masters has never been surpassed. During the 1980s, in addition to those mentioned above, Joan Ullyot, Diana Palmason, Evy Palm, Antonio Villanueva, Gunther Mielke, Ron Hill, Taf Davies, Pierre Voets, Derek Fernée, Herb Lorenz, Fritz Mueller, Bruce Mortensen, Dave Sirl, Ron Robertson, Shirley Matson, Ruth Anderson, John Gilmour, Clive Davies, John A. Kelley, Ed Benham, and Ruth Rottfarb all redefined what aging means. It was an exciting era to be part of.

More recent feats by older runners, apart from Whitlock, include Eamonn Coghlan as the first man over forty to run a sub-four-minute mile (1994), Constantina Diță, who at age thirty-eight became the oldest runner ever to win the Olympic marathon (2008), Deena Kastor, who sustained a stellar career that started at high school to set world and American masters records after turning forty, and Meb Keflezighi, who was two weeks away from his thirty-ninth birthday when he won Boston so heroically (2014, chapter 20) and has kept racing at elite level into his forties.

Through forty years of such role models, and merely by giving older runners a significant place, running has been a leader in a profoundly important process of change in social attitude to aging. We're still in the early stages. A recent development in novels and movies is a willingness to represent older characters and build the narrative on a new awareness that older people's lives are still in active process, following them as they confront challenges, forge or renew significant relationships, deal with emotions, reaffirm their sense of identity, or learn new forms of self-expression and achievement. Masters running was way ahead on all those.

29. Libby James, age eighty, makes history at the US Masters
5K Championships, 2016. Courtesy of Gavin Liddell/Syra-
cuse Festival of Races.

Let me finish with a recent experience. In October 2016, I won the
over-seventy-five race in the USA Masters 5K Championship at the Festival of Races in Syracuse, New York. After collecting a dry top, I went
back to watch the women's race finish. True to the theme of this book, I
found myself witness to history: Kathryn Martin of Northport, New York,
became the first sixty-five-year-old woman anywhere in the world to run

faster than twenty minutes for 5K (19:57). Even more transformational, Libby James of Fort Collins, Colorado, ran 25:11, at age eighty. That's the best at that age by more than three minutes, a breakthrough on a Whitlockian scale. I watched Libby walk away from the finish line with the spring and verve of a teenager stepping onto the dance floor.

The significance of such a performance goes beyond the statistics of sport. It recalibrates human potential. It should transform how society perceives old age. It confirms that when I was eight, I was right, as I wrote in closing the introduction to this book, that a race can mean more than just a race. It can show that human beings are still capable of attaining pure beauty through arduous endeavor. It can revive the spirit of that wonderful image of old runners as "a sunny day in winter." I thought of the two stumbling, over-eighty women and the jeering young men in the sad scene in Fanny Burney's novel, and how that has been the prevailing image of old age through most of human history. Libby and Ed have overturned centuries of stereotyping.

Once more, I thought, in yet one more way, the sport I discovered at age eight is making history.

Appendixes

Bibliography

Index

Timeline 1: The Running Boom, 1960–1982

1960   Abebe Bikila's barefoot world record victory in the Olympic marathon in Rome catches the world's imagination.

1961   Mihály Iglói, a refugee from communist Hungary and a brilliant coach, establishes a distance running "school" at the Los Angeles Track Club, introducing European interval-training methods.
Le Cross du Figaro is created in Paris; open to many categories, it is the first popular "fun run."
More than 600 road races are held in the United States, as reported by Road Runners Club of America (RRCA, founded 1958).

1962   Auckland Joggers Club is founded in New Zealand by Arthur Lydiard and Colin Kay.
The Auckland Marathon (founded 1959) is the first race known to secure a commercial title sponsor, other than a sports newspaper.
Lydiard's *Run to the Top* is published, becoming internationally influential on training methods.

1963–65   The world marathon record (officially, still "world best performance") is broken in three successive years in England's Polytechnic Marathon (Windsor to Chiswick) by runners from the United States, Britain, and Japan.
Entries steeply increase in all road and cross-country races in the United Kingdom and Europe, and in marathons in Japan.

1963   Buddy Edelen is precursor of the American upsurge in distance running when he sets a world marathon best at the Polytechnic Marathon.
Merry Lepper and Lyn Carman defy officials to run the Western Hemisphere Marathon in California.

Hal Higdon publishes "On the Run from Dogs and People" in *Sports Illustrated*, expressing the appeal of running to nonelite runners.

1964   Dale Greig officially runs the Isle of Wight Marathon in 3:27:45.
Seoul's Dong-A race, established in 1931, becomes a full marathon.
Bill Bowerman and Phil Knight found Blue Ribbon Sports in Oregon and begin selling running shoes.
Fred Wilt's *Run Run Run*, with contributions by major coaches like Arthur Lydiard and runners like Vladimir Kuts, adds to Iglói's work in bringing international knowledge to American runners.
At the Tokyo Olympics in October, Billy Mills wins the 10,000 m and Bob Schul the 5,000 m, the first Americans to win long-distance gold medals since Johnny Hayes in 1908, and still the only Americans to win those events. A generation of American boys is inspired.
America's first "fun runs" are founded by RRCA to implement its national "Run for Your Life" campaign.

1965   The first new-wave marathons are founded: Harlow in the United Kingdom and Hamilton and Rotorua in New Zealand. Tourist-center Rotorua will become a "destination" marathon.
Run for Your Life by Arthur Lydiard and Garth Gilmour publicizes jogging for health.

1966   Having visited Lydiard, Bill Bowerman (with Dr. W. E. Harris) publishes *Jogging*. More than a million copies are sold.
Boston Marathon entries top 500 for the first time.
Roberta Gibb unofficially runs the Boston Marathon.
Bob Anderson starts *Distance Running News*.

1967   Kathrine Switzer, wearing a bib number, is attacked by an official during the Boston Marathon.
At Japan's Fukuoka Marathon, now "International Marathon Championship," Derek Clayton (Australia) runs the first sub 2:10 world record.

1968   Kenneth Cooper publishes the first version of *Aerobics*, merging with Lydiard and Bowerman to create a mass cult of fitness, especially in America, with running at the center.
IGAL (Association of Older Long-Distance Runners) is founded in Germany and holds the first masters marathon championship (in Holland).

1969   Browning Ross's magazine *Long Distance Log* receives support from
        United States Track and Field Federation.
        Boston Marathon tops 1,000 starters.

1970   The New York City Marathon, Seattle Marathon, and Peachtree 10K
        Road Race (Atlanta, Georgia) are founded.
        Distance Running News, now bimonthly and with 3,000 subscribers,
        becomes *Runner's World* with Joe Henderson as editor.

1971   Alan Jones in Vestal, New York, devises a way of measuring courses,
        hiring his nine-year-old son Clain to help make the bicycle-mounted
        gadget. The "Clain Jones Counter" makes road courses accurate for
        the first time.
        Bill Bowerman messes with his wife's waffle iron to design the first
        "waffle" shoes. They are made and marketed by Blue Ribbon Sports.
        Adrienne Beames in Australia runs 2:46:30, the first sub-three
        marathon by a woman.
        At the Boston Marathon, Harry Cordellos becomes the first blind
        marathoner.
        Chris Brasher, Olympic gold medalist and sports journalist, opens a
        sports store with an emphasis on running in Teddington, England,
        that becomes The Sweatshop, a major franchise.

1972   Frank Shorter wins the Olympic marathon in Munich.
        New marathons are founded in Portland, Oregon, and Vancouver.
        Athens Classic Marathon is founded, partly by the Greek Tourist
        Board, the first marathon conceived as incentive for international
        destination tourism.
        Boston Marathon accepts women as official entrants.
        New York Mini 6 mi. (now 10K) is founded, the world's first open
        women's-only road race. It is sponsored by "Crazylegs" women's
        shaving cream, the first road race sponsorship in America other than
        by newspapers.
        Auckland Joggers Club founds Round the Bays, the first so-named
        "fun run."
        Spiridon, a French-language running magazine, is founded in
        Switzerland by Noel Tamini with the mission of "democratizing"
        running for women as well as men.
        Bob Schul, Olympic 5,000 m winner in 1964, opens a sports store.

1973   Honolulu Marathon founded. Entries will double every year, and it becomes the major destination marathon for the Pacific Coast and Japan.

Cherry Blossom Ten Miler founded in Washington, DC, and the Falmouth Road Race (7.3 mi.) on Cape Cod.

World's first women's marathon organized in Waldniel, Germany, by Dr. Ernst van Aaken.

Olympian Jeff Galloway founds Phidippides as a specialist community running shoe store.

1974   Virginia Ten Miler (Lynchburg), Hospital Hill Run (Kansas City), and the Berlin and Christchurch (New Zealand) Marathons are founded.

Ernst van Aaken and Manfred Steffny found the German edition of *Spiridon* magazine.

Jim Davis founds MarathonFoto, creating the running photography business.

1975   Marine Corps and Amsterdam Marathons are founded.

George Sheehan's first book, *Dr. Sheehan on Running*, is published. Sheehan, with his homey eloquence, becomes the best-known speaker on the new circuit of prerace lectures and panels.

1976   New York City Marathon celebrates America's bicentenary with a new course, passing through all five boroughs. This is the first "city marathon" of the new movement. Entries leap to more than 2,000. Bill Rodgers and Michiko Gorman win, becoming new marathon heroes.

The Liberty Torch Relay also celebrates the bicentenary, with thirty-three runners covering nearly 9,000 miles through fifty states; it is a precursor to the Sri Chinmoy runs and relays founded in 1977.

Paris Marathon is founded.

1977   New York City Marathon doubles entries to 4,823 starters, the biggest footrace in history.

Chicago, Grandma's, and Toronto Marathons founded.

Lilac Bloomsday and Bobby Crim road races founded.

Avon Women's Running circuit founded.

James Fixx's *The Complete Book of Running* gives running a best seller and bible.

Running Times first published.

Sri Chinmoy Marathon Team founded to put on noncompetitive "peace runs," relays, and (from 1985) "Peace Miles" worldwide. Thom Gilligan takes a Boston group to the Honolulu Marathon, creating the destination marathon travel business that eventually becomes Marathon Tours and Travel.

1978   First Avon Women's Marathon, Atlanta.
Utica Boilermaker 15K Road Race founded.
Grete Waitz runs a world record 2:32:30 at the New York Marathon.
First Sunday Times Fun Run in London, which quickly becomes the biggest British version of the "fun run" phenomenon.
Blue Ribbon Sports of Oregon changes its name to Nike Inc.

1979   Tokyo Women's Marathon founded.
Grete Waitz is the first woman to break 2:30 for the marathon, with 2:27:33 in New York.
RRCA establishes the "National Run for Life Day."
RRCA introduces liability insurance for clubs and events in the United States.

1980   The American-led boycott of the Moscow Olympic Games focuses running's energy, and public attention, on the US road circuit.
The Avon Women's Marathon in London has runners from twenty-seven countries.
Dublin Marathon is founded, with 2,100 entries the first year, a record inaugural field.
Terry Fox, age twenty-one, who has lost one leg to cancer, sets out to run a "Marathon of Hope" across Canada to raise money for cancer research. Public acclaim makes this the first major charity run.
Gary Fanelli is the first elite runner to compete in, and win, a road race in full costume, running as "Elwood Blues" (of the Blues Brothers), in Bowmansville, Pennsylvania.

1981   At the Boston Marathon, more than 320 men run faster than 2:30 (the most ever to run this fast). Nearly all are Americans.
In the World Cross-Country Championships, Ethiopia and Kenya compete for the first time. They place first and third teams.
The London Marathon is founded and makes charity fundraising an explicit part of its mission.

Across Canada, the first fundraising Terry Fox Run is held in the hero's memory, respecting his wish that it be a noncompetitive run/walk.

The Beijing and Rotterdam Marathons, and England's Great North Run Half-Marathon, are founded.

City road races become the biggest and most public sporting events of the modern world.

At the New York City Marathon, Alberto Salazar and Allison Roe run world records.

The same 1981 New York City Marathon is broadcast live for the first time on ABC television. Worldwide, in just over two hours of an October morning, road running becomes epic mass entertainment.

In Christchurch, New Zealand, despite distance and cost, the fourth World Masters Championships is the biggest participant adult track and field meet in history.

The International Olympic Committee (IOC) votes to add the women's marathon to the 1984 Olympic Games in Los Angeles. Proposals to end the constraints of compulsory amateurism are put formally before the International Amateur Athletics Federation (IAAF) and are being debated when, two months later in Portland, Oregon, the Cascade Run Off 15K under race director Chuck Galford defiantly awards prize money. Soon the world's best runners can be openly remunerated. The new professions of running agent and manager are created.

1982   Recognizing the emergence of running as an industry, Phil Stewart starts *Road Race Management* newsletter, initially as an offshoot from *Running Times*, establishes an annual race directors' conference, and begins to publish *Road Race Management Guide* (the industry's annual bible). The sport is maturing economically and operationally. The Association of International Marathons (AIMS) is founded, the first attempt at federation for road running outside IAAF, and an important source of guidance and consistency for race organizers. Rome Marathon founded.

Appendix B

Timeline 2: Women's Running, 1896–2017

1896   Stamata Revithi (sometimes inexplicably referred to as Melpomene, name of the Greek muse of tragedy) may have run a version of the Athens Olympic Marathon course, but accounts vary wildly as to whether, when, where, and why she did it. Claims that she was excluded overlook the fact that trials were held for the Greek team on March 10 and 24, 1896, so it would have been unjust to accept her last-minute application (if she made one).

1903   A 12K race for female store assistants from Paris to Nanterre attracts 2,500 runners.

1917   Alice Milliat founds La Fédération Sportive Féminine de France, the first governing body for women's sport.

1918   Marie-Louise Ledru runs a "marathon" in Paris, reported as 5:40, the first documented performance. But at that date there is no certainty, as "marathon" meant any long road race, and France still preferred 40 km as standard for a "marathon race."

1918   The Dipsea Race, founded 1905 on rugged trails in Marin County, California, adds a Dipsea Women's Hike. Although it is a fully timed running race, it is called a "hike" to evade criticism. Fields are larger than for the well-established men's race, but after five years conservative opposition forces its cancellation (Spitz, 1993).

1922   Alice Milliat extends her French federation to become La Fédération Sportive Féminine Internationale and creates the Women's Olympic Games (later retitled Women's Games). This pressures the IOC into including some women's track and field events for the 1928 Games, including the 800 m, though at the last minute they cut the events from ten to five, prompting the British women's team to withdraw in protest.

1923   First national cross-country championship for women is held in France.

1926   Violet Piercy runs what was long accepted as the first world marathon record, supposedly on the Windsor–Chiswick course. In fact, it was a solo run over 22 mi. (35.4 km) on a similar but different route.

1927   England follows France in establishing a women's national cross-country championship.

1928   The women's 800 m is included in the Olympic program, and the first three break the world record. When one Canadian runner falls at the finish, it is widely misreported that "several women collapsed." This calculated fiction incites outrage about women suffering inappropriate, "terrible exhaustion," and gives the IOC a pretext to remove the event. The only Olympic race for women is 100 m until 1948, when 200 m is added.

1931   Gazella Weinreich (age sixteen) attempts to enter a marathon from Laurel to Baltimore, but is excluded by the Amateur Athletic Union (AAU). Later reports suggest she may have run, starting behind the men.
The first international cross-country race for women, Belgium versus England versus France, is run in Douai, France, and won by Gladys Lunn of England.

1933   Piercy runs another "marathon" on an uncertified route from Windsor to London, ending with a theatrical entrance when she runs onto the stage of the Golders Green Hippodrome. Her time for the unspecified distance is recorded as 4:25.

1936   Two women reportedly run the 13 mi. race up Pike's Peak.

1954   Diane Leather (later Charles) is the first woman to run a mile in under five minutes. She runs internationally many times, usually over 880 yd. She also wins the English national cross-country championship five times.

1959   Arlene Pieper completes the full Pike's Peak Marathon, a course with 7,000 ft. elevation change, in 9:16.

1960   The 800 m is reintroduced into the Olympic program.

1961   Julia Chase is the first American woman to finish a road race,
         running the Manchester Thanksgiving Day 5 Miler at 7:10 per mile
         pace. Chris McKenzie and Diane Lechausse also ran.

1963   Merry Lepper and Lyn Carman jump into the Western Hemisphere
         Marathon, Culver City, California. After dodging officials, Lepper
         finishes in 3:37:07, though the course is believed to have been short.
         Judy Mitchell is an accepted entrant in the new Equinox Marathon
         in Alaska. On a very difficult, uncertified course, she runs 7:15:04.
         Women will run this race every year, steadily improving their times.

1964   (May) Dale Greig is accepted as a runner in the Isle of Wight
         Marathon, though she must start ahead of the men. She finishes in
         3:27:25, the first documented world best on a certified course.
         (August) Mildred (Millie) Sampson runs 3:19:33 in the Owairaka
         Marathon in Auckland, New Zealand. Like Leather and Greig,
         Sampson is a well-established track and cross-country runner and
         a several times national champion. She runs against men, strongly
         encouraged by her clubmates.

1965   Road Runners Club of America introduces a women's cross-country
         championship, over 2.5 mi, despite objection from the AAU.

1966   Lyn Carman wins the Santa Barbara Marathon, the first of her three
         victories there.
         Debbie Hayes also wins the first of three, at Alaska's mountainous
         Equinox Marathon, in 5:24:30.
         Roberta (Bobbi) Gibb mails an entry to the Boston Marathon, but
         it is rejected. Hiding in bushes near the start, she joins the field and
         runs 3:21:14, now recognized as an inaugural race record. *Sports
         Illustrated* runs a feature article on Gibb's gate-crashing run.

1967   Kathrine Switzer sends a formal entry to the Boston Marathon,
         as "K. Switzer," and receives bib number 261. At two miles, race
         co-director Jock Semple violently tries to rip off her numbers and
         eject her. He is repulsed by a shoulder charge from her boyfriend.
         Photographers capture the confrontation. Huge publicity ensues for
         women's access to the marathon and other sports. Switzer finishes
         in approximately 4:20 but is suspended from the AAU. Gibb again
         unofficially runs a slightly shortened course, in 3:27:17.

A semi-official women's race is added to the international cross-country championship at Barry, Wales, and is won by Doris Brown (later Heritage) of the United States.

Maureen Wilton, age thirteen, runs a 3:15:22.8 world best marathon in Toronto, Canada, with Switzer also present to make it a genuine women's race.

Anni Pede runs 3:07:26 in a mixed marathon in Waldniel, Germany. She is a protegé of the enlightened Dr. Ernst van Aaken, who advocated that all humans should train for endurance as part of healthy living.

1968–71   Gibb again runs Boston in 1968, and other women run in the years following, the most being five in 1970, when Sara Mae Berman wins for the second of three victories. They agitate for official status.

1970   The Road Runners Club of America holds the first championship marathon for women (September 27), won by Sara Mae Berman.

Two rival international cross-country championships for women are held, one in Maryland, USA (supported mostly by English-speaking teams) and one in Vichy, France.

Nina Kuscsik's entry to the first New York City Marathon is accepted, but she is ill and does not finish.

1971   A special committee is established in San Francisco to discuss long-distance running for women. The AAU women's committee increases the officially permitted distance for women to 10 mi. and provides for "selected" women to run marathons.

The new Triple Cities Runners Club 12-Mile Road Race in Vestal, New York (June 26), states "Women welcome" on its entry form, the first known to have accepted women from the inaugural running.

Four women officially run the New York City Marathon.

Adrienne Beames in Werribee, near Melbourne, Australia, is the first woman to run a marathon under three hours, with 2:46:30. (Some lists discount this performance. It was accurate, on a certified course, and officially timed, though effectively a time trial. It was disregarded by some because the officials were drawn from professional athletics; the women's amateur association had refused to sanction a women's marathon. In the State of Victoria at that time, the two branches of the sport were fierce rivals.)

Those who reject Beames's time credit the first sub-three women's marathon to Beth Bonner (USA), 2:55:22 in New York, September 19, 1971; and Cheryl Bridges (now Treworgy; USA), 2:49:40 in Culver City, December 5, 1971.

1972 The Boston Marathon makes women official, though they have to meet the men's qualifying standard of 3:30:00, and the AAU rules that they must run "separately from the men." The women meet this requirement by lining up in single file at one side of the start. Nine women run. The winner is Nina Kuscsik of New York.

The Vancouver Marathon accepts women from its first running.

Women's 1,500 m is added to the Olympic Games program in Munich.

Women are again accepted at the 1972 New York City Marathon, but are required to start ten minutes ahead to meet the AAU "separate" rule. Led by Kuscsik, the six women entrants, with other supporters, protest the ruling with a ten-minute sit-down at the start. They then bring legal action against the AAU for discrimination.

Title IX mandates equality for women in federally funded education, and thus sports.

1973 The dispute in women's cross-country is resolved when the IAAF takes over the International Cross-Country Union's annual event as a full world championship. The inaugural women's race is won by Paola Pigni (Italy), with England the winning team.

The first women's-only marathon is held in Waldniel, Germany, on the initiative of Dr. van Aaken.

1974 The world's first national marathon championship for women is the American AAU race in San Mateo, California, won by Judy Ikenberry in 2:55:18.

The first international marathon championship for women is the IGAL World Masters Championship (over thirty-five) in Paris, won by Dale Greig (Great Britain/Scotland), age thirty-seven.

The second Waldniel Women's Marathon attracts an international field.

Alan Blatchford organizes the Masters and Maidens Marathon in Guildford, England, to defy restrictions against women. Leslie Watson, a former track and cross-country runner, enters because "it might be slimming." She becomes a prolific marathon and ultra runner, winning an unmatched sixty-eight marathons and inspiring many British women.

1975   Jacqueline Hansen is first to run under 2:40, with 2:38:19 in Eugene, Oregon. She had been first under 2:45 the previous year, and in all won twelve marathons. She was the second official Boston winner in 1973.

1976   Joan Ullyot's *Women's Running* is published.
"The New York Academy of Sciences on Marathoning" conference unanimously passes a resolution drafted by Nina Kuscsik advocating the inclusion of the women's marathon "as well as other long distance races for women" in the Olympic program, forwarding it to all official bodies.

1977   Kathrine Switzer joins Avon Cosmetics to oversee sports promotions and creates the Avon Women's Running Global Circuit. In seven years, this takes well-organized and sponsored road running to women in thirty-seven countries on six continents.

1978   The first Avon International Women's Marathon is held in Atlanta, Georgia, and is won by Martha Cooksey (USA).
Grete Waitz (Norway) wins the New York Marathon in a world record 2:32:30.

1979   Second Avon International Women's Marathon in Waldniel, Germany, is won by Joyce Smith (England), who like Waitz is a world-class track and cross-country runner.
Tokyo Women's Marathon is founded in imitation of Avon. Joyce Smith wins in 1979 and 1980.
Grete Waitz is the first woman to break 2:30, with 2:27:33 at the New York City Marathon.
Jacqueline Hansen (president) and others form the International Runners Committee (IRC) that, with support from Nike, lobbies for "parity for women distance runners."

1980   The third Avon International Women's Marathon closes the inner-city streets of London for the first time for a sports event, attracts global television coverage, and draws runners from twenty-seven countries and five continents. It surpasses IOC requirements for a sport to be added to the Olympic Games.

The IAAF makes the women's 5,000 m and 10,000 m official distances and adds the women's marathon to the program for the first world championships in 1983.

1980   RRCA introduces its annual Women's Distance Festival, to compensate for the lack of Olympic opportunity in long-distance races.

1981   After lobbying by Switzer, with evidence from the 1980 Avon race, backed by a medical report from Dr. David Martin and van Aaken's earlier research, and continuing pressure from the IRC, the IOC agrees to include the women's marathon in the 1984 Olympics.

1982   The first official international women's championship marathon (other than masters) is the European championship in Athens, won by Rosa Mota of Portugal.

1983   The first IAAF world championship marathon for women, in Helsinki, is won by Grete Waitz. Marianne Dickerson (USA), a beneficiary of the Avon development program, is second. The track program includes the women's 3,000 m, the first at a world event. The IRC continues to lobby for the full program of distance races in the Olympics, and it approaches the American Civil Liberties Union, which files suit "on behalf of all women distance runners." The judge in 1984 rules that the suit "has not yet proved the Olympic rules discriminate," a decision upheld on appeal.

1984   The first Olympic marathon for women, in Los Angeles, is won by Joan Benoit (now Samuelson) of the United States.
The first Olympic women's 3,000 m is marred by the fall and injury of prerace favorite Mary Decker.
The sixth and last Avon International Women's Marathon, in Paris, is won by Lorraine Moller of New Zealand.

1985   *Das Laufbuch der Frau* (The Woman's Running Book) by (the late) Ernst van Aaken and Karl Lennartz is published in Germany.

1988   Team in Training begins when Bruce Cleland, of Rye, New York, forms a team to train for the New York City Marathon, raising money for the Leukemia and Lymphoma Society. This charity training program grows into the world's largest, bringing many beginners, especially women, into the marathon.
The women's 10,000 m is added to the Olympic program.

1994	Tegla Loroupe (Kenya) is the first African woman to win a major marathon (New York City). She wins again in 1995. In 1996, Fatuma Roba (Ethiopia) is the first African to win the Olympic women's marathon.
	Television celebrity Oprah Winfrey runs the Marine Corps Marathon, inspiring many women to try running.
1996	The 5,000 m replaces the 3,000 m in the Olympic Games.
1998	The first Rock 'n' Roll Marathon is held in San Diego, California. With a party atmosphere and emphasis on entertainment, music, and costume, the series attracts large numbers of women participants.
2001	Naoko Takahashi (Japan), the Olympic champion in 2000, runs 2:19:46 at the Berlin Marathon, the first woman to break 2:20. She becomes a national idol, arguably the first woman to achieve heroic status in Japan.
2002, 2003	Pam Reed is twice the overall winner of the Badwater Ultramarathon in Death Valley, California; she runs for more than twenty-four hours in extreme heat, confirming earlier research about women's endurance.
2003	Paula Radcliffe runs a world record 2:15:25 at the London Marathon.
2008	The women's 3,000 m steeplechase is added to the Olympic Games, at last making the range of distance races for women the same as for men.
2017	Women equal or outnumber men in most road races in the English-speaking world, and worldwide the balance is shifting. More than half of regular runners in North America are women.

Timeline 3: Masters Running, 1909–2008

No up-to-date global history exists for masters running. Several items below come from personal contacts and may prove to be typical of their era rather than inaugural. Breakthrough performances are not included because there are too many if all age groups were surveyed. For a summary of pre-twentieth-century historical and literary references to older runners, from Homer on, see my essay, "The Seasoned Runner as Hero, in History and Literature," in King and Cumming (2005).

1909	South London Harriers versus Blackheath Harriers cross-country match includes a separate race for "veterans" (c. over thirty-five).
1910	Peter Foley, a regular Boston Marathon contestant, has his entry rejected because at fifty-four he is "too old." He disguises himself by shaving off his copious beard, runs anyway, and is acclaimed by the crowds. He reportedly continued running Boston most years to the age of eighty-five.
1931	Veterans Athletic Club is founded in the United Kingdom as the world's first sports association for seniors. (The American Senior Golf Association followed in 1935.)
1947	Hamilton Harriers (New Zealand) hold a club veterans championship.
1961	*Le Figaro* newspaper in Paris creates Le Cross du Figaro cross-country, with many categories, including "seniors masculins" and "seniors feminines." The Romford Half-Marathon in England offers "prize to the first unplaced veteran."

1962   Canterbury Veterans Athletic Association is founded in Christchurch, New Zealand.
Auckland Joggers Club is founded, serving mostly older, noncompetitive runners.

1965   Arthur Lydiard and Garth Gilmour publish *Run for Your Life* on the health benefits of jogging for all ages. Lydiard tours New Zealand for a "Get Fathers Fit" campaign.
David Pain in San Diego begins to put on "masters miles."

1967   The third Rotorua Marathon in New Zealand introduces awards for over forty, forty-five, and fifty.
Bill Bowerman and W. E. Harris publish the best-selling *Jogging*, which attracts many older Americans.
Chandler Road Race in British Columbia gives masters awards.

1968   David Pain's initiative leads to the creation of the US Masters Track and Field Championships in his hometown of San Diego.
Ken Cooper publishes *Aerobics*. In a few years, it popularizes jogging and walking for all ages.
In Germany, Interessen-Gemeinschaft Älterer Langstreckenläufer/ Association of Older Long-Distance Runners (IGAL) is founded. A masters marathon is held in Holland.

1970   On the initiative of the Canterbury Veterans Association, an over-forty race is added to the official New Zealand cross-country championships, the world's first nonstadium national masters title.

1971   Fort Stanwix thirteen-miler in Rome, New York, offers separate age-group awards.
David Pain takes his first tour group to Europe for masters races, the first such international track events.

1972   The Veterans 25K Grand Prix is founded in Bruges, Belgium, by Jacques Serruys, with awards in all five-year age groups. For two decades, it serves as an unofficial European, and sometimes world, championship.
The inaugural Vancouver Marathon offers awards for masters, as well as women, the first race to do so from its inception.

1973   *Veteris* begins publication in the United Kingdom as the first magazine covering masters running.

1974   IGAL organizes the first world masters road championships, 10K, and
          marathon, including a women's marathon.

1975   David Pain's pioneering work culminates in the first World Masters
          Track and Field Championships in Toronto, with thirty-five nations
          competing.

1976   New Zealand adds a national marathon championship for masters.

1977   World Association of Veteran Athletes (WAVA) is founded at the
          second world championships in Gothenburg, Sweden.

1979   The American Fifty-Plus Fitness Association is founded, hosting
          annual conferences and "fitness weekends."

1980   James Fries publishes an article in the *New England Journal of
          Medicine* that articulates the principle of "Compression of Morbidity"
          (COM): maintaining quality of life as long as possible instead of
          submitting to conventional senile decline.

1981   The advent of professionalism brings money awards for masters for
          the first time in several major road races and marathons.

1982   The new Twin Cities Marathon (combining the City of Lakes and St.
          Paul's marathons) under the innovative Jack Moran offers age-group
          awards and masters prize money on an age-graded basis, the first
          major race to do so.

1985   World Masters Games founded in Toronto, since held every four
          years, with participant numbers typically more than 20,000.

1986   The Boston Marathon adds a prize purse, with generous awards for
          masters.

1987   National Senior Games founded in the United States.

1992   WAVA takes over international road events from IGAL, with the
          first world championships being a notably ill-organized event in
          Birmingham, United Kingdom.

1996   Walter Bortz's *Dare to Be 100* develops the work of Cooper and Fries
          on the value of running or walking in maintaining quality of life.

2000   Leonard T. Olson's *Masters Track and Field: A History* is published.

2001   WAVA becomes World Masters Athletics, the current world
          governing body, affiliated with IAAF.

2008   Eliza Chakravarty and co-authors publish "Reduced Disability and Mortality among Aging Runners" in the *Journal of the American Medical Association Internal Medicine* (formerly *Archives of Internal Medicine*), the results of a twenty-one-year longitudinal study that shows conclusively that active runners live longer, by seven years on average, and suffer few debilitating disabilities.

Bibliography

Many articles in *Running Times* (including the website), *Marathon & Beyond, New Zealand Runner, Canadian Running,* and *Runner's World* have been relevant, but except when cited in the text are not included here. Nor do I include my own publications in those magazines and websites, which have often been part of the process of developing this book.

As a lifelong scholar of literature, I tend to draw on literary writers to clarify my thoughts or sometimes to express them better than I can. I do not think it would be useful or possible to list all these influences, but I gratefully acknowledge them all.

Bale, John. 1994. *Landscapes of Modern Sport.* Leicester: Leicester Univ. Press.

Beck, Jason. 2016. *The Miracle Mile: Stories of the 1954 British Empire and Commonwealth Games.* Halfmoon Bay, BC: Caitlin.

Beverly, Jonathan. 2017. *Run Strong, Stay Hungry.* Boulder, CO: Velopress.

Bortz, Walter M., II. 1996. *Dare to Be 100.* New York: Touchstone, Simon & Schuster.

Boyle, Vince. 2006. *The Fastest Old Man in the World: The Derek Turnbull Story.* Tussock Creek, NZ: Pat Turnbull.

Carnegie, David, Paul Millar, David Norton, and Harry Ricketts, eds. 2011. *Running Writing Robinson.* Wellington: Victoria Univ. Press.

Chakravarty, Eliza F., Helen B. Hubert, Vijaya B. Lingala, James F. Fries. 2008. "Reduced Disability and Mortality among Aging Runners: A 21-Year Longitudinal Study." *Archives of Internal Medicine* 168, no. 15:1638–46.

Chataway, Chris. 1956. "Introduction." In *Franz Stampfl on Running.* London: Herbert Jenkins.

Clerici, Paul C. 2013. *History of the Greater Boston Track Club.* Charleston, SC: History Press.

Cooper, Ken. 1969. *Aerobics,* rev. ed. New York: Bantam.

Cooper, Pamela. 1999. *The American Marathon*. Syracuse, NY: Syracuse Univ. Press.

Depping, Guillaume. 1871. *Wonders of Bodily Strength and Skill*. Paris.

Doyle, Arthur Conan. 1899, 1922. "The Croxley Master. A Great Tale of the Prize Ring." In *Tales of the Ring and Camp*. London: John Murray.

Fenton, James. 1993. "War in the Garden." *New York Review of Books*, June 24, 1993.

Fixx, James. 1977. *The Complete Book of Running*. New York: Random House.

Glickman, Marty. 1999. *The Fastest Kid on the Block: The Marty Glickman Story*, rev. ed. Syracuse, NY: Syracuse Univ. Press.

Halberg, Murray, and Garth Gilmour. 1963. *A Clean Pair of Heels*. Wellington: Reed.

Hall, Harry. 2014. *The Pedestriennes: America's Forgotten Superstars*. Indianapolis: Dog Ear.

Jennings, Andrew. 1996. *The New Lords of the Rings: Olympic Corruption and How to Buy Gold Medals*. New York: Pocket Books, Simon & Schuster.

Jones, Bill. 2011. *The Ghost Runner: The Tragedy of the Man They Couldn't Stop*. Edinburgh: Mainstream.

Keston, John, and Richard A. Lovett. 2011. *Expressions of Aging*. Bend, OR: 42K Books.

King, Steve, and Dan Cumming. 2005. *Running in the Zone: A Handbook for Seasoned Athletes*. Victoria, BC: Trafford.

Lundgren, Mike. 1999. "The 'Greening' of a Marathon." *Marathon & Beyond*, September/October 1999.

Lungqvist, Arne. 2011. *Doping's Nemesis*. Cheltenham: SportsBooks.

Lydiard, Arthur, and Garth Gilmour. 1962. *Run to the Top*. Wellington: Reed.

Maraniss, David. 2008. *Rome 1960: The Olympics that Changed the World*. New York: Simon & Schuster.

McHugh, Betty Jean, and Bob Nixon. 2011. *My Road to Rome: The Running Times of BJ McHugh*. Burnaby, BC: Skep Media.

Moore, Kenny. 2006. *Bowerman and the Men of Oregon*. Emmaus, PA: Rodale.

Moore, Richard. 2012. *The Dirtiest Race in History: Ben Johnson, Carl Lewis and the 1988 Olympic 100m Final*. London: Bloomsbury.

Murphy, Frank. 1972. *A Cold, Clear Day: The Athletic Biography of Buddy Edelen*. Kansas City: Windsprint.

Nabokov, Peter. 1981. *Indian Running: Native American History and Tradition*. Santa Fe: Ancient City Press.

Neutra, Richard. 1954. *Survival through Design*. New York: Oxford Univ. Press.

New Zealand Amateur Athletics Association. 1981. *New Zealand Amateur Athletics Association 94th Annual Report*. Wellington.

Olson, Leonard T. 2000. *Masters Track and Field: A History*. Jefferson, NC: McFarland.

Orwell, George. 1971. "The Sporting Spirit." In *Collected Essays, Journalism and Letters of George Orwell*, vol. 4. London: Mariner.

Pindar. 1969. *The Odes of Pindar*. Translated by C. M. Bowra. Harmondsworth: Penguin Classics.

Pitarresi, John. 2002. *The Utica Boilermaker: America's Premier 15k Road Race*. Utica, NY: North Country Books.

Robinson, Roger. 1989. "How the Olympics Ought to Be." *New Zealand Runner*, October/November 1989.

———. 2003. *Running in Literature*. Halcottsville, NY: Breakaway.

———. 2011. *Heroes and Sparrows: A Celebration of Running*, rev. ed. Auckland: Streamline.

———. 2013. *Young Sam Butler and the Origins of Modern Running*. Cambridge, UK: St. John's College.

———. 2014. *Spirit of the Marathon: The Challenge and the Journey*. New York: Humphries.

Rosa, Gabriele. 2014. *Correre la vita: Sulla storia della maratona moderna*. Genova, Italy: Il Nuovo Melangelo.

Sandrock, Mike. 1992. "Forest of Champions." *Running Times*, May 1992.

Sherman, Gabriel. 2003. "Miles through the Years: The History of Running in Central Park." *New York Runner*, Summer 2003.

Simson, Vyv, and Andrew Jennings. 1992. *The Lords of the Rings: Power, Money and Drugs in the Modern Olympics*. London: Simon & Schuster.

Snell, Peter, and Garth Gilmour. 1965. *No Bugles, No Drums*. Auckland: Minerva.

———. 2007. *Peter Snell: From Olympian to Scientist*. Auckland: Penguin.

Spitz, Barry. 1993. *Dipsea: The Greatest Race*. San Alselmo, CA: Potrero Meadow.

Straub, Rudy. 1979. *The Brooks Guide to Long-Distance Footrace Administration*. Lynchburg, VA: Rudy Straub.

Switzer, Kathrine. 2007. *Marathon Woman: Running the Race to Revolutionize Women's Sports*. New York: Carroll and Graf.

Switzer, Kathrine, and Roger Robinson. 2006. *26.2 Marathon Stories*. Emmaus, PA: Rodale.

Tulloh, Bruce, and Sue Tulloh. 2001. *Running Over Forty*. Marlborough: Tulloh Books.

Ullyot, Joan. 1976. *Women's Running*. Mountain View, CA: Anderson World.

van Aaken, Ernst, and Karl Lennartz. 1985. *Das Laufbuch der Frau*. Aachen, Germany: Meyer u. Meyer.

Vitiello, Gregory. 1979. "Running On." *Pegasus XVII*, New York: Mobil Services Co. Ltd.

Wroblewski, A. P., F. Amati, M. A. Smiley, B. Goodpaster, V. Wright. 2011. "Chronic Exercise Preserves Lean Muscle Mass in Masters Athletes." *Phys Sportsmed* 39, no. 3: 172–8.

Index

Italic page numbers denote illustrations.

Roger Robinson is a rare combination of literary scholar, award-winning writer, and longtime elite runner. He represented England and later New Zealand in world championships, set records as a master at the Boston, New York, Vancouver, and other marathons, and returned after a knee replacement to set more records in the over-seventy age group. Author or editor of works such as the *Oxford Companion to New Zealand Literature*, and now emeritus professor, he was also senior writer for *Running Times*, is known for writing on running's history, and has published often in *Runner's World*, *Canadian Running*, and European magazines. He lives in New York State and Wellington, New Zealand, with his wife, running pioneer Kathrine Switzer.